AF473668

LILIANA PORTER

IN CONVERSATION WITH / EN CONVERSACIÓN CON

INÉS KATZENSTEIN

---

introductory essay by / ensayo introductorio de
Gregory Volk

LILIANA PORTER

IN CONVERSATION WITH / EN CONVERSACIÓN CON

INÉS KATZENSTEIN

introductory essay by / ensayo introductorio de
Gregory Volk

Fundación Cisneros/Colección Patricia Phelps de Cisneros
New York ▪ Caracas

Fundación Cisneros
2 East 78th Street
New York, NY 10075
www.coleccioncisneros.org

Distribution in North America:
D.A.P. / Distributed Art Publishers
T 212.627.1999, F 212.627.9484
www.artbook.com

Distribution in Latin America and Spain:
Editorial RM
info@editorialrm.com
www.editorialrm.com

Library of Congress Cataloging-in-Publication Data
Porter, Liliana, 1941– interviewee.
Liliana Porter : in conversation with = en conversación con Inés Katzenstein / introductory essay by = ensayo introductorio de Gregory Volk.
pages cm
English, Spanish.
ISBN 978-0-9823544-7-6 (alk. paper)
1. Porter, Liliana, 1941—Interviews. 2. Artists—Argentina—Interviews. I. Katzenstein, Inés, interviewer. II. Volk, Gregory, writer of added commentary. III. Fundación Cisneros. IV. Title. V. Title: Liliana Porter : en conversación con Inés Katzenstein.
N6639.P67A35 2013
709.2—dc23 2012041161

Cover [Portada]: *Untitled* (Self-Portrait with Square) [*Sin título*] (autorretrato con cuadrado), 1973
Title page [Portadilla]: *Red Shoes* [*Zapatos rojos*], 2010
Contents page [Índice]: Portrait of Liliana Porter in her studio in [Retrato de Liliana Porter en su taller de] Rhinebeck, New York [Nueva York], 2010
Pages [Páginas] 96–97: *To Bring Him Back* [*Traerlo de vuelta*], 2010

Produced by Marquand Books, Inc., Seattle
www.marquand.com

Series editor: Gabriel Pérez-Barreiro
Selection of artworks: Inés Katzenstein, Liliana Porter
Editors: Ileen Kohn, Donna Wingate
Copyeditors: Carrie Cooperider, Audrey Walen [English], Mariana Barrera Pieck, María Esther Pino, Amelia Sosa-Zimerman [Spanish]
Translator: Kristina Cordero
Translator introduction: Cristian Pietrapiana
Proofreader: Elizabeth Chapple
Series design: Zach Hooker
Volume design: Ryan Polich
Typesetting: Brynn Warriner
Color management: iocolor, Seattle
Printed and bound in China by C&C Offset Printing Co., Ltd.

Contents

Índice

INTRODUCTION

This book, the seventh in the Fundación Cisneros (FC)/Colección Patricia Phelps de Cisneros (CPPC) Conversaciones/Conversations series, explores Liliana Porter's trajectory from the 1960s to the present, and reveals her working process through an illuminating conversation with curator Inés Katzenstein. It may be surprising to find that her intellectually rigorous artworks so often evince a humor that ranges from dry wit to something akin to intellectual slapstick. Porter's work, from the multiples and mail art created in the New York Graphic Workshop she founded in the 1960s with Luis Camnitzer and José Guillermo Castillo to her more recent short videos, rewards our careful consideration. The techniques utilized, whether printmaking, drawing, photography, painting, or video, are specifically determined by the ideas she seeks to express.

Gregory Volk's thoughtful introduction underscores both the inventive and interventionist tendencies of Porter's work and her ability to reconcile dialectic oppositions, such as an antic sensibility with sophistication, hopefulness with sorrow, the tiny with the immense, the commonplace with the unique, silence with communication. These apparent contradictions are what make the work so "richly human."

Inés Katzenstein describes Porter's oeuvre as an act of knowledge that employs humor as its methodology. In her wide-ranging conversation with the artist, Katzenstein elicits insights into Porter's biography; her working methods and conceptual processes; personal and professional partnerships; artistic influences; her identification with her native Argentine culture; and her appreciation for New York, her adopted home for the past forty years, as a place where "everything is possible." In the course of the conversation, it becomes clear that, for Porter, it can equally be said that, "everything has possibilities"—objects and gestures, the conventions of art making, all are transformed through the artist's juxtapositions, reconstructions, and recontextualizations.

I am deeply grateful to Liliana Porter for agreeing to undertake the creation of this document in partnership with the CPPC. It is profoundly gratifying to add her voice to others in this series in fulfillment of the Colección Patricia Phelps de Cisneros's mission to commission and preserve firsthand accounts from leading Latin America artists and intellectuals. Inés Katzenstein, long a champion of Porter's work, proved to be an extraordinary interlocutor for the project, and Gregory Volk, who has written with great insight and precision about Liliana Porter elsewhere, contributed an excellent framework for Porter's own words, which have not previously been published on this scale. I extend my sincere appreciation to Satoshi Tabuchi, the CPPC's librarian, for his diligence in researching the remarkable additional material for the e-book version. The e-books are an exciting new venture for us that will bring the work and words of our Conversación / Conversation artists to an even wider audience, in greater depth. I would also like to thank Donna Wingate and Ileen Kohn for realizing the CPPC's mission through its publishing program and, once again, Marquand Books for their continued dedication to producing fine printed volumes.

Gabriel Pérez-Barreiro

Director, Colección Patricia Phelps de Cisneros

A TERRIBLE SIMPLICITY
On the Art of Liliana Porter

Gregory Volk

Many of Liliana Porter's signature works from the late 1960s and 1970s arose from her sustained, risk-taking engagement with experimental printmaking. Many also involved what Porter terms in her interview with Inés Katzenstein *arte boludo,* or "dumbass art." What this means, for Porter, is a willingness to use simple, quotidian, seemingly meaningless things in her prints, as opposed to things gorgeous, luscious, or jam-packed with content. Typically, these mundane things (a nail, a screw, a single drawn line, a dangling bit of thread) retain their normalcy while they are jarred into startling new contexts—with wonderment, humor, catharsis, and especially with Porter's kind of keyed-up thoughtfulness and intelligence. An early work from 1968 called *Wrinkle* [*Arruga*] features ten prints of the successive stages of a single sheet of paper as it was repeatedly creased, folded, wrinkled, and crumpled into a ball. A crumpled sheet of paper, of course, is about as banal as you can get, and happens all the time. However, painstakingly preserving, recording, and transforming this throwaway thing is another matter entirely. In Porter's prints, destruction shades into supple beauty. A single sheet of otherwise ruined paper encapsulates transformation per se while suggesting topography and geology, the landscapes of distant planets seen through powerful telescopes, magnified photographs of the skin's contours, and even the stages of a human life, ranging from smooth youth to wrinkled old age. Responding to this work, the tremendous Fluxus poet/artist Emmett Williams aptly likened it to "still-lifes of action paintings," "a still life of a dynamic process," "earthquakes," "ripples on the water," and "the mountains of the wrinkled earth and the valleys of the moon."

In the 1970s Liliana Porter also liberally intervened in famous art-historical images. Part of the charm of these works involves their antic sensibility, while they constitute a sophisticated investigation of originals and reproductions, paintings and doctored prints. For her print *The Magician* [*El Mago*], 1977, Porter took as her source a reproduction of René Magritte's painting *The Magician (Self-Portrait with Four Arms)*, 1952, in which Magritte is simultaneously eating, cutting meat on a plate, and pouring a glass of wine, and superimposed her own hand holding a fork and attempting to feed Magritte a small piece of real cake. We've seen this work by Magritte dozens and probably hundreds of times before, mostly as postcards, posters, and reproductions in books, which means that the original painting has long since become a found, reproducible, increasingly commonplace object. Porter's absurd attempt to feed cake to a famous image remakes the commonplace Magritte image as something nutty and unique, further exaggerates what is already a surreal exaggeration, and results in a loopy conflation of the practical and the fantastical. It is also a total riot.

When you compare these relatively early works with Porter's work since the 1980s and the 1990s, you see how much she has gradually, yet decisively, migrated from printmaking (however eccentric and experimental) to an expanded practice that includes prints, photographs, paintings, drawings, sculptures, videos, and installations; moreover, hers is a practice marked by constant risk, exploration, and a kind of go-for-broke verve. Of special importance is Porter's decision in the 1980s to work in various ways with an eclectic (and ever-expanding) assortment of toys, animals, cartoon figures, and household items found at flea markets, antique stores, and souvenir shops. In Porter's studio, several shelves are densely packed with this cast of characters and objects, which includes figurines of bears, ducks, cowboys, and German soldiers, knitted bottle cozies, miniature ballerinas, windup tango dancers, a drum-playing fox, penguins, pigs, clowns, Japanese Buddhists, Chinese revolutionaries, and Che Guevara, among many others. Sometimes Porter's various figurines appear as actual objects in her work; sometimes they are photographed, painted, or drawn; and sometimes they appear as actors in videos. They can occur singly, which tends to emphasize the aura of loneliness and solitude often pervading Porter's works, in pairs, or in groups. Liliana Porter's human figurines and animal curios often seem to be operating in some immense and empty expanse, without touchstones or anything to provide guidance or direction. This is accomplished with minimal means, for instance photographing objects within white fields (usually a piece of paper in Porter's studio) or placing objects on a white shelf, but it has a profound impact. Her little figures seem enmeshed in distances, haunted by immensities; they are at once thoughtful, purposeful, and bewildered in a big world that far exceeds any real understanding, any sense of order that they can bring.

Wind, 2011, is a photograph of a solitary, fluffy toy chick standing in a white zone strewn with tiny shreds of seemingly wind-strewn paper. You register that this is a mere toy positioned in a mediated and manipulated environment, but there remains something achingly poignant about this chick standing in this particular way: it's at once stalwart and vulnerable, hopeful and sad, and it seems to have poised midroute toward some uncertain destination. This is exactly the kind of thing that really gets to me with Porter's art. An image that could easily be cheesy, breezy, and ironic isn't at all. Instead, it is lovely, and searing, and mysteriously imbued with humanity, responding to our collective aspirations and frustrations, our aptitude for wonderment and frequent consternation, our interest in freedom and our painful experience of limitations, restrictions, and doubt.

In the excellent interview Inés Katzenstein conducted with Liliana Porter, Katzenstein inquires, "What was it about New York that left such a big impression on you?" Porter responds in this way: "What struck me most was the feeling that one sometimes gets in New York, that 'everything is possible,' and that if there were any obstacles to making something happen, they had more to do with me than the environment." This "everything is possible" awareness (or influence, or breakthrough) that Porter experienced as a young Argentine recently arrived in New York and energized by the bountiful city very much characterizes her art. At other points in the interview, Porter specifically reveals something of her artistic process and ambitions. "I still have to go through this process in which I feel that I am doing something else, something different that I don't fully understand, something that has yet to reveal itself to me," she announces, and then later memorably declares, "what art gives me is awareness. Awareness of this short period of time that we have, on one hand, and on the other hand a way of understanding reality. It may sound corny or dramatic, but for me art is a form of salvation."

Reading what Porter has to say about her artistic process, in particular her comment that art is a form of "salvation," I am struck by how much this expatriate Argentinian connects not only with an "everything is possible" ethos in New York City but also with a visionary strain in American literature and art leading all the way back to the noted nineteenth-century Transcendentalist poet-philosopher Ralph Waldo Emerson, an enduringly influential figure who greatly affected the writers and artists around him in Concord, Massachusetts, such as Henry David Thoreau, Margaret Fuller, Walt Whitman, the Hudson River School painters, painters of the American West, and the Luminist painters, as well as later artists and writers including Edward Hopper, Barnett Newman, Agnes Martin, and Sol LeWitt. "Conceptual artists are mystics rather than rationalists," LeWitt wrote in *Sentences on Conceptual Art*, sounding frankly Emersonian. "They leap to conclusions that logic cannot reach." As the former Unitarian minister Emerson gravitated to poetry and art for his spiritual inquiry, he tended to make enormous claims on art, seeing it as inseparable from questions of individual character, psychological growth, revelation, and redemption. Emerson was typically dismissive of art that did not arise from the galvanic inspiration that he sought, advocating instead a kind of untrammeled wildness, an organic fusion of art and the total person, and a thorough willingness to take risks. He believed that formalism itself would solve nothing; however, "the instant dependence of form upon soul," as he wrote in his 1844 essay "The Poet" (incidentally the first great statement in the United States about radical and experimental art-making strategies), could offer a great many possibilities—artistic forms that would elastically take the shape of the artist's own psyche; and an art that is cerebral, impassioned, risky, experimental, extraordinarily open to the world, and willing to find new forms (no matter how unorthodox) capable of conveying driving ideas.[1]

Also in "The Poet," Emerson further addressed his approach to artistic materials and themes, announcing, "Thought makes every thing fit for use," and then adding a bit later, "Small and mean things serve as well as great symbols. . . . We are far from having exhausted the significance of the few symbols we use. We can come to use them yet with a terrible simplicity."[2] This is not exactly a nineteenth-century precursor to Pop, Minimalism, and Conceptual art (all of which duly influenced Liliana Porter), or to Porter's work per se, but then again Porter and Emerson are not far from one another. For Emerson, familiar things, things humble and seemingly inconsequential, could easily be matters for an especially searching, psychologically (and perhaps also spiritually) charged art. This seems especially pertinent for the likewise searching Porter, who employs a remarkably democratic array of oftentimes "small and mean things" (such as a fluffy toy chick) as well as "great symbols" in her work.

On one level, Porter's sprawling collection of international bric-a-brac remains kitschy and debased: cheap souvenirs purchased in gift shops; an elderly auntie's cherished, but vaguely creepy, tchotchkes; forgettable prizes won at the local carnival; plastic wedding cake decorations. Porter finds rich, evocative potential in all these oddball items that would otherwise be so much mass-produced jetsam sloshing around the world. One senses that she adores them. They speak to her. You get the feeling she's held them a lot, scrutinized them, studied their expressions, seen them as individuals, lived with them at close quarters. They are mute, but communicative. They seem to not really tell but emanate stories, or rather, scraps and excerpts of silent stories, hints of memories, snippets of dreams. It's absolutely correct that Liliana Porter works with found objects, but she does so with a rare and peculiar devotion and intensity, and it may well be the case that these found objects function as

1. Ralph Waldo Emerson, "The Poet" (1844), in *The Portable Emerson*, ed. Carl Bode, in collaboration with Malcolm Cowley (New York: Penguin Books, 1981), 242.

2. Ibid., 245.

her surrogates and ambassadors, which she uses to explore the full range of the psyche, including childhood and memory, connections to and alienation from others, love (and its breakdown), purposefulness, alienation, fear, occasional exhilaration, the raw experience of political crisis and injustice. Porter's work is never overtly autobiographical, yet it seems animated by a profound, deeply felt psychological and social inquiry: the deep self in relation to a fractious and conflicted society.

In *The Explanation*, 1991, two figurines face one other: a solemn man in a black suit and hat and a cute yellow duckling with extra-long eyelashes. They connote not only different milieus but different worlds or universes, yet they are nevertheless trying for some mutual understanding. The same goes for *Dialogue with Alarm Clock*, 2000, in which a woman in a pink gown (who looks as if she's been plucked from atop a wedding cake) seems to be earnestly conversing with a mother pig and her piglet who double as an alarm clock. Surprising, often freakish interpersonal encounters abound in Porter's work. Empathy also abounds; it is astonishing how one feels such tenderness and affection for her characters even though they are ignoble little knickknacks.

When you see works such as these, and contrast them with Porter's works from the late 1960s and 1970s with a focus on prints, it is tempting to divide her oeuvre into a "before" and "after": back then, prints; now, toy (or otherwise found) figures incorporated in various media. However, this easy division tends to obscure how consistent (and consistently explorative) Porter's approach has been through the years, in the midst of her obvious changes. One unifying connection has to do with exactly what Inés Katzenstein so insightfully suggests in the introduction to her interview with Porter. Katzenstein writes, "Porter's work, in my opinion, is an exhibition of her relationship with life in a specific artistic terrain." She goes on to discuss what this relationship might be in the form of several questions: "Where are we going and where do we belong? How do we relate to the people we encounter along the way? How can we communicate with one another when we are essentially distant beings? How can we possibly function socially through such artificial codes without wondering about them? What is knowledge? What is the relationship between the practice of art and happiness?" Inés Katzenstein is right; these have always been Liliana Porter's driving concerns, and while she has used diverse means to explore them, they remain at the core of her art. Another important connection has to do with precisely how Porter uses found objects in a wonderfully idiosyncratic, downright visionary way, creating a profound, humanly searching visual poetry crafted from, among other things, rudimentary hardware and miscellaneous doodads, which she imbues with a curious double identity, at once resolutely quotidian and quietly spectacular.

In fact, throughout Porter's work, the objects as they normally are and as they've been decisively transformed and mediated coexist. It is for the viewer to constantly move between these two contexts, the one mundane and the other skewed, weird, at times humorous, and psychologically complex. At first glance *Scratch*, 1974, an etching and aquatint print, reveals a single nail puncturing a wall at an angle and the nail's cast shadow; it is tough to imagine a more banal image than this. It takes time to discover a single (and actual, not printed) scratch starting from the point of puncture, angling across the paper, and also the surrounding mat; visible, tactile "damage," such as could easily have been caused by the sharp nail, which also looks lustrous and even bejeweled. Presence and absence, agitation and repose, all converge while the nail, shadow, and scratch also loosely suggest a clock face, one of many references to time throughout Porter's work. *Key Ring*, 2011, a photograph from Porter's recent exhibition at Hosfelt Gallery in New York, is equally marvelous. A key ring (with attached key) sports a miniature plastic Jesus in a white frock with a red sash. This trinket Christ, this pocket or pocketbook Redeemer, dragging a burdensome key through an empty, white expanse, is altogether riveting. Porter's photograph focuses attention on the absurdity of Jesus reduced to a mass-produced practical gadget, but also makes this gadget seem oddly sacred, as well as deeply (and painfully) human. The key is a heavy burden, and almost as big as Jesus's body, but also a great promise, as in "the keys of the kingdom of heaven" (Matthew 16:19). This image also resonates in our immediate lives as we move through the world, looking for loveliness, while encumbered by memories, worries, losses, and fear.

The Russian literary critic Mikhail Bakhtin's theory of the carnival also illuminates certain kinds of visual art—and may usefully apply to Liliana Porter.[3] In Bakhtin's terms, the "carnivalized moment," or the "carnivalized situation," is that moment when the normal rules, values, hierarchies, and modes of apprehension are temporarily suspended in favor of a brand new freedom, which can be simultaneously ungainly and exhilarating, bewildering and liberating. Excess, exaggeration, hyperbole, exuberance, and parody are intrinsic to these carnival situations, which do not seek to transcend normal life; they don't try to substitute a keen new consciousness for an enervated one. Instead, both mundane and carnivalized life exist together, and one moves between the two, entering the outrageous or distorted carnivalized situation in order

3. All quotes from and references to Mikhail Bakhtin are from his *Problems of Dostoevsky's Poetics*, ed. and trans. Caryl Emerson (Minneapolis: University of Minnesota Press, 1984), 122–24.

to be tested and transformed, and then return to one's normal life—perhaps shaken, perhaps deepened—with some wisdom gained. I'm not suggesting that Porter is somehow beholden to Bakhtin, which in any event is not that important. I am suggesting that an eccentric carnival inclination—one that involves free-spirited play and buffoonery, which, in Bakhtin's terms, "combines the sacred with the profane, the lofty with the low, the great with the insignificant, the wise with the stupid" and that temporarily replaces normal life with all its rules, categories, hierarchies, and stratification—is essential in her work, and is a major reason why her works, which almost always reference familiar, found objects, are so engaging, cathartic, and liberating. Also, while Liliana Porter is not an obviously political artist in the sense of addressing this or that issue, or this or that perceived societal wrong, there is a deep and implicit politic operating in her work that has everything to do with the joyous suspension of, in Bakhtin's terms, "socio-hierarchical inequality," as well as with a fundamental interest in freedom. And then there's the fact that many of Porter's projects really do have a carnivalesque appeal and excitation, complete with gaudy costumes, masks, animals that have human attributes and vice versa, processions, performances, and wondrous, logic-warping events.

Consider Porter's photograph *Dialogue (with Penguin)*, 1999, which is an unlikely encounter between Jesus and a penguin. In the photograph, Jesus (who is a plastic lamp, complete with an electrical cord wrapped around his torso) gazes at a wide-eyed wooden penguin, who stares back with a look of pure astonishment mixed with nervousness, embarrassment, and excitation. On one level, this encounter isn't all that far-fetched; both interlocutors are mass-produced figurines, and therefore share a certain context. On another level, the encounter is frankly bizarre, namely between a Savior and a bird from Antarctica, yet this bizarre meeting also succinctly evokes age-old conflicts and dichotomies: religion and nature, humans and animals, heaven and earth, us and them, you and me. Jesus, with calm demeanor and downcast eyes, seems to exude serene wisdom even though he is truncated, immobile, and clearly ridiculous, while the penguin, leaning slightly forward, is all eyeballs and ears. There is something comical about this weird meeting, which seems to be taking place in a void, yet is seriously captivating, its unlikely humanity compelling. Porter's outlandish image taps into our own frequent uneasiness with others; the strangeness and mystery of other people, other lives; the fissures that often exist, even between friends, family members, or lovers; and the flowing ease of communication when such fissures are bridged.

This photograph of a plastic night-light Jesus seemingly in discussion with a cute wooden penguin emphasizes exactly what this particular Jesus and this particular penguin really are—knickknacks, or store-bought kitsch. They are objects, and Porter's photograph highlights their objecthood, in a way very similar to her earlier work that accentuates the objecthood of, say, a nail or a screw. But at the same time, the arrangement of both objects into an intense, interpersonal encounter transforms things entirely, and both figures are perceived—against all evidence, and against all logic—as live, inquiring beings, with their own complex inner lives, thoughts, and nuanced emotions. There is something dear and kind about this Jesus lamp; something hopeful, fragile, fearful, and eager about this toy penguin. Although aware that one is looking at a photograph of two cheesy items, there is something really special and evocative about these two figures in particular, which seem to have miraculously entered another plane of experience and comprehension altogether.

For several decades Liliana Porter has been fashioning an idiosyncratic and admirable art with a peculiar, richly human effect: it helps us to live more abundantly in a time (like all times) that is painful and hopeful, maddening and enticing. Her art deals in tough and enduring questions, while it also traffics in available wonder, and you go to it not merely for delectation but for wisdom and nourishment.

Parts of this essay originally appeared, at times in somewhat altered form, in "Five Sections for Liliana Porter," *Liliana Porter: Línea de tiempo* (Mexico, D.F.: Museo de Arte Contemporáneo Internacional Rufino Tamayo, 2009).

LILIANA PORTER

IN CONVERSATION WITH

INÉS KATZENSTEIN

PROLOGUE

"Signification is the result of the will."
—Jacques Rancière, *The Ignorant Schoolmaster*

The more one explores the work of Liliana Porter, the clearer it becomes that each and every one of her images is the result of an interrogation of the world around her. Hence, the objective of this conversation was to unfold the thought processes of an artist who assumes the construction of her oeuvre as an act of knowledge; to open it up in an effort to understand her relationship to the objects reflected in her work. If the conversation with Liliana Porter here presented seems at times to err on the side of the biographical and anecdotal, the "error" was intentional and consistent with the belief that personal stories lend a special kind of vitality to memories, and that by reconstructing the artist's experience of those memories, we may arrive at a clearer definition of the artistic and ethical perspective implicit in her works.

Throughout these six chapters, organized in a loosely chronological order, Porter's story has a way of approaching and then retreating from her works, of traveling from a social and cultural context to technical reflections, and then from the technical to personal aspects of her private life. Thus considered, her idiosyncratic private life becomes exemplary of the thoughts and experiences of a Latin American artist who has been based in the United States for more than forty years, during a time that saw the emergence and predominance of multiculturalism and its subsequent backlash and fallout. Nevertheless—and this is what makes the relationship between art and life so particular and distinct in the case of Liliana Porter—the artist makes it clear that her life is characterized by the decision to build slowly her own form of personal expression and to pursue an artistic practice that is informed by the belief that art embodies a real possibility for communication, even communion, with objects, ideas, reality, and people.

This interview evolved over a number of sessions in various circumstances. It began with an intensive series of conversations over the course of four days at Porter's home in Rhinebeck, New York. Our discussions ranged from family stories to historical analysis, from confession to theory. On each of these topics, Porter ignited a spark between jokes and truth, details and morality, personal and political life—and it is my hope that this publication reflects all of these nuances. Following those early sessions, we spoke on a few occasions in Buenos Aires, but our conversations took place primarily via e-mail, a format in which I aimed to maintain the freshness and intimacy of our face-to-face conversations, even imposing upon myself as interviewer a terse, colloquial style directed by the paths that my curiosity traveled as our conversation continued evolving.

For me, a number of important discoveries about Liliana Porter emerged from this dialogue. First, I was surprised by the intensity of her relationship to Argentina, and her pragmatic—though not necessarily uncomplicated—relationship to the United States. Perhaps more significantly, these talks gave me the impression that Porter is an artist who has focused on translating what she thinks, questions, and feels into a code that takes on the form of what we call art. While her work has certainly changed over time, and has echoed the different languages and trends that have predominated at different moments, each variation has always underscored her most essential themes. I write this and it feels like a cliché. Can this be said about all artists? I don't believe so.

Porter's work, in my opinion, is an exhibition of her relationship with life in a specific artistic terrain. The questions are few and simple, arising from the very particular kind of distance (at once immersive and alienated, tender and lucid) that exists between her and the world. Where are we going and where do we belong? How do we relate to the people we encounter along the way? How can we communicate with one another when we are essentially distant beings? How can we possibly function socially through such artificial codes without wondering about them? What is knowledge? What is the relationship between the practice of art and happiness? Once again, they sound like elemental questions, almost clichés. But they aren't. The truth is that few artists concern themselves with such matters; this conversation reveals a constant reflection on these themes.

I sense that this very particular relationship between art and life is what differentiates Porter from her fellow artists and contemporaries. Although she is among the most industrious of artists, and absolutely integrated into the contemporary art world, I would like to underscore the fact that her work is quite distinct from that of her contemporaries. We could situate her in different "isms," trace her influences, and deconstruct her context, yet her work establishes a differential with respect to the most common forms of art, which places her at an unusual margin: it is a marginality that, rather than inching toward the obscure and the hermetic, retreats from the central or the canonic through its tendency to move toward the horizon of communication.

This distinction, I believe, stems from the theatrical component of her strategies. From the outset, Porter's attitude has always been more rhetorical than direct. In her first phase as an established artist (which I identify as the mid-1960s through the late 1980s), a pseudo-pedagogical tone emerges in her work, a desire to make an image no longer for its formal appearance but in order to reveal some kind of discovery, with the wagging finger of a stern schoolmistress or the gaze of an innocent schoolgirl; something that the artist herself pretends to not understand entirely but whose importance she can sense. Let's take, for example, the *Magritte* series. The artist exposes her relationships with the image, she wants to show that she knows, she understands. This demonstrative quality is also key to the conception of her paintings in the 1980s. In those pieces, when Porter paints—that is, when there is material—the nature of the gesture is so conventional in its "expressionism," and the material treatment surges so surprisingly and emphatically, that they almost become parodies. Here, Porter paints by acting like a painter. Each technical change in the picture exists to highlight its difference from the rest. When she stops working in parody, when she stops being pedagogical, she begins to explore a genre of "little objects" from street fairs devalued and anachronistic from the start, and makes them operate on a theatrical plane (with the photograph or the video as the representation of that theater), challenging the viewer to establish animistic relationships that are normally repressed or relegated to the realm of childhood. There is something here of the sociological experiment that to me also sounds like a gentle disruption of the aesthetic conventions of art.

Finally, perhaps the most transgressive aspect of her work is the deployment of humor as a methodology of knowledge, as an emancipating methodology, in the sense that Rancière alludes to when he speaks of the "blurring of the border between those who act and those who watch."[1] In Porter, laughter—when it emerges—has a way of eliminating all inequality between artist and viewer. The communion occurs instantly. Humor is what drives the artist's radical and fundamental position, and is consistent with the way in which quotidian philosophical problems are manifested in her work. But there is no translation from the heights of philosophy to the depths of laughter—just the adventure of experiencing it all together.

Inés Katzenstein

1. Jacques Rancière, *The Emancipated Spectator* (New York: Verso, 2009), 19.

STARTING OUT

INÉS KATZENSTEIN What is your first memory as an artist?

LILIANA PORTER I think it might be from 1958, when I was still a student at the Universidad Iberoamericana de México, and some articles about my work were published in the newspaper [Fig. 1]. As you can see, I remember when others used the word "artist" to speak about me. But as for me defining myself as an artist—that's something I definitely don't remember. It's hard to say whether "artist" is a positive or negative word, wouldn't you say?

IK What makes you say that?

LP Because the word "artist" has something of "actor" in it. In other words, something kind of fraudulent, and it's also the kind of word used by someone who wants to define oneself as different, which is not very appealing. Whenever someone categorically announces "I am an artist," I immediately begin to suspect that he or she must be kind of stupid, or at the very least there is a high probability that his or her work is a bit mediocre. It's like answering the question "What do you do?" by saying "I am wise."

IK There is something that struck me more and more as I got to know you, and that is the fact that your perspective on the world, in an everyday sense, is as intense, lucid, and humorous as the world vision that your artwork manifests. The surprise, innocence, or cruelty exuded by those little dolls in your photographs is the same surprise, innocence, or cruelty with which you gaze at what's going on in your garden through a window in your house. Is your work the consequence of a gaze that reveals a previously felt sense of alienation with the environment around you, or was that gaze something you slowly built and cultivated, until it became who you are?

LP I may be too close to myself to be able to realize or analyze what you are asking. In reality I think everyone is like that, because how can you dissociate what you are from what you do? It would be so much work!

IK What I am trying to say is that your work, to a greater degree than the art of other more formalist or content-driven artists, seems to be the direct

Fig. 1. Liliana Porter at the Taller de Grabado, Universidad Iberoamericana, Mexico City, 1958.

Fig. 2. From left to right: Julio, Margarita, Luis, and Liliana in Buenos Aires, 1955.

consequence of a clear transposition of a particular way of looking at reality. At the same time, of course, we can also ask ourselves to what degree that way of looking at the world is informed by the work.

LP You must be right. I was also probably influenced by the atmosphere in which I was raised, by an intelligent father with a tremendous sense of humor and a mother who reinvented her reality because of some terribly difficult childhood experiences. I believe it was very influential to witness how my mother, instead of becoming a bitter, angry, or negative person, built a life with a great deal of compassion, in a perpetual state of awe for, or awareness of (though it may sound corny), the mystery of the perfection that one finds in nature. I was also very influenced by the way she developed a kind of basic faith in human beings, or in life, or maybe it was simply just a basic, abstract faith [Fig. 2].

I think all those things helped me to perceive the world and the things in it. Then, as I grew up and began to develop my artistic practice, themes began to emerge on their own that I found interesting—both in my life and in my work at the same time.

IK Reading some letters you wrote to your family when you were very young and living in New York, in 1964, it is clear that you already possessed a very sophisticated sense of humor that must have come from your father, a famous writer and humorist. Can you tell us who Julio Porter was, and what he did?

LP According to Wikipedia (and this is true), "Julio Porter (July 14, 1916, Buenos Aires–October 24, 1979, Mexico City) was an Argentine screenwriter and film director and known as one of the most prolific in the history of the cinema of Argentina. He wrote scripts for over 100 films between 1942 and his death in 1979. He directed 25 films between 1951 and 1979."

He was that and much more . . . I got along very well with my father. He was a lot of fun, and very smart, and he supported me unconditionally. He was not, exactly, an archetypical father, in the sense of someone who would go around giving you transcendental advice or anything like that. That role was fulfilled by my brother or my mother. My father was a well-known figure in Argentine film, radio, and theater. I was very proud of my family, of my house, and of him, and I felt very lucky to be his daughter. My father loved his friends, their parties, restaurants, and people in general. He was a lot of fun, but he could also be very irresponsible and uncontrollable. Being with him was not always fun or easy for my mother, most likely because she was desperately in love with him, even after they separated. They would write poems and letters to each other, they were always creating dramas, fighting and then getting back together . . . they were straight out of an Italian movie!

IK Can you recall any situations from your life as a child that might give a sense of the atmosphere in your house?

LP The first thing that comes to mind is a conversation I often had with my brother Luis when we were very little and still slept in the same room (Luis is three years older than me). Everything was dark, and each time I heard a noise, maybe because he had shifted in bed or something like that, I would ask him:

"Luis?"

"What?"

"Is that you?"

"No. I'm someone else."

"No! Come on!"

"I'm someone else."

"Cut it out. Is it you?"

"I'm someone else. Otherwise how do you explain these long black hairs growing on my hands?"

"Mamaaaaaaa! Mama!!!!"

The incredible thing about this was that it was actually a game that we would play over and over, in the same or a very similar way.

Another interesting fact of my life is that my grandparents were Russian, from the Ukraine. Sometimes they would put me to bed singing songs in Russian. On the other side of my family, my mother's parents were from

Romania and my mother would sing songs to us in Romanian. I didn't understand either language, but as I listened to the songs, very specific scenes would unfold in my mind. The first song I ever composed at the piano was called "The Russian Indians." I was very distressed when my grandmother informed me that "in Russia we don't have Indians."

IK The connection to strange languages that deny access to meaning and separate us from the supposed truth of things, and at the same time that terribly powerful relationship between the "amusing" and the "horrifying," are key to your contemporary work. To what degree do you feel that the world of your childhood shaped you as an adult?

LP For me, the world of one's childhood clearly has a profound impact on the personality that one assumes as an adult. Personally, all of my early experiences at home, at school, with my parents, my brother, my friends, are very present.

IK When toys finally appear in your work starting in the 1970s, then assume a central role in the 1990s, do you think that the world of your childhood is revealed even more explicitly? In other words, did the toys help you reclaim something from your childhood?

LP To tell you the truth, though it may sound strange, I don't connect the toys or those objects that I use in my work with my childhood. That is, I don't associate them with anything from the past, if the past is understood as something that no longer exists. I don't feel that I have "reclaimed" anything when I choose to work with those elements. If anything, I feel that now, simultaneously, I *am* all the stages of my life. As if I never lost anything, really, just accumulated experiences without the need to substitute one phase for another in a consecutive sense. In fact, I don't think that my relationship with those objects is childlike at all. There is no nostalgia. It's really something more analytical. I confront the object and I take the time to see it.

IK You began studying art when you were around twelve years old, in an arts-oriented secondary school program. How did you come to choose this vocation at such an early age? What models of women artists were meaningful to you?

LP In those days you could go straight into fine arts after primary school. I loved it, even though I lived quite far from the school until I was fourteen, in the neighborhood of Florida. To be honest, I don't have a clear memory of wanting to be an artist. What I do remember is that I loved drawing, painting, and the whole atmosphere of the school. The projection room where they taught art history was very old, with dark red velvet curtains and wood everywhere, and it smelled like a piano.

During that time, I don't remember having any one model in particular of a female artist, though I was aware of the existence of Raquel Forner.[2] I liked [Lino Enea] Spilimbergo[3] and the drawings of [Juan Carlos] Castagnino,[4] and later on I discovered modern art and became interested in Braque, Gris, and Picasso.

IK Before we continue talking about your early years, I'd like to ask you some general questions that, I hope, might address your entire trajectory, and serve as an introduction to the way you think and work. Does your working method involve processes of searching that culminate in a work of art, or are they more like sparks, encounters? Is there a moment in the game when everything stops and the final work comes together?

LP By now I am already engaged with the themes that, I know, will keep coming up again and again. And so the method is more about "letting things happen." I allow things to happen on their own, and then I "adjust everything" as little as possible.

For example, I once had a pre-idea of making a porno movie. Well, it wasn't really a porno, but for now let's call it that. What do you do in this kind of situation? I had no clue how it might turn out, nor did I really understand why I was so interested in doing it. All I knew was that I wanted to put situations together in such a way that, at a certain point, even if I was just filming a teaspoon, or some other everyday object, the viewer would perceive it as a kind of pornography. Because it isn't the object that you need to transform, it's the gaze of the viewer. Anyway, go figure out how to do that! And, though it was difficult, I would program it in my brain. If there were signs of something that might work, I would be on the lookout. I would start this way: first I would look at the figures in my doll collection, and after studying them closely it would soon become clear what kind of thing one of them might do, with whom, and how. Friends could participate in the process, too—it would be fun for others to suggest scenes for the "raw material."

Then, let's say that at a certain point the piece became more sophisticated

2. Raquel Forner (1902–88) was an Argentine painter and sculptor.

3. Lino Enea Spilimbergo (1896–1964) was an Argentine painter and engraver.

4. Juan Carlos Castagnino (1908–72) was an Argentine painter and illustrator.

and one began to understand the purpose of what one was doing, as well as the hidden moral. But, then, if the piece were to be a "success," these things would reveal themselves on their own. When you begin to understand what you are doing, you can manage the formal aspects to drive the idea forward.

I always know that the result will be consistent with my previous work, yet I still have to go through this process in which I feel that I am doing something else, something different that I don't fully understand, something that has yet to reveal itself to me.

IK I can't help but laugh, thinking of you in front of the shelves with your dolls, looking at your poor little slaves with lust! This idea of "allowing things to happen," was it similar to when you arranged objects for your still lifes in the 1980s? Did the narrative and emotional dimension of those works make the process different from what you just described?

LP I think the process was similar. Those "preferred" elements were there at that moment (certain books, the little boats, some postcards) and I would arrange them until I felt that everything was right, that everything was true, so to speak.

IK The technical processes of your work have changed considerably, especially if we compare the pieces from the 1980s (for which those countless, complex processes that included photo-engravings, objects, drawings, paintings, and more were central to the meaning of each piece) to your photos from the 1990s, which were much simpler, technically speaking. I wonder if the process of the "conception" of the work also evolved over time.

LP Each technique requires a different kind of effort. And your working conditions slowly adapt. When I began making videos, I was absolutely clear about what I wanted to do, so it was very easy for me to get technical assistance. The photos were trickier because I never studied photography, and I wanted to take them myself without actually learning the meaning of all those little numbers on the camera. So, little by little, I took the photos, operating on instinct. How they actually came out is still a mystery to me. I learned what I had to learn, but in a very partial, kind of absurd way. Going back to the concept itself, in the paintings there was more technical complexity because I was trying to deconstruct the different levels of representation. In the photographs, however, those levels become one, and that one level is contained in the object itself. Of course, the gesture becomes less complicated technically. And the object, perhaps, becomes more complicated.

IK You have shared your life and work with other artists (Luis Camnitzer, Alan Wiener, and, more recently, Ana Tiscornia). What is the place of their [respective] collaborations in your life as an artist and how do you regard each of these collaborations, which are surely quite different from one another?

LP Luis and I were very young when we first met. I was twenty-two and he was twenty-six, so we grew up together. We were both very hardworking and we complemented each other quite well. We supported one another and had extremely useful conversations about our work. I could invent pieces for him (and vice versa) without any problem. Our individual bodies of work were very different, but we had a deep understanding of the other's work and mentality, so we helped each other a lot. It was a very positive relationship. Things always worked out well for us. With Al Wiener the relationship did not revolve around art. Plus, Al was not really interested in "being an artist." That said, he was perfectly able to criticize my work, not so much from a formal or conceptual perspective but with more distance, focusing more on aspects of my personality and the context that we were living in. Al was someone who, like nobody else I have ever known, lived absolutely in the present. He didn't look back and he didn't plan anything for the future. "Sufficient unto the day is the evil thereof," as the Bible says. I learned a great deal from Al's unusual quality.

I met the Uruguayan artist Ana Tiscornia in 1990 when we were both invited to Cuba as judges for the *Joven Estampa* contest at Casa de las Américas. We became very close friends while working together during those days. Later on, we met in Uruguay and then, when Al and I separated, I rang her up in Montevideo from New York and said, "Why don't you come?" And we've been living together ever since.

Ana understands my work, my way of thinking, and my tastes to such a degree that sometimes she knows in advance what I am trying to do. She is more organized and systematic, and she also has had more formal training (architecture, semiotics, and other subjects). Sometimes, when I'm talking about something I've just done, I'll ask her: "So what is this?" and she'll explain it to me, because she seems to know the answer before I do.

Though our work and our activities are different, she's helped me a lot with the videos, and she is the co-director on the last two because she became so completely involved in the work with me. We have also collaborated on public artworks, and together we conceived two exhibitions that were extraordinary experiences, because in reality neither of us sacrificed anything—we just superimposed our two worlds, one on top of the other, and created a third world that was new for both of us [Fig. 3].

Fig. 3. Ana Tiscornia and Liliana Porter, Galería Casas Riegner, Bogotá, 2011.

IK Yet it's clear that you always chose to share your life with people who were more or less involved in the same things as you, and who formed something of a team with you. Why do you think this is so?

LP I've never thought about it, but I think that a shared life in all its dimensions is, at least in my case, the direct consequence of common concerns, thoughts, and interests. To tell you the truth, I create most of my works alone. I made only one work in collaboration with Luis Camnitzer and José Castillo [in the exhibition *Information*, in 1970], and in recent years, some with Ana. Soon we are going to open a fifth show of collaborative works, and we are writing a piece for a book on the art of the future. We also created a heteronym, Alicia Mihai Gazcue,[5] who is still alive and kicking and more and more active all the time, so she's giving us a lot to do. In any event, what I enjoy most is working with other people who are doing things alongside me even if they are working on their own project. It's stimulating to interrupt one's activity, discuss, and exchange ideas.

IK Looking back on your career, it's clear that you are an artist who is tremen-

5. This character was conceived in response to an invitation from the magazine *Otra Parte* (Buenos Aires: Summer 2007–8) to create a fictitious artist for a special issue focusing on criticism and fiction. Porter and Tiscornia created the images and I wrote a short piece on the life of Alicia Mihai Gazcue. Since then Porter and Tiscornia have continued to give life to the artist, who has participated in various activities, exhibitions, and publications.

dously active, prolific, and committed to her work. Have you ever gone through bouts of creative depression?

LP I think that the period I worked the least was when I was playing the role of "stepmother." Al, my second husband, had a son from a previous marriage, and since I hadn't had children myself, I was charmed by the idea of Eric coming to live with us. So he did, and during those three years I did a lot less artistically. Eric was something of a sad child. I wanted him to be happy, and I did everything imaginable to make him happy. During that time my head was very immersed in that relationship; but I don't recall ever having had a real creative "depression."

IK You never thought of doing something else? You never lost your faith in art?

LP No. All the "other things" I thought might interest me were always within the realm of what we call art. I think I might have liked to be a writer.

NEW YORK IN THE 1960s
A Critique of the Print

IK At age sixteen you and your family moved to Mexico. Why did you go and what did you glean from the years you lived there?

LP My father loved gambling. And on a gamble he bet our house, and wouldn't you know, he lost. He was a complicated guy, but since the stars were always on his side, he quickly got a contract to work in Mexico, and that's how we ended up there.

Fig. 4. Liliana Porter and Juan José Arreola at the opening of Porter's first solo exhibition, *Óleos y grabados*, Galería Proteo, Mexico City, 1959.

I gained a lot from my years in Mexico. At first, it was the experience of getting to know another country, with a different geography, customs, and another way of looking at life. Then, I developed friendships with José Emilio Pacheco and Carlos Monsiváis, who were around my age, and who are now very respected writers. I also got to know Juan José Arreola, Emilio Carballido, José de la Colina, Homero Aridjis, Juan García Ponce, Octavio Paz, and Alfonso Reyes, among others . . . and, of course, the visual artists of those days. When I arrived in Mexico I saw Antonio Seguí a lot because we went to the same printmaking workshop in La Ciudadela.

Mexico was where I developed my printmaking technique and where I had my first solo show, when I was seventeen, at Galería Proteo [Fig. 4]. The Mexicans were very generous with me. Even though I was so young, they published a lot of articles about me in the newspapers—they took me seriously. I have a marvelous article by Juan José Arreola that I could recite to you by heart. In those days, Mrs. Margarita Nelken, the art critic in vogue at the time, wrote about my work on several different occasions. I have three personal diaries from that period, so I can reconstruct it almost day by day. Whenever I re-read them, I am always struck by how persistent and disciplined I was, and still am, with my work.

IK Why did you decide to return to Argentina, especially when your parents and brother stayed on in Mexico?

LP I went back because I really missed my friends, my city, everything. So when I was nineteen, three years after leaving, I returned to Buenos Aires to live with my grandparents (my father's parents). I also returned to the Escuela de Bellas Artes (Fine Arts School, which by then was called Escuela Nacional de Bellas Artes Prilidiano Pueyrredón), and my professors were Ana María Moncalvo and Fernando López Anaya, both marvelous teachers and magnificent people [Fig. 5]. I had an excellent relationship with my grandparents. My grandfather was a formidable character, a very sweet man who in his heyday had been the owner of the Porter Hermanos printing press, which published the works of young writers and printed the legendary magazine *Martín Fierro*. He was full of the most wonderful anecdotes and always gave me books. My grandmother was a spectacular Russian lady.

Fig. 5. From left to right: Fernando López Anaya, Liliana Porter, Eduardo Levy, and Ana María Moncalvo, Galería Galatea, Buenos Aires, 1961.

IK New York is a city that you came to as a tourist, and where you would ultimately remain for the rest of your adult life. Was staying there an immediate and lasting decision, or was it a series of decisions? Did you ever fantasize about returning to Buenos Aires, or maybe Mexico?

LP By 1964 my parents had already returned to Buenos Aires, but my brother stayed behind in Mexico to finish his architecture degree. I went to Mexico to visit him and Guillermo Silva Santamaría, who had been my printmaking professor; he suggested that I go to Europe to visit the museums. I was twenty-two years old. Antonio Seguí was in Paris, so the plan was that he would show me around during that first European visit. But while I was still in Mexico, an old classmate of mine from Bellas Artes, Carlos Stekelman, who lived in New York with his sisters (Ana, a dancer, and Marta, a doctor), invited me to stay with them for a week so that I could see the museums and the World's Fair before going on to Europe. I accepted the invitation and I was so astounded by the city that I decided to postpone my trip to Europe and stay in New York for a while.

IK What was that like?

LP Four days after I arrived, I signed up for a printmaking workshop at the Pratt

Fig. 6. From left to right: Luis Camnitzer, Liliana Porter, and Luis Felipe Noé in New York, c. 1965.

Graphic Arts Center in Manhattan, and that was where I met Luis Camnitzer and, through him, Luis Felipe Noé; they shared an apartment on Sullivan Street in the West Village. I had always been a great admirer of Noé, but had never met him personally, so it was all quite amazing. The three of us spent a lot of time together: we went to exhibitions, we talked about art, and so on [Fig. 6]. Then my romance with Luis began, and in 1965 we got married. Luis always said that we were in New York temporarily: there was never an intention to stay, and we existed in a kind of transitory state. But we also never decided to return to Argentina or Uruguay, either.

The only time it ever crossed my mind to leave New York was in 2001 when the twin towers fell, but I decided to stay. And the one thing I always knew that I wanted, from the beginning, whether consciously or unconsciously, was to maintain my relationship with Buenos Aires—to not lose my identity as an Argentine, even if that definition is totally abstract, subjective, and very difficult to explain. It's kind of like saying I wanted to "keep my last name," I don't know.

IK What was it about New York that left such a big impression on you? What was it that made you decide, at that moment in 1964, to stay? What exhibitions do you recall as having made an impression on you?

LP What struck me most was the feeling that one sometimes gets in New York that "everything is possible," and that if there were any obstacles to making something happen, they had more to do with me than the environment. In

Fig. 7. Liliana Porter in front of her *Wrinkle Environment Installation I*, Museo de Bellas Artes, Caracas, Venezuela, 1969.

other words, it was the feeling of being in a place that was overloaded with stimuli—things to see, study, experiment with, and learn. It was also the sensation of being in the twentieth century, of living in the present moment. The exhibitions that left the greatest impression on me were those at the Castelli Gallery, works by the Pop artists and Minimalists.

IK Once you arrived in New York, your work went through a rapid transformation: one might say that you stopped being an art student and adopted a more reflexive language and conception of your work. What was that change about, and through which artists, works, or ideas did you arrive at this?

LP I believe I arrived at that change through printmaking. That is to say, I realized that revolutions in art, new movements and concepts, always occurred through painting and sculpture, but rarely from printmaking. And when I analyzed this, I concluded that this problem is due to the technique, which in the case of printmaking is a very involved process. In other words, the traditional printmaker is sometimes just an excellent technician; that is the sum total of his or her merits. Luis and I began to study this precisely at that moment in which we were both about to give in to the problem: Luis was making those gigantic linoleum pieces with images influenced by German Expressionism and I was working with etching plates that were growing bigger and more technically complex as time went on. We both began to analyze the most important characteristics of the print, and we reached the conclusion that it was its status as a multiple. And that was the genesis of all the ideas that we developed in the New York Graphic Workshop [NYGW].

Just like all other movements throughout art history, there was a context that needed a specific language. And at that moment, the gestation of Pop, Minimalism, and Conceptual art was in the air. Pop emphasized serialized objects taken from the market, like Warhol's Campbell's soup cans, which were a perfect multiple. We realized that only an artist like Warhol, who was not a printmaker, could have had the mental freedom to choose the silkscreen technique, which was totally consistent with his concept—a technique used by the industry and scorned by the world of "fine arts." On the other hand, we also had political ideas (taking art out of the realm of the elite) and, for that purpose, the democratic techniques of printmaking couldn't have been more ideal. Based on these ideas, I made mail exhibitions, using commercial techniques, such as offset, and disposable pieces (environments like those I created based on the image of a wrinkled piece of paper at the fine arts museums in Chile and Venezuela [Fig. 7]), and, later on, photo-silkscreens that I printed directly on the wall and which were later erased when the exhibition ended. Emphasizing the concept rather than the technique, or, in other words, putting the technique at the service of the idea, was what enabled me to transcend the simple, singular category of "printmaker."

IK It was a process of self-criticism with respect to the discipline within which you were framing your work.

LP Exactly. With regard to the artists who had a direct influence on me, those whom I found the most interesting include Lichtenstein, Warhol, Oldenburg, Dieter Roth, and, later on, the Italians of the Arte Povera group.

Minimalism and Pop, at the same time, made us very conscious that what we were witnessing was a very local kind of art that was not exportable to developing countries. A typical minimalist work of art would have been inconceivable, absurd, and I would even say ethically questionable, if created in a Latin American country. These artworks were very expensive to produce, and made possible by very advanced technologies. They were only able to exist within an economic structure that was able to assimilate them from different points of view, including the art market, society, etc.

On the other hand, Pop works were also the direct result of a hyperdeveloped consumer society. All of those materials that were used for advertising in supermarkets and on the streets simply did not exist in our countries, where we still carried a little cloth bag to go out and buy our bread. The United States, however, was the epitome of waste and excess. The funny thing is that now everyone is being encouraged to use those little reusable cloth bags when they go out to buy their bread. What our countries imported of Pop and Minimalism are only apparent visual conventions, hybrids influenced by reproductions—an interpretation based on the visual and not the concept.

Seeing those exhibitions at that time confirmed our suspicion that the thesis of international art is a fallacy, and that aspiring to it in order to arrive at the mainstream requires a kind of negation of one's own context, to put on a costume in order to be validated by the predominant trend. In that sense, I think the path I opted for was the best one of all: to continue being who I was and to incorporate everything naturally that seemed consistent with my ideas.

IK I'd like to ask you about the cyclical stereotypes that are created with regard to Latin American art in the United States. In an earlier conversation, you mentioned the exhibition *The Geometry of Hope* [2007] and the first Pinta show in New York [2007] as milestones in recent history in that they offered a new perspective on Latin America; a perspective that underscores the constructive tradition and, as such, is closer to the Argentine model, which is stereotypically more rational and "European" than the previous stereotype, which was connected to the natural or "marvelous" realm. With respect to your work, how did you feel about the way that the United States looked at Latin America throughout these different historical phases? How do you feel now, with regard to this new geometrizing tendency?

LP To me it doesn't matter what the trend of the moment is when it comes to defining what is Latin American. In other words, it's the same to me with respect to the production of my own work, because no matter what happens, I will keep doing what I'm doing. I have no need to "design" my identity, and controlling other people's perception of who I am and what I do is something I cannot do, nor does it interest me. Over the years I have participated in many, many roundtables and panel discussions on this topic, reflections aimed at defining the essence of Latin American art, identity, globalization, and other clichés. Of course, there are different points of view on the matter. But I most definitely could never forgive myself if I stopped being who I am so that others might accept me. I think in Spanish and I can think in English. That, in my opinion, is an enriching situation. What spoils things is when you voluntarily hide who you are in a quest to join the mainstream—or the opposite, when you transform yourself into a stereotype in order to enter the mainstream. Luckily, the younger generations are getting past those issues. And in general I feel that there is a more open attitude with regard to the integration of other cultures.

IK Luis Camnitzer says that his audience is Latin American because he believes that a certain level of mutual comprehension is generated among people who share the same language. Would you agree with this concept? Do you feel greater empathy in the communication of your artistic ideas with an Argentine or Latin American public?

LP When I show my videos (you may notice that I typically write all my texts and subtitles in both English and Spanish), I feel that some parts will be understood better in this context and other parts can only be understood by an Argentine. For example, in *Drum Solo / Solo de tambor* [2000], the segments entitled "Coro Argentino" and "Gaucho" are obviously more easily understood by an Argentine. I think that all works of art are perceived according to context. For example, at the Sharjah Biennial, in the United Arab Emirates, the curator selected *Forced Labor (Red Sand)* [*Trabajo forzado (arena roja)*, 2008]; there, that work suddenly took on meanings that it did not have in New York or Buenos Aires, and that I couldn't have possibly predicted.

To answer your question: my work encompasses, within its concept, the understanding that things change and re-signify depending on the context and the person looking at it. So, what Luis says is true.

IK Were you in touch with what was going on in Argentina while you were in New York?

LP I had an idea of what was going on in Buenos Aires, but I was focused on my own work. Many of the events that occurred were very far removed from the themes that had begun to interest me. That did not make them, from my perspective, better or worse. They were things that were happening at a time when I was concentrated on other things. That's not to say that I didn't find certain projects relevant, such as that of the Instituto di Tella in Buenos Aires, a very provocative and controversial place that had its frivolous side, but also generated ideas. The thing is, with respect to what I was saying before about Latin America and the United States, I think the essential concept of North American Pop was not exportable. That it was a local phenomenon, absolutely born and bred in the United States. What was called "Pop" in our countries was a translation from a formal perspective: primary colors, the use of images from popular culture. . . .

I still remember the impact that the graphic force of the billboards and other advertising media had on me when I first arrived in New York in 1964. The food packaging in the supermarkets had the same effect. Pop art appropriated that language, almost literally, and simply placed it within the context of fine arts. And if one of these things was powerful in and of itself, it was even more powerful on the walls of a gallery or museum.

IK The mid-1960s mark the start of a gradual process of visual reductionism in your work. Did this occur simultaneously with the criticism of the print that you mentioned earlier?

LP When I became aware of the trap of technique, I decided to stop and try to address ideas that were as unostentatious as possible, technically speaking. The value of the work had to lie clearly in what I was addressing, not how I was expressing it. To start, I selected images with the least charged meanings. Only now do I realize that it was an impossible task, or at the very least somewhat strange. Still, in those days, for me, the most "insignificant" elements were objects that I might find, for example, in a hardware store: a little nail, a hook, a thread, and also, later on, the corner of a folded sheet of paper, a tiny wrinkle, and then shadows, for creating absences.

One explanation for these decisions might be that when I was a little girl I thought that the merchandise sold in hardware stores was free, because I couldn't believe that people were actually supposed to pay money for things like a single nail. That must be why, subconsciously, I chose those materials. I couldn't think of anything more trivial. At that point the empty space appeared, the monochrome white backgrounds. By removing an object's context, there was no need for a background that defined a place: things were not occurring in a real space, or in a copy or representation of real space, but in an abstract space.

In *Stitch* [1970], the real thread is connected to a thread that is only represented [Fig. 8]. An infinitesimal situation, but one that reveals themes that concerned me at the time and that I've continued to explore since: the issue of time, the substance of reality, my relationship to things, meanings, and so on. And that was how the images in my work evolved.

I think that the voluntary "visual reductionism," as you refer to it, served to hone or reveal the way in which I looked at the world around me. Meaning that if, at that particular moment, I consciously chose elements that I perceived as insignificant (in every sense of the word), I was clearly not talking about a

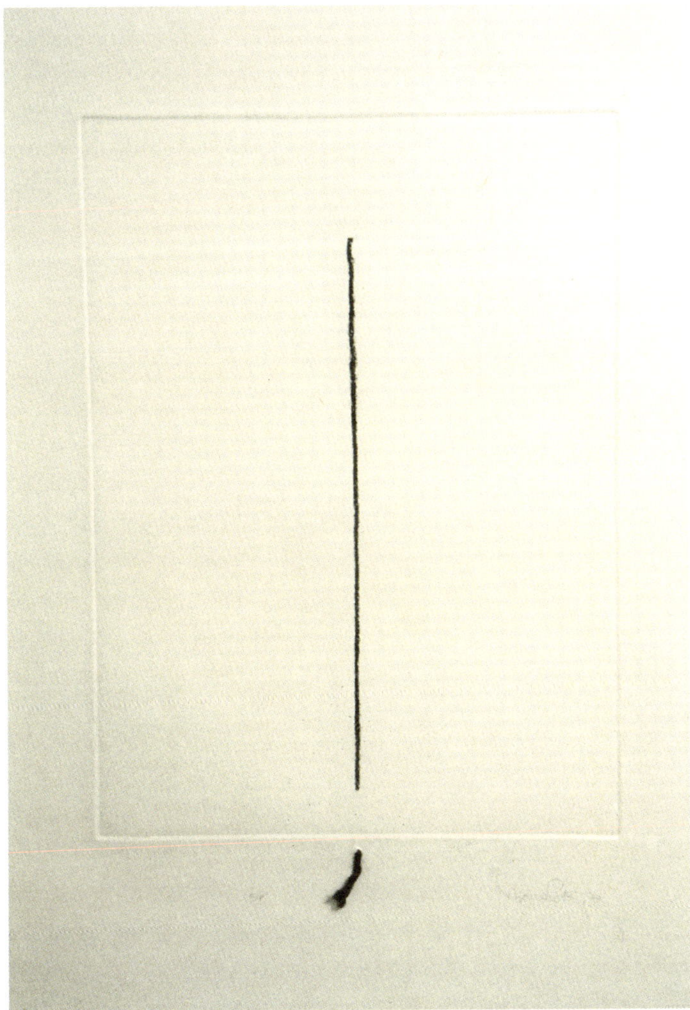

Fig. 8. *Stitch,* 1970.

nail or a shadow or a hook. The final meaning did not emerge from the thing, the "little object," or even the gaze. In a sense they created a space for silence, a place, a reflection that had absolutely nothing to do with the hardware store.

IK It seems that at the moment you made a discovery, paradoxically through the supposed "iciness" of the laboratory upon which you represented those trivial little components (the white of the wall, the white of the untouched paper, and, later on, when you started taking photographs, the depth of the void of the photo studio), some expressive aspect of the object jumped out. I wrote about this in the essay for your show at the Centro Cultural Recoleta in Buenos

Fig. 9. *La lune* [*The Moon*], 1977.

Aires, in 2003: "The more 'objective' the focus on the thing, the more perfect and unreal the emptiness in which it is found, and the more 'affective' our gaze becomes. Camnitzer maintains that 'White lends sadness to objects—even a nail. [Liliana's] is not a rational minimalism but rather an attempt to distill the magic that is hidden inside the *little thing*.'"[6]

LP At this point I know that white space is essential in my work. It takes the object out of any and all contexts and temporalities. I don't know if this is entirely possible, but I'm trying to eliminate the distraction between "oneself" and the thing. I don't know if that choice of space is intuitive or rational, or the two categories simultaneously. What I do know is that when the curtain goes up, the object is no longer on the table in my studio in Rhinebeck. I voluntarily situate it in another place (or non-place) because I perceive that it will be easier to "see it" that way. There, the subjective is simultaneously objective. The relationship one establishes with "the little thing" becomes more real. If it seems "magical," it's because we are not accustomed to that way of looking. With respect to the scale of the object in relation to its space, the smallness serves to underscore the infinite nature of the "place" and the "aloneness" of any entity or person.

IK Did you ever feel tempted to take the linguistic route?

6. Conversation with Luis Camnitzer, New York, July 2003. Cited in *Liliana Porter: Fotografía y ficción* (Buenos Aires: Centro Cultural Recoleta, Malba-Colección Costantini, 2003), 21.

LP The only texts that appear in a painting or mural were quotes excerpted from other texts (Borges or *Alice in Wonderland*) or images of open books. But I never replaced images with texts. I also recall the print I made in the *Magritte* series [1977], entitled *La lune* [*The Moon*], in which words were obviously important; but the words were Magritte's, not mine [Fig. 9].

IK You've said many times that meeting Luis Felipe Noé was a pivotal experience in your life as an artist, not just because of your friendship but because of an idea: what he called "broken vision," a concept that suggests a social state of chaos, which the work of art has to represent structurally: "As I thought about the Nueva Figuración [group] on my way to Europe, I came to the conclusion that until that moment, our goal had been to depict an image of the relationship only through fusion. Today, however, an important aspect of the relationship develops through opposition or through tension."

This observation led Noé to carry out various experiments with the structure of the painting, dismantling the conventions of the picture with a language that, at the time, the conservative American critic Hilton Kramer characterized as "undigested expressionism" [Fig. 10]. Analyzing artworks from this period, it would seem that this concept, paradoxically, led you to make decisions that were the opposite of Expressionism, and closer to the cleanliness of the image. Could you speak a little about this?

Fig. 10. Luis Felipe Noé, *Introducción al desmadre* [*Prologue to Holy Mess*], 1964.

LP In 1964 Luis Camnitzer shared an apartment in the Village with Noé. Both of them were in New York on Guggenheim fellowships. We spent a lot of time together; in the beginning we had studios in the same building in Little Italy. Noé was a lot of fun, very lucid, very passionate about everything he did, and because I was only twenty-two, I felt our age difference a bit more acutely—I perceived him as mature (he is eight years older than me), as someone I had a lot to learn from. In those days, he was making pieces in which he combined old, unframed oil paintings that he found at street fairs with something that he made himself (sometimes on the other side of the stretcher), with crazy arrangements and collages, fluorescent paint, etc. I was fascinated by that combination of elements from such divergent sources, yet that came together to create a new situation. It was a "broken vision" in the sense that it did not possess a linear logic—the piece came together through a number of different techniques and codes, and questioned certain ideas, such as that of authorship or beauty.

The freedom that I saw in Noé was very stimulating. But in 1964 I still hadn't begun making those empty, minimalist pieces that you were referring to. At that time, I was working on semi-Expressionist prints with a lot of texture. To give you an idea, these are some of the titles: *Fragmento de una multitud* [*Fragment of a Crowd*, 1966]; *Exquisito a caballo con cielo* [*Exquisite Rider with Sky*, 1965], a title that was suggested by Noé around that time; *Retrato de nadie* [*Portrait of Nobody*, 1964]; *Development of a Cube* [1965]; *About Geometry with Fruit* [1965]; *The Duchess Rides the "D" Train* [1964]; *The Duchess Says: Eat this Apple* [1964]; *Cedar Bar 1 pm* [1964]; or *The Pop Duchess of Alba* [1965], all of which reference things I saw around me. The Cedar Bar was an artists' hangout in those days (actually I think it was called the Cedar Tavern); the Duchess of Alba was a theme I had been working on in Buenos Aires before coming to New York, and now she was on the subway or selling apples in a calendar (thematic influence from Pop art); and the *Fragment of a Crowd* was a direct consequence of the impact of people in the city, and so on.

Later on, when Camnitzer, José Castillo, and I established the New York Graphic Workshop [NYGW], and began to analyze and question what we were doing, I realized that technical display was a trap, and decided to create pieces avoiding that typical habit that printmakers have, which is such a point of pride. Luis was making work that was very influenced by German Expressionism, and was going through a similar process: first the impact of the technical possibilities that existed in New York, and then the profound shift inspired by thinking about the notion of editions.

IK In what sense do you believe, as you have said on many occasions, that "broken vision" is something that you are still working on today?

LP A conversation between a Renaissance man who is inside a postcard and "looks" at a plastic character taken from the twenty-first century is a form of broken vision. The line that begins on the hand in virtual space and then continues on to the real space of the paper is also broken vision. Maybe Noé would disagree! That would be a classic situation of broken vision. . . [Fig. 11].

IK From 1964 to 1970 you were part of the printmaking laboratory the New York Graphic Workshop, along with Luis Camnitzer and Venezuelan artist José Guillermo Castillo [Figs. 12 & 13]. Reading the catalogue that the Blanton Museum published in 2008 on the group, one gets the feeling that you had serious ideas about what you were doing despite the fact that you used the conventional formats of avant-garde groups (group, name, acronym, manifesto) almost with the spirit of a parody. I wonder if you could speak a bit about the topic of humor—for example, the manifesto and the so-called cookie,[7] or the notion of "contextual art," and to what degree the use of those conventions was a strategy on your part.

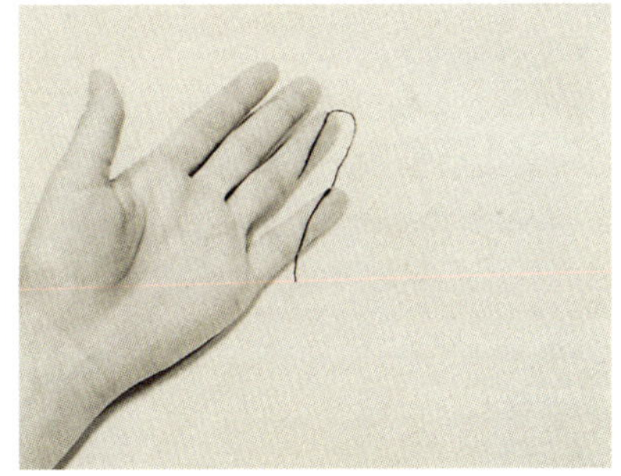

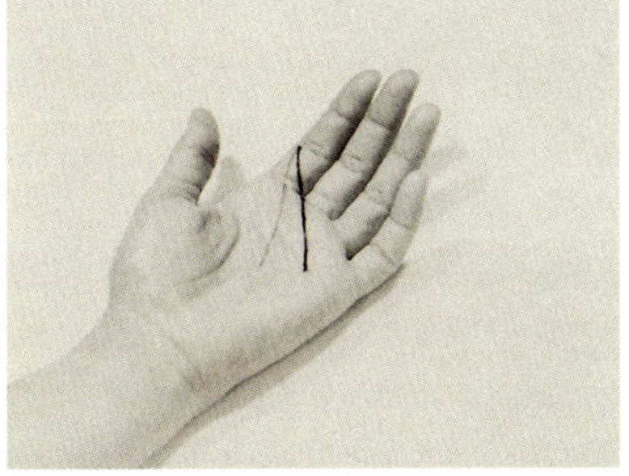

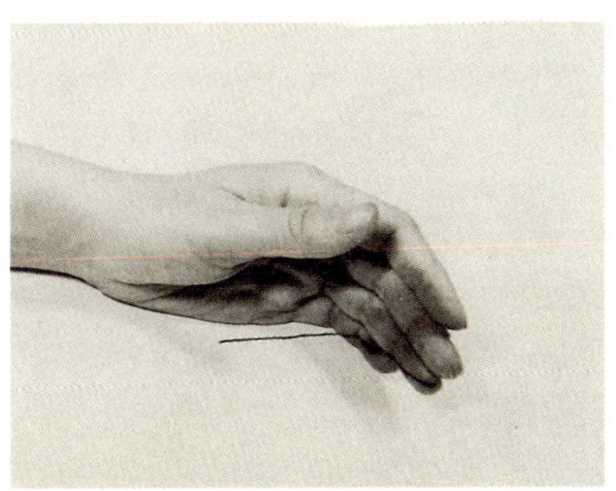

Fig. 11. *Untitled I, II,* and *III*, 1973.

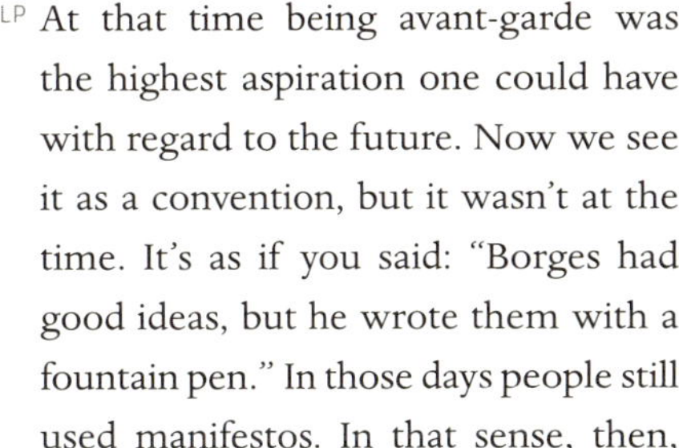

LP At that time being avant-garde was the highest aspiration one could have with regard to the future. Now we see it as a convention, but it wasn't at the time. It's as if you said: "Borges had good ideas, but he wrote them with a fountain pen." In those days people still used manifestos. In that sense, then, yes—it's a bit like what you just described: what we did was very planned. Luis contributed his theories and José, his canny strategies and total cynicism. I think that José was conscious of all those conventions (of the manifestos, etc.) and was skeptical of them. He had a tremendous capacity for analyzing the age he lived in, and I think he was moved by Luis's seriousness. Luis would come in and sit down to read "the brick" (that was what we called his analytical texts)

7. The "cookie" was a cookie that the group's members sent by mail in lieu of a Christmas card. "We made a mold [woodcut] and we took it to a bakery and asked them to make a special edition of long-lasting cookies. We put them in cardboard boxes, to mail them, and included the FANDSO manifesto, signed by the three of us." E-mail from Luis Camnitzer to Liliana Porter, August 2011.

Fig. 12. The New York Graphic Workshop studio, c. 1965.

and José would look at him, amused and charmed, and he would say to him in his Venezuelan accent and with a smile: "Don't worry so much, kiddo," because he didn't believe in any definitive philosophical, political, or aesthetic theory. He accepted everything, but he also knew that none of it "was such a big deal." He was very lucid in that sense. Looking back now, I think that he understood how everything becomes convention, and any affirmation is essentially transitory in nature. Precisely because he was that way, I think that José benefitted from a certain rigid quality that Luis had; it balanced his sense of reality.

Fig. 13. From left to right: José Guillermo Castillo, Liliana Porter, and Luis Camnitzer, 1970.

IK What were the main theses that held NYGW together? What was FANDSO?

LP The main ideas of NYGW placed an emphasis on the edition, on the multiple work, which involved a desire to make a more democratic art form. On the other hand, we were very aware of the need to emphasize the concepts and proposals, not the technical prowess. Printmakers have always been very rigid with respect to the laws of the *métier*, and we sought to broaden the possibilities that were offered by the prospect of multiple-work production. That was what led us to environmental pieces, mail art, three-dimensional art, the use of non-traditional materials for printmaking, and ideas like editing a gesture—for example, the act of folding in *Wrinkle* [*Arruga*] from 1968.

FANDSO, literally, was Free Assemblable Non-functional Disposable Serial

Object. This was the acronym for the concept of the new print that, perhaps in a slightly forced way, reflected the interests of each of the three members of the group. José was drawn to the notion of *modules*; interchangeable modular units like those he exhibited at NYGW's show at the Museo de Bellas Artes in Venezuela in 1972. The *disposable* part referred to the mail exhibitions and environmental pieces like my wrinkled murals or the murals with Luis's words in Xerox copies; the notion of *serial object* encompassed all the multiple works.

IK Why did you start doing mail exhibitions and what did they consist of?

LP What most captivated me was the poetry of sending something like a shadow by mail. Today Luis says (and I don't know where he gets this from) that we made mail art because we couldn't get a gallery, but I think that we were trying to get by without the galleries, they seemed antiquated and we were against the idea of making objects. You see, the great thing about NYGW was that different visions of art were able to coexist without friction. José was marvelous but totally skeptical: he believed that the thing was meaningless; for me, the issue was not to determine if it had meaning but to invent the meaning; and Luis, of course, believed that it did have meaning, and so he theorized and wrote about it. But to get back to your question, when we started out we wanted to make artwork that was not "sellable." Also, unwittingly, mail art was like an extension or expansion of the print, it employed mass production techniques such as offset instead of etching or woodcut. The idea was to create less-precious pieces.

My first piece of mail art included an instruction/title that said: "To be wrinked and thrown away." This instruction was accompanied by another piece of paper with an image of crumpled paper printed on it. The idea was that the recipient was to crumple the paper and throw it away. The work would self-destruct. It was the edition of a gesture in which the viewer participated. What I was doing was shifting the meaning of the fact just a bit. Normally, when you crumple and throw out a piece of paper you don't think about it. In this case, the gesture, within the context of art—the context of the useless—becomes poetic. The important thing is that there was no reason behind it, no connection to the practical realm.

Later on, in 1969, I showed a series at the Instituto Torcuato di Tella that consisted of sending "shadows" by mail: *Sombra para dos aceitunas* [*Shadows for Two Olives*], *Sombra para boleto de colectivo* [*Shadow for a Bus Ticket*], *Sombra para un vaso* [*Shadow for a Glass*], and *Sombra para una esquina doblada* [*Shadow for a Folded Corner*] [Figs. 14–17]. In this, work time was inverted: the first thing that existed was the printed shadow that you received by mail, and then the person

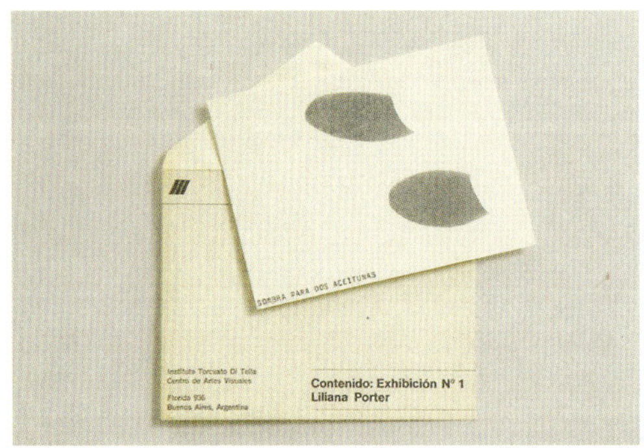

Fig. 14. *Sombra para dos aceitunas* (exposición por correo) [*Shadows for Two Olives* (Mail Exhibition)], 1969.

Fig. 15. *Sombra para boleto de colectivo* (exposición por correo) [*Shadow for a Bus Ticket* (Mail Exhibition)], 1969.

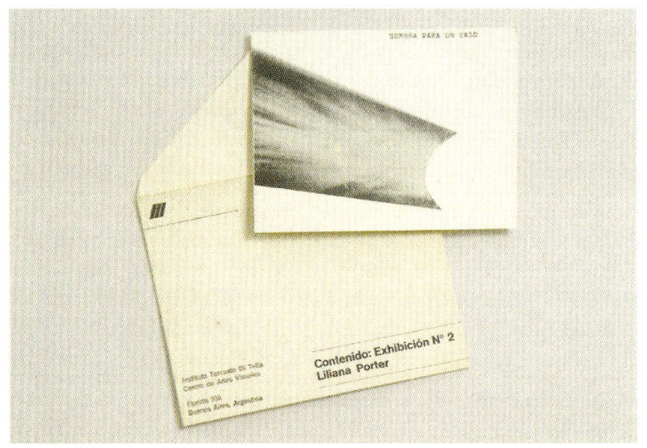

Fig. 16. *Sombra para un vaso* (exposición por correo) [*Shadow for a Glass* (Mail Exhibition)], 1969.

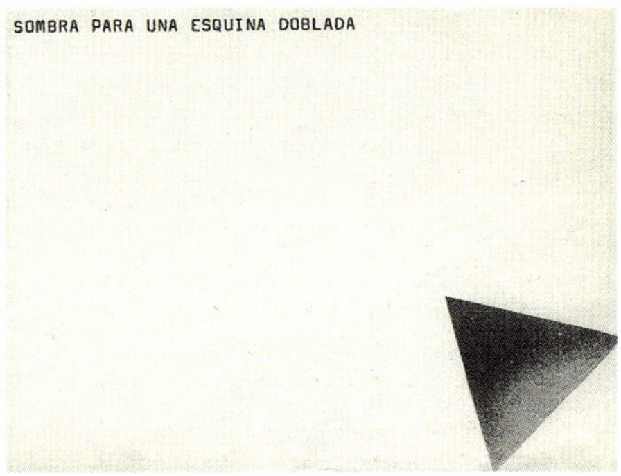

Fig. 17. *Sombra para una esquina doblada* (exposición por correo) [*Shadow for a Folded Corner* (Mail Exhibition)], 1969.

who received the postcard, if they wanted, might place the olive, the glass, or the bus ticket on top of, or next to, the shadow. . . .

IK I wonder if anyone actually put the olive next to it?

LP Who knows; I would have. . . .

IK What other examples of mail art were you familiar with?

LP We knew of a few practices; but the fantastic thing was that Ray Johnson was our neighbor, and he was making mail art long before us, and we had no idea! It was very funny when we found out. The mailman had all these opinions about the works that we were receiving. It was clear that he understood how the pieces of mail that came from both Ray's place and ours were something else, and he began to wait for them with a certain degree of anticipation.

IK When you invented the character of Juan Trepadori at the NYGW, a fascinating facet of the group's history emerged, which had to do with making fun of the art world and expressing solidarity with artists at the same time. Could you explain Trepadori and the ideas behind creating such a character?

LP Juan Trepadori was an artist we invented at the workshop. This is the story: in the beginning, when our work was still somewhat expressionist and we were making prints with color and texture, there were publishers who would buy entire series of prints. But when we began to be more "ascetic" in terms of form, the works turned out to be unsellable, much less in full editions. So one time, when an artist friend had run into financial trouble, we decided to invent a printmaker artist who could respond to the aesthetic/commercial desires of a publisher named Barton, who was thrilled with the work by this invented artist from Paraguay, Juan Trepadori. They were modern works, but comprehensible, sophisticated, and at the same time happy pieces—in other words, ideal.

So any friend who came by and needed money would make a Trepadori. The work would sell and the artist would win their little Trepadori grant, which served, among other things, to free works of art that were being held up in customs (that was the situation with the first Trepadori), to cover the costs of an art class, or to pay for materials. Lots of artists made Trepadori pieces because it was a very easy style to follow. The beauty of all this was that our "accomplices" (from the very first one, whose own work was dramatic, Francis Bacon–style work) got into the Trepadori spirit and actually had a great time when they made these prints, even though they were the exact opposite of their own personal aesthetics. As time went by, Trepadori became more and more human, and quite adored. He was a basically derivative, not at all brilliant, artist who, curiously, gave the artists who participated in the enterprise the freedom to create without pressure and to experience an unprecedented, almost unspeakable kind of pleasure.

IK The group's last official activity was its collective participation in the now-legendary exhibition *Information*, at New York's Museum of Modern Art (MoMA), in 1970 [Fig. 18]. What was this work all about?

LP The project consisted of a page mounted on the wall that said, "The New York

Fig. 18. Installation view of New York Graphic Workshop's project featured in *Information* at The Museum of Modern Art, New York, 1970.

Graphic Workshop announces its First Class Mail Exhibition #14." Next to it there was a table with pens and envelopes so that people who wanted to receive the work might write their address on an envelope. Instead of this poster, what the public received was a very similar one that replaced the word "announces" with the same word in the past tense: "announced."

IK Once again you created a work of art that attempted to poke fun at the art system and at the same time make a donation (in this case, the piece was donated to the public). The group wanted to give the work away as a gift, but also (according to the NYGW's book) play a game that would supposedly wreak havoc on the finances of the museum, which would be forced to assume the costs of sending thousands of works through the mail. Could you expand on the relationship between the tautological circuit (since people were receiving the announcement of a work of art that consisted of the mailing of the announcement), the anti-institutional spirit, and the concept of edition?

LP I see this work less as a joke and more as a game with time—as a game with the non-material nature of the thing. And the part about how the mailing costs were going to be very expensive for the museum is typical Camnitzerian mischief, a sardonic way of resisting the institution and its implications.

IK How long did NYGW last?

LP Until around 1970. The group split when José began working at the Center for Inter-American Relations [now the Americas Society], as director of the institution's literary division (among other activities, he founded the magazine *Review* and was instrumental in translating García Márquez into English). It was then that a group of artists, myself included, staged a boycott of the institution because we disagreed with the policies of the art program and the organization in general. We decided that, personal relationships aside, it would be strange to continue functioning as a professional group, and so we distanced ourselves from José.

After 1970 we continued to make some work together, or we put the NYGW stamp on some things, but that was usually Luis and me. José was less connected.

IK In 1971 you and Camnitzer founded a printmaking school in Italy. How did this project come about [Figs. 19 & 20]?

LP In 1971 we went to Europe together for the first time, and stopped in Lucca, Italy, on the invitation of the Uruguayan artist Gonzalo Fonseca. We saw a house for sale there, an old chestnut mill with a vineyard and a barn on the banks of a river, and Luis suddenly came up with the idea of putting together a summer school. I remember that the house (which Luis still has) cost $8,000, and we made a down payment of $1,000 that Luis's father gave us. We went back to New York and sent two prints from Picasso's *Suite Vollard* to auction, along with a lot of other artworks that we had acquired through bartering. That's how we were able to buy the house. We started renovating it, and then we got to work putting the school together. We began holding classes there every summer, with a maximum of twelve students. They came from all different countries, and either stayed at a little hotel nearby or camped out. They ate their meals with us, and worked very hard. It was all very intense. I remember Luis was quite hard on them and so it was my role to calm the atmosphere a little.

IK What were the classes like? Did you try to transmit the ideas of FANDSO?

LP The way we taught was as follows: first we would analyze a student's ideas and proposals from every possible perspective, and then, once we had arrived at a relevant proposal, together we would analyze the various possibilities for formal and technical solutions. In no way did we try to get them to adopt our ideas or be influenced by our work. Very much the opposite: we wanted to help our students discover their own interests, their own voices, their own questions and solutions.

IK Salvador Dalí played an unexpected role in your life.

LP In 1964, when Luis was at Pratt Graphic Arts Center, Dalí arrived at the school, talking about wanting to make a three-dimensional print. Since nobody could understand anything he said (he spoke a combination of Spanish, Catalan, French, and English), they called Luis to translate, and he ended up becoming something like Dalí's assistant. It was all unpaid, but who cared? It was Dalí!

Then the possibility of making prints for him came about. He made the plate with us, but just when we were ready to print the edition the publisher told us that Dalí was going to Europe and there wasn't enough time to produce and sign them. He proposed making the prints in Europe, but in that case a golden opportunity would slip from our grasp. And so, totally spontaneously, I made the rather outrageous suggestion that before leaving for Europe Dalí could sign all the sheets of paper before the prints were made. I also suggested that a mask, or stencil, be prepared so that Dalí might always sign at the very same spot on each page. Can you imagine? The publisher just stood there staring at me in shock, as if to say "that's like signing blank checks!" Then he began to laugh. Luis did not like that little laugh, so he immediately rang Dalí at the St. Regis Hotel (where Dalí had his studio and stayed six months every year), and presented the idea to him. And Dalí, as spontaneously as I, said "Bring me the papers so I can sign them right away!" And that was exactly what we did.

Fig. 19. Camnitzer and Porter's house in Lucca, Italy, c. 1971.

We assumed that the matter had ended right then and there, but Dalí kept this up for the rest of his life, and there is a famous story about how a truck full of signed papers got stolen, and after that hundreds of fake Dalís began to turn up in the market. The interesting thing about it, of course, was that it was the images that were false, while the signatures were original.

IK What role did Dalí play in the purchase of your first home in New York?

LP In those days we were renting a house in Locust Valley, Long Island, close to the university where Luis taught. One day the person who had handled the rental for us, and who had become a good friend, came by very excited and told us that there was a house nearby for sale and the owners needed to sell fast. The only thing we had was a Dalí watercolor, about two meters high; it had been the backdrop of a kind of diorama that Dalí was putting together, with Luis's help, for the cover of a magazine. Dalí had given it to us as a gift. So when the possibility of buying this house materialized, all we had to do was get Dalí to authenticate the watercolor. And that was how, all of a sudden, somewhat unwittingly, we had two houses, one in Italy and another in Long Island. That was how our life together always was—whatever we touched turned to gold.

Fig. 20. Road sign for Camnitzer-Porter, Lucca, Italy, 1975.

IK Was your life always like that?

LP Yes, but those were decisions that I probably never would have dared to make on my own.

IK You need partners.

LP Definitely.

IK How long were you married to Camnitzer?

LP Until 1978.

AN ARGENTINE IN NEW YORK
Identity Experiences

IK In 1973 you had an exhibition at MoMA in the Project Room [Fig. 21]. How did this show come about? What did it consist of? What repercussions did it have?

LP In 1972 I exhibited a series of installations that were photo-silkscreens printed directly onto the walls at Galleria Diagramma in Milan. The silkscreens were images of nails and hooks with their shadows, connected to real threads that I affixed to the floor, hyper-realistically. They were minimal situations that deluded the viewer, and yet the really important thing for me wasn't just about confusing space and perception, it was about the kinds of images I used. These were elements that, in and of themselves, had no meaning and that I installed in the empty white space, creating a poetic situation on the basis of that silent space. After the Milan show, I began to work with the Hundred Acres Gallery in New York, a gallery I adored that was owned by Ivan Karp and run by Barbara Toll. One week later I received an invitation from Riva Castleman, the chief curator at the Department of Prints at MoMA, to show my work in the museum's Project Room. So, when I got the invitation, I went to the gallery to thank them for interceding for me, because I had imagined that the proposal had come from them. But as it turned out, they had had nothing to do with it. . . . What they did do was program a solo show to coincide with the MoMA show, and instead of one floor they gave me two. I never did find out how that invitation came about. . . .

There is a curious situation connected to this exhibition. On the gallery wall, in a brief essay, I dedicated the exhibition to the struggle of the Latin American people. In those days we believed that Latin Americans had to take advantage of any situation to transmit messages of consciousness-raising. The idea wasn't so bad. This kind of discourse was very much in the zeitgeist, in the way that people today talk about women's or immigrants' rights. You have to consider the context: the Vietnam war, the hippie movement, and Latin American thought united in a kind of utopia. (That was the year [1973] of the coups in Uruguay and Chile.) In one way or another, all young people were rebelling against the establishment, and as Latin Americans we saw all associations with institutions as a source of conflict. On the other hand, I was living with Luis, who was very political, and in general he was the one who structured whatever

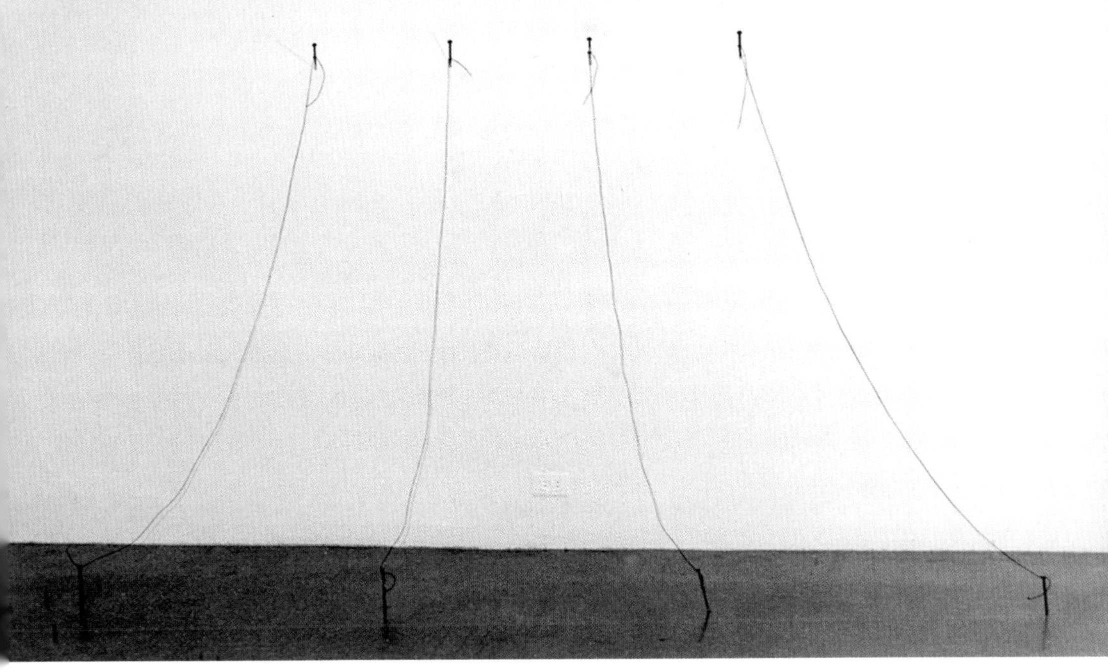

Fig. 21. *Untitled* (Nails), The Museum of Modern Art, New York, 1973.

discourse was needed. So, naturally, when the MoMA invitation arrived, he was ready to write the "little brick" in which I would directly reject the proposal.

Luckily, in the middle of all this, José Castillo showed up for a visit and convinced both of us that if I were to turn down this invitation, I would also have to say no to the gallery that I had just begun working with, and Luis could forget about teaching at the university, since everything, in some way or another, came from the same source. So I ended up doing the show, but with a statement on the wall.

IK In the NYGW book, Camnitzer states that the text said that you knew your invitation to the museum was the result of being a Latin American woman.

LP The text has been lost and I don't remember it very well. I checked with Luis and he says it definitely said both things. You have to keep in mind that this was a very particular kind of situation. And being here, precisely here, one felt guilty not just for being so far away but also for being in a territory that clearly was associated with the dictatorships. Every act became symbolic. So, on one hand, I felt happy to receive an invitation from MoMA, and on the other hand I questioned the institution, given that many of their board members were implicated in the United States' policies in Latin America. For that reason, when

Fig. 22. Liliana Porter in her Locust Valley, Long Island studio, with *The Line* in the background, 1973.

I finally decided to exhibit there, I did it with an announcement that recognized the conflict.

At the same time, in New York there was a struggle to integrate minorities and recognize their equal rights, and this had a way of forcing institutions to offer a quota for minorities in order to demonstrate their political correctness. I believe Riva Castleman was truly interested in my work, but I am also sure that the institution benefitted in some way from that double representation: woman and Latin American [Figs. 22 & 23]. The purpose of my declaration was to make that benefit a little more complicated.

IK What was the exhibition like?

LP In this exhibition there were photo-silkscreens printed directly onto the wall, as well as real objects. The printed elements were a little nail, a rope, a shadow, and a hook, which were integrated with the real things.

IK The matter of visual deception, of trompe l'oeil, was somewhat important to your work at that time, and this continued to be true in the works on canvas that you made later on. How important was that deception, in which the public would confuse a painted shadow with a real shadow, or a silkscreened nail with a real nail?

LP The trick itself did not interest me. What seduced me was the way in which the

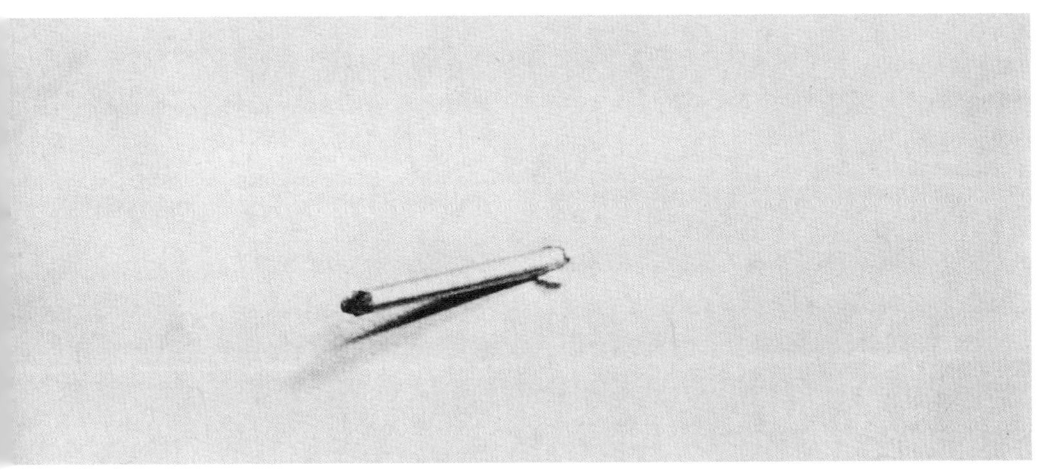

Fig. 23. Announcement card (front and back) for Porter's solo exhibition, The Museum of Modern Art, New York, January 11–February 13, 1973.

real came together with the virtual (the silkscreened nail with the real thread), and the perplexity, or the agitation, that the nakedness of those pieces aroused in me. One factor that did become very important—and that took on a central role—was the empty space. I also think that these were works that functioned according to an important law, which is that of the *boludo*, the "dumbass." *Arte boludo*, dumbass art (which is what Luis and I called it) works as follows: you pick things that mean nothing (which we know is impossible) and opt for the least mysterious elements in the world, even though in fact they end up being mysterious. Look for the most neutral, least expressive things: a little hook, a shadow, a tiny thread. . . .

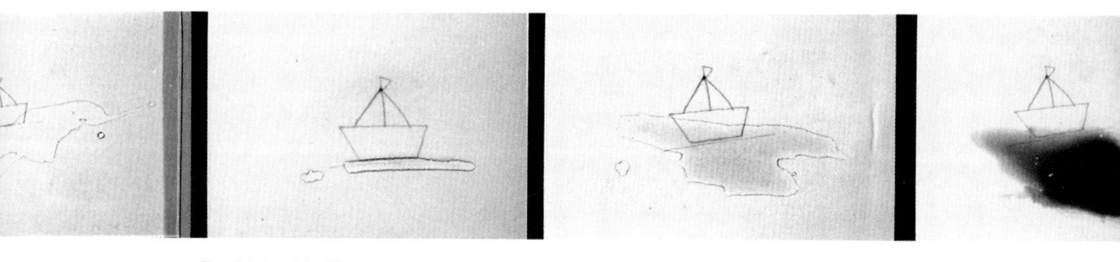

Fig. 24. *Untitled* (contact strip – boat), c. 1976–77.

IK In the same way, the scale of the materials in relation to the space was significant. There is a reason you speak of them in the diminutive. There is expressiveness, a particular kind of poetry of the small.

LP The scale is real. The nail is the size of a nail, the noose, the size of a noose. They seem small only because of the empty space surrounding them. (Recently I altered the scale when I made videos, to adjust for the dimensions of the projection.)

IK Yet there is a particular expressiveness that each element exudes when it appears alone in a huge empty space. Would you say that the relationship of scale elicits feelings for the objects?

LP The empty space is like a silence that surrounds the object, isolating it from everything else so that we may see it better. I believe that being alone, without context, emphasizes and enhances the true condition of the element.

IK During those years, you went through a very difficult personal crisis. Can you talk about the effect this crisis had on your work?

LP In 1976 I had some serious health problems that coincided with my separation from Luis. It was a very rough time, and I felt myself confronting death in every sense. And that became connected to the tragic story of my mother, and her way of being positive in spite of her circumstances. During those years, I was forced to reorganize my life, and that gave me a kind of wisdom, as corny as it might sound. Not long afterward, I married Al Wiener, and we lived together for twelve years. From the perspective of my art, during the beginning of the crisis, I began to work on a series of drawings that were like sentences in which certain images replaced the words. The protagonist was a little boat made out of paper that went through some terrible tragedies: it caught on fire, it sank, and it broke apart [Fig. 24]. Looking back now, those drawings did not reflect any theory of art. They were really like writing in a diary. It wasn't literature. It didn't matter if they were good or bad. They were absolutely true. From that point on there was less control over the content, it was less stiff, less ascetic, and it became more personal. I didn't care too much whether what I was doing was art or not.

IK What was your role in the New York art scene at the time? Did you show your work more or less where you wanted to show? Did you feel some degree of marginalization because of your nationality?

LP Now I realize that you can live here a thousand years, but you will always be a foreigner. If you look at my CV, it's striking to see what a large percentage of my collectors and shows have to do with Latin America. There's no way around it: people are separated into categories here. But that's not my problem, and I don't have time to fight it. Not long ago, someone asked me when I finally became integrated here, and I replied that the interesting thing about living here is that you don't have to integrate.

People have the right to continue being different, to live in their own unique, personal countries; here you can invent your own country. But to answer your question, I don't really know what role I play or where I am. Only recently have I started to sense a broader recognition of my work.

IK Are you referring to recognition beyond those identity-based classifications?

LP That's right. What has become very clear to me—and this is interesting—is what happens with artists from the United States. You tend to think: "Well, the guy owns the place," but it's not like that. It turns out that they regard you as having an advantage, in the sense that I am known not just in New York but also in Argentina, Peru, and Spain, and who knows how many other countries, while in general the North American artist has a very local impact. In general terms, I would say that the art world here is very big and has various levels of integration and recognition, even for locals. In any event, regarding my status in the art system back then, like a lot of young people, I was very content: I had a show at MoMA, and I had a gallery. . . .

IK How is the category of *arte boludo* (dumbass art)[8] related to the purported intellectuality of conceptual art?

8. See Luis Camnitzer, *De la Coca-Cola al arte boludo* (Santiago, Chile: Editorial Metales Pesados, 2009).

LP The dumbass quality that we were talking about had a moral edge: it was a stupid kind of art, but not that stupid. The question of the empty space and the little thread, or any other insignificant object, had to do with the discovery that silence was more important than the word, and silence could be the waiting room of genius. I am thinking of Giorgio Morandi as a model. What I am trying to say is that there is nothing all that intelligent, because we haven't arrived at the definition of anything, and philosophy comes up against that limitation. So I think the best thing to do is find a way to be silent for a while, a method in which space is the protagonist, so that the object is barely a presence.

IK Let's move into the 1980s, when two things were happening simultaneously in New York: on one hand, a group of critical, conceptual artists (with a lot of women at the forefront), who worked with the appropriation of images from mass culture, emerged during this period. And on the other hand, there was a return to painting and a boom in the art market.

LP The moment when painting returned is relevant, because everyone began to want to paint again. I was very interested in some of these painters, like David Salle, mostly because of the way he superimposed different images on a single canvas. And I always found the photographer Cindy Sherman to be remarkable, a strong artist. I loved the idea of the stereotypes from movies, and how she would isolate one image from a narrative whole. It isn't just about the image you are looking at, but what you're not looking at, too, an imagined narrative.

IK Barbara Kruger, Jenny Holzer, and Cindy Sherman are artists who appropriated and used languages from mass culture, and they are related to certain aspects of your work, specifically with the critique of representation that appears in your use of icons from mass culture. What was your relationship to that scene?

LP Directly or emotionally, nothing. They sometimes had exhibitions that seemed original or that opened my eyes in some way, but I can't tell you that they were important to me, as I was influenced by [Luis Felipe] Noé years earlier, for example. The artists that really made an impact on me were Lichtenstein and Warhol.

IK Did that happen just once, in the 1960s, or did they continue to influence you over time?

LP They continued to influence me. Lichtenstein continued having these sensational shows, he kept coming back with new work that I found surprising. Another artist I was very interested in was Joel Shapiro: I thought it was magnificent how he could spend his entire life on the image of a person who is on the verge of falling down. I remember how I approached him once and told him that I loved his work, and that I thought it was incredible how he kept working on that character who was about to fall down, in different ways and positions. Another important artist for me is Richard Artschwager. I love that useless table he made out of a cube with the space below drawn in.

IK What is it about Warhol, specifically, that appeals to you?

LP Mostly the repetition. He makes you see that repetition, and instead of emphasizing something, it's ultimately voided, like when you repeat the same word over and over until it doesn't mean anything anymore. But I also really like his portraits, which in reality are not portraits of any one specific person because they are all the same. Warhol is about transforming everything into a product, and in that sense his figures are terrifying. That, in some way, is also why I am so fascinated by Lichtenstein's crying woman, which is the coldest thing imaginable from the perspective of language; and yet at the same time, it can be so sad.

IK You explore some similar issues to what you're describing—and not just the meaning of images and symbols in their existence as merchandise (I'm thinking of your Mickey Mouse or Che Guevara pieces from 1995) but in relation to that terrifying quality that you just spoke of, which has to do with the contextualization of the images. In your recent work, it's incredible to see what happens with objects that we normally see in innocent contexts, which are depicted in a way that displays all of their monstrosity.

LP Yes, and in the case of Warhol, the genius is that his work becomes more and more dramatic without any need for blood or cliché. For example, I'm thinking of his image of Marilyn. All the sadness and drama is in our heads. That's how everything is.

IK Well, I don't know if *everything* is like that. I think Pop's specific job is to radicalize the relationship between symbol and neutrality.

LP That's a good word, neutrality. In addition to Warhol, I liked Jonathan Borofsky, and I also loved Richard Prince's jokes. They really are jokes, some of them written by hand on a piece of paper that is framed and hung on a wall. What makes them interesting is that they're the kind of jokes you'd tell in a bar: racist, fascist, macho, or just in bad taste. But within the context of a gallery, they are fantastic. He had a show in which the jokes were painted in an Expressionist style. Now that was completely, totally absurd due to the dislocation between humor and painting—fantastic! Then there is a very interesting piece by Artschwager, in which he used a plastic rectangle with very rounded edges, almost an oval, which he used as a stencil to draw on the wall and floor. He drew it all over the city, so that you might just be walking down the street and happen upon it, for example, drawn on the ground. What I found so clever about it was that you inevitably recognized it, which set into motion a very affectionate kind of complicity between the unknown artist and the everyday citizen, as if he were saying to you: "I'm with you."

IK Toward the late 1970s you began to work on canvas. In this sense, I'd like to know what happened with the FANDSO utopia. Did you ever feel that you had betrayed the quest to produce unlimited editions and the interest in broadening access to the work of art in favor of a single work of art aimed at the market?

LP No. You see, on one side you have the idea, and on the other you have reality in constant motion. Concepts cannot be fixed points forever. For example, who would have predicted that, now, some of those pieces conceived to be thrown away would be valued in the art market at such high prices? Someone might consider it a betrayal or a failure of the original plan. I, on the other hand, think that the original idea remains untouched and clear in its idealistic, utopian proposal, and the work itself (for example, the mail exhibitions) is not a living work but a document of itself. And in their condition as documents, I believe it is correct, natural, and inevitable that they have a relatively high market value.

IK At the same time, the late 1970s marked the beginning of the boom in postmodernism, which was very connected to the theoretical foundations underlying your work, especially the thesis that any object is necessarily sign and merchandise at the same time—in other words, the idea of the image as spectacle. How did you relate to that theory?

LP Personally I never really agreed with the thesis that one trend or movement came after another one, that the person who speaks first wins and everyone else is derivative, or that if you don't do something in a certain way you are out of line. Postmodernism, to a large degree, was the opposite of that idea of evolution, and in this sense it was very close to my natural inclinations: everything was allowed, there was no such thing as old, modern, or fashionable. So it was very interesting, even in a political sense.

IK You've described the text that accompanied your MoMA exhibition as a very clear manifestation of identity positioning. I wonder if you might expand on how you were affected by the issue of multiculturalism and the struggle for the representation of women and Latinos that was so prevalent in New York.

LP I have attended many conferences, roundtables, and lectures dealing with these topics, and to tell you the truth, I never felt represented by the feminists in the United States. I come from a different cultural experience, and there were a lot of situations that I just couldn't abide. I would even say that, for me, the feminists in the United States demanded the power men had instead of questioning it.

IK How do you feel about the opportunities you had as a professional artist, being an Argentine woman living in New York?

LP At the time, I felt that I was doing what I wanted to do, and that I wasn't being discriminated against for being a woman. But looking back on it now, I sense that I was wrong. If you compare my career with that of men at my level, it's clear that the men have made progress much faster. But, in general, I felt that things had gone pretty well for me, and I didn't feel oppressed by my husband or by anyone else. I was certainly aware of discrimination, the difference in salaries and opportunities, and the roles that had been established, and I knew that the men grossly outnumbered the women represented at exhibitions and galleries. I understood that there were many things that needed to change, but I didn't feel integrated into feminism as it was being proposed in the United States. Plus, I was very young and quite a novice.

IK What was your impression of feminist art?

LP During that time a group of women artists came of age who were doing work that was overly autobiographical and, to my mind, quite corny—very literal and illustrative things, many of which I found gratuitously aggressive. In reality, I think that I was a little prejudiced and unable to properly digest all of that work; although, of course, there were also some strong pieces that did resonate with me. For example, Martha Rosler's *Semiotics of the Kitchen*, from the 1970s, which is brilliant. There are some relevant figures from that early group, like Lucy Lippard, Nancy Spero, Miriam Shapiro. . . . To give you a better idea of my perspective: the most interesting thing I saw in all the American feminist activism was the Guerrilla Girls,[9] who appeared later on, in the 1980s; and in fact they're still active. From the outset I was inspired by their intelligence and humor, as well as their anonymity. I attended a lot of their conferences and activities; without a doubt, they are very effective and brilliant. They dress up as gorillas (to preserve their anonymity) and their interventions cause one to reflect on issues like sexism, discrimination, exploitation, corruption, etc. They are radicals, true fighters for human rights. Radical and intelligent.

Now I realize that, beyond certain limitations that kept me from connecting with certain works of art, I just didn't agree with an essentialist idea of the woman. The [feminist] works that really impressed me were those that addressed the issue from a perspective of social construction.

IK Could you expand on this point, on the social construction of womanhood?

LP There is an idea of the woman, which is the result of a social construct that operates according to political interests and cultural patterns. The feminist approach that most interests me has to do with revealing and questioning this construction.

IK To what degree did your friendship with the artist Ana Mendieta influence your perspective on these issues?

LP During those years my friendship with Ana Mendieta was a very enriching experience. She was a feminist, someone I admired a great deal; she made very brave, difficult works. Her oeuvre was based on performance, and therefore it didn't have a market because the documentary photograph had not yet come into vogue.

I met Ana through Hans Breder, in 1965. He had been her professor at the University of Iowa, and then they had an affair. Ana came to the United States from Cuba, and she was sent straight to an orphanage in Iowa when she arrived.

9. In 1985 a group of female artists, incensed by an exhibition at the Museum of Modern Art that included 165 artists, but only 17 women, founded the Guerrilla Girls. Dubbing themselves "The Conscience of the Artworld," they produced posters to convey information and provoke discussion, utilizing humor and bold statements, such as "Do women have to be naked to get into the Met. Museum?" They assumed the names of dead women artists and began wearing gorilla masks when appearing in public to preserve their anonymity. To date, the Guerilla Girls have produced over ninety posters, actions, billboards, postcards, books, and magazine projects, examining discrimination in art, culture, and politics.

In 1975 she left Iowa and came to live in New York, which at the time was the center of the art world. She wasn't afraid of anything; in the beginning she worked cleaning houses and at a bar, and at a restaurant in Soho called Food.[10] Ana could put away an entire bottle of rum with no problem. Completely the opposite of me! She always talked about how, as a child at the orphanage, she would say to herself: "I'm either going to be a criminal or I'm going to be an artist." Thank God she became an artist! I admired her precisely because she was so different from me, and in comparison I felt absolutely bourgeois.

IK It's clear that you were never drawn to participate in activism. Is there any cause that you have ever felt especially moved by or committed to?

LP Yes, art. I think art is a cause that can be viewed as political. Art is a form of constant questioning; if you embrace that process, you inevitably position yourself in front of life and society.

There are artists whose work directly addresses political issues. In my case, politics is not a theme, although it's manifested in many ways. For example, I've tried to be consistent with regard to the many contexts in which my work circulates. In other words, when there was a dictatorship in Argentina, I was invited to represent the country; obviously I declined. And then there were situations like the *Contrabienal*,[11] in which I participated actively and contributed by writing a declaration [Fig. 25]. There were many other specific situations in which I took a public stance—sociopolitical struggles, such as the opposition to the Vietnam war. In 1970 I made a silkscreen print from a photo that was published in the *New York Times*, which depicted the murder of a Vietnamese woman, and beneath it I wrote: "This woman is North Vietnamese, South African, Puerto Rican, Colombian, Black, Argentinian, my mother, my sister, you, I [*sic*]" [Fig. 26].

IK What was your experience with respect to the emergence of so-called multiculturalism?

10. Food restaurant opened at 127 Prince Street on the corner of Wooster Street in October of 1971, founded by Gordon Matta-Clark, Caroline Gooden, and Tina Girouard. Approximately sixty artists worked as cooks, waiters, and busboys over the first three years. It was a community-based business whose goal was to support and sustain the art community of downtown Manhattan. The group was also successful at developing a creative environment where artists were guest chefs, films were made, dancers performed, and art was discussed, inspired, and produced.

11. *Contrabienal* was a book published as a response to the 1971 São Paulo Biennial, which was designated by many as the Dictatorship Biennial. *Contrabienal* was organized by radical Latin American artists in New York, the Movement for Latin American Cultural Independence (MICLA), and the Museo Latinoamericano.

Liliana Porter

El artista, como todo ser humano, no está al margen de la realidad social que lo envuelve. La posición de "no comprometido", es en sí un compromiso, pero con la reacción.
Para quien hace arte, la forma de hacerlo, las situaciones en las que acepta o renuncia su exhibición, implican una forma de manifestar una posición política, consciente o inconscientemente.
Participar en esta contrabienal es una forma de precisar esta conciencia, y también una forma de comunicación con compañeros alrededor de esa conciencia.
Quizás, de este enfoque común, puede salir un nuevo lenguaje.

Liliana Porter.

Fig. 25. Cover of *Contrabienal* and Porter's declaration, 1971.

LP When the Bonino Gallery was in New York, in the 1960s, nobody ever talked about whether Noé was Hispanic or not. It was during the Nixon years that you had to start filling out the form and putting an asterisk in that category.

This reminds me of a story that Luis Cancel, the curator at the Bronx Museum, once told me. Cancel's background was Puerto Rican, and he had been living in New York for many years when he received an invitation to go to Buenos Aires for the first time. After he returned, he told me that every time he spoke about the "Hispanics," the Argentines would say that they had no idea there were so many Spaniards in New York. He didn't realize that Argentines don't use that word to define everyone who speaks Spanish; they had no idea what he was talking about.

IK Was this new situation something you were able to take advantage of in any way?

LP The thing is, Americans are used to these kinds of classifications: if you speak with an accent (and I do), people sometimes talk to you in a louder voice, or they think you don't understand them, and many people believe themselves to be superior. That situation is very difficult to change, but it's their problem. And if I have an exhibition in Houston, for example, and the museum buys one of my pieces, it's going to be for a Latin American collection, even though I have done all my work in the United States. There are very strict categories, but in some sense I tell myself: All right, fine—after all I am from Argentina!

IK In the United States, has your work ever circulated outside the category of Latin American?

LP Yes. The Hundred Acres Gallery, in SoHo, which I joined in 1972, not only did not emphasize the fact that I was from Argentina, they went to the other extreme. On certain occasions, I actually think it was convenient for them that my last name sounded completely English.

Also, when I exhibited at the Project Room at MoMA in 1973. The invitation came about because I was proposing something new in the field of printmaking. In that circumstance, I was the one who presented myself as Latin American.

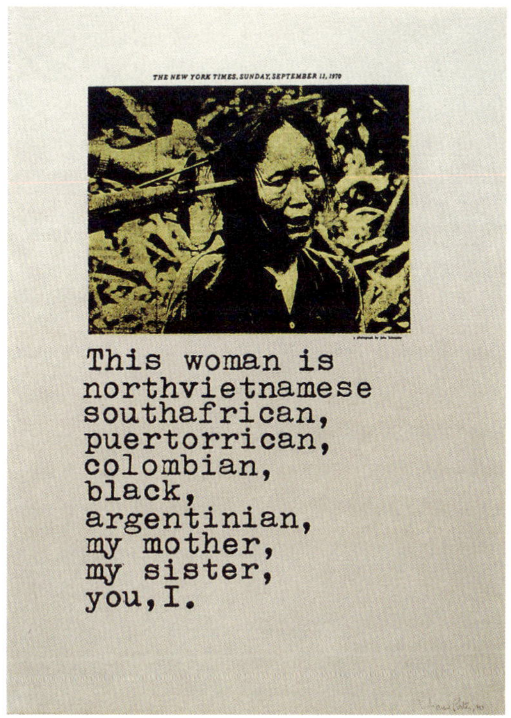

Fig. 26. *The New York Times, Sunday, September 13, 1970*, 1970.

And there are times when you're invited to participate in a thematic exhibition and you're there not because you are Latin American. Although you never really know if you are filling a politically correct slot. . . . On the other hand, when I talk to American artist friends of mine, I can tell that many of them, except the very famous ones, don't feel integrated either.

IK What you're saying is that it is a paradoxical characteristic of New York that makes you feel that you're never at the center. . . .

LP Unless, I don't know, you're Cindy Sherman. But you'd have to ask her. . . .

PHOTOGRAPHY AND FICTION

IK Let's talk a bit about photography, the central theme of the retrospective that you and I worked on together, *Fotografía y ficción* [*Photography and Fiction*], which was shown at the Centro Cultural Recoleta in Buenos Aires in 2003. The main concept behind the exhibition was to reveal the presence of photography in your oeuvre since the late 1960s, specifically since 1968 (when you made your first photogravure, *Wrinkle* [*Arruga*]) and how this technique, with its capacity to "literalize" things, as Baudrillard would say, tacitly defined the foundations of your work as a reflection on the relationship between objects and technical reproducibility [Fig. 27]. The exhibition showed how photography has been present throughout the evolution of your work, despite the fact that for over twenty years it remained hidden in what you considered scarcely more than a phase in your production process, and photos were treated as "unpretentious makeshifts meant for internal use,"[12] just as they functioned originally, when painters used them as the basis for their frescos.

LP I perceived the photograph as the most objective kind of image possible, an instrument that allowed me to appropriate objects from reality (for example, a nail) and then print them on a wall; or I could put situations together, take a photograph of them, and insert the photograph into a print. It was a time in which photography was still quite separate from the other visual arts. And so I used it as a vehicle for displacing images into and between my pieces, but I still hadn't ventured to show the photographs on their own. Before the 1990s I had only exhibited a few, very few, pieces with photographic support. There wasn't a context for that kind of work at the time. Much like what Ana Mendieta experienced, the galleries were not receptive. I didn't have much faith, either; because if I had had faith, I'd have said: "This is art, enough already!"

IK When did you present a photograph as a photograph for the first time?

LP I took my first photos, in black and white, between 1968 and 1977, and the majority were images that included my hands—whether wrinkling a photograph, as

12. Walter Benjamin, "Breve historia de la fotografía," in *Discursos interrumpidos I* (Buenos Aires: Aguilar, Altea, Taurus, Alfaguara, 1989), 65. Published in English as "Little History of Photography," in *"One-Way Street" and Other Writings* (London: NLB/Verso, 1979, 1985). Originally published in German in *Die literarische Welt* (September–October 1931), *Gesammelte Schriften*, vol. 2, translated by Edmund Jephcott and Kingsley Shorter.

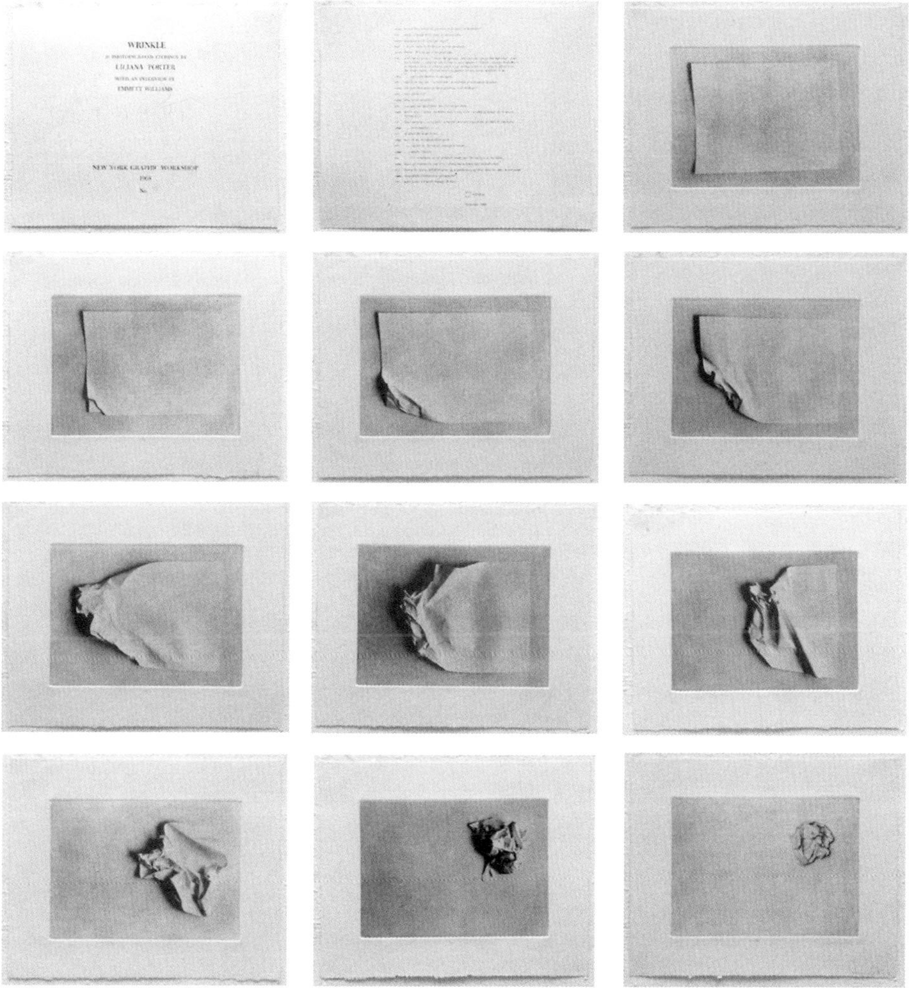

Fig. 27. *Wrinkle*, 1968.

in *Arno* [1968], or drawing ink lines that would continue on the wall or onto another piece of paper. I also made photographs that featured my face, and Luis's face, with ink lines that connected forms on different surfaces.

I've taken a lot of photographs, but mainly to turn them into photo-silkscreens or photogravures. In 1995 I decided to use the medium as is. I remember one of the first photos was a triptych, *Dialogue with Petrus Christus Postcard*. In 1994 I had an exhibition with Leandro Katz and David Lamelas in Buenos Aires, at the Instituto de Cooperación Iberoamericana, and my work, which was a wall installation, included a shelf where I put together three "dialogues." One of them was a postcard of *Portrait of a Young Lady*, by the Flemish

Fig. 28. *Dialogue with Petrus Christus Postcard,* 1995.

painter Christus, of a girl looking out of the corner of her eye at a Brazilian soccer player made of plastic, standing on a little wooden cube. I took a black-and-white photograph of the scene, which, the following year, became part of the triptych *Dialogue with Petrus Christus Postcard* [1995] [Fig. 28]. Then there is *Gaucho* [1995], which was originally a silkscreen, then a painting, and, finally, I went back to the negative, and printed the photograph. I decided to make the photo because I realized that it was enough on its own.

Before then, I was prejudiced—I felt that I couldn't take photographs because I wasn't a photographer. It was a disciplinary prejudice that probably came from my training as a printmaker. Before long I came to realize that a perfect technical understanding wasn't necessary. Suddenly, my head was free from confusion and I began to understand that if you don't think so much about technique and just do the work, you produce images that, in the end, may be more original than they would be if you were a professional photographer.

IK There is a piece, a painting, that I like very much. It is called *The Photograph II* [1996], and shows a series of figurines posing for a still camera [Fig. 29]. The image is very funny because the characters are posing quite seriously, facing the camera that appears in the painting like yet another character in the scene. In reality, it is a dialogue between the figurines and the camera, looking at one another very solemnly. What's interesting is that it's a painting on canvas that comes from a print that comes from a photograph, the topic of which is photography. Another curious aspect about this piece is that, unlike other work you've done that includes your hand or the paintbrush as traces of the process of production, this picture no longer includes the body, only the camera.

LP The story behind that painting is from an exhibition at Monique Knowlton's

Fig. 29. *The Photograph II*, 1996.

gallery in New York: I wanted to show photographs, but she asked me to include at least a few pieces on canvas, so I made two paintings that I called *The Photograph* that document a photograph.

IK Little by little you began to broaden the repertoire of images in your work[13] until a certain moment arrived when something clicked and you became a toy collector. More than just a run-of-the-mill collector, you turned into what Walter Benjamin defined as a "physiognomist of the world of things,"[14] someone capable of extracting all the metaphysical and sentimental potential of objects. How did that itinerary toward collecting begin?

LP I remember the sequence: boat, books, Alice rabbit, Mickey, jugs, Donald, postcards. Very slowly, other characters were added. For example, there was José

13. In an essay on Porter, I wrote that Magritte's *Familiar Objects* would be fundamental because, in establishing a dialogue with it, Porter would begin to expand her repertoire of images. Magritte's work presents a group of men in front of whom he places the image of certain objects. Porter replaces these images with others, putting photos with images of different objects on top of them. Figures already used by the artist, such as the triangle, the cube, and the pyramid reappear, but the boat, cloud, and moon appear for the first time. These figures would become essential in the repertoire of images in the artist's next stage and, fundamentally, they would gradually take on the status as symbol. In Katzenstein, *Liliana Porter: Fotografía y ficción*.

14. Walter Benjamin, *The Arcades Project* (Cambridge and London: Belknap Press of Harvard University Press, 1999), 207.

Gregorio Hernández, a nineteenth-century doctor who was canonized by the Venezuelan and Colombian people, and who looked like the Magritte character. He is a Surrealist character. A saint with a tie! And that, I think, was where the *Dialogues* series began.

IK A number of processes come together here: the repertoire of objects grows, the *Dialogues* series comes into being, you begin to exhibit photographs, and humor takes on a central role for the first time. With regard to this last point, while the toys you collect refer to the past, I get the feeling that there is a clear rejection of a certain kind of melancholy and an emergence of humor, which brings with it a number of discoveries relating to toys. Would you agree?

LP It's true. I think the humor came about unconsciously. Confrontations between objects, even when they are old objects, occur in the present, while in my previous paintings it seemed that the elements couldn't extricate themselves from the past.

IK There is an issue that is very important, particularly during a time in your evolution that has to do with the political symbology of objects. I'm referring to those works in which the images have highly charged cultural connotations—such as *Minnie/Che* [2003–6], a plate featuring the image of Che [Guevara] with Minnie Mouse on top of him, madly in love [Fig. 30].

LP There are a number of elements in these images that seduce me, specifically, the way in which someone is alive one moment and then suddenly becomes a plate, or the image on a package of cheese, as in the case of a cheese sold here called Juana de Arco. In the *Minnie/Che* piece you mention, certain clichés are at work as well. Che represents communism, and Minnie, capitalism, and I love the idea of them suddenly falling in love, or of Minnie sneaking a kiss with Che. In the film, the work is presented in two takes: one, when she gives him the kiss, and another, when she turns around and looks at us and the music grows louder, to the point that maybe it's even a bit moving. . . .

There is a photograph in which Che appears gazing at Alice's rabbit and both are on the same plane, the plane on which we situate, for example, San Martín or Evita: people whom you no longer know whether to classify as part of history or mythology.

IK Do you think that your shift to a different medium in the 1990s, from silkscreens to photographs, transformed your perception of the expressiveness of your figures?

Fig. 30. *Minnie / Che*, 2003–6.

LP Definitely. The image in a photograph is more concrete than in the print, more real. You could also say that from the shift from photography to video, the relationship to the images is even more direct. I moved progressively closer to the object. Then the shelves appear with the live objects, and when you reach that point, you realize that they continue to be a representation. . . .

IK I think it's important to point out that it is precisely in the 1990s, a time of explosive development in digital technologies, that you abandon the semiotic problem you had been exploring in the years up until then (that didactic experimentation with different planes of virtuality and presence) and you put other components into play.

LP That's right, because what technology does, in the first place, is question the objectivity of photography. When all the digital possibilities appear, the concept of what is real is destabilized. In other words, the viewer relates to the representation to such a degree that, if you go out to buy toothpaste and you have never seen it in a photo, you don't buy it, because you say: "That doesn't exist." Nowadays, the thing is a by-product of its representation.

IK How did the idea of filming your first video come about?

LP It was based on a Pinocchio toy that plays a drum when you wind it up. What interested me was the expression on Pinocchio's face when he finished playing. And the only way to represent that silence is with the noise and gestures that come before. It was then that I decided that the ideal thing would be to film him. In general, video art was not something I liked, but I needed that temporal element.

IK The cinematographic format that you used in each of your films, characterized by the montage of a series of scenes or *tableaux vivants*, preceded by texts and accompanied by music, is very unusual. How did you arrive at this?

LP I arrived at it directly from the experience of color photography, meaning that the video segments are like photographs in which more things happen. I have the album with all the notes and letters and material from when I made *For You / Para usted*, my first film [1999]. The album begins with a letter that I wrote to Juan Mandelbaum, who has a video production company, explaining what I wanted to do.

This is a transcription of the first part of my letter to Juan [late 1997]:

> *The idea is based on the following format: a series of vignettes or situations that occur one after the other, coming together to form a whole, which will have a general title. Some will be in color, some in black and white. Some will be silent, others will have sound, and they will each be preceded, definitely, by a text or a title.*
> *I can picture it better on film, or at least I want it to be able to be seen on a large screen with the lights out. Also, it's important that it be done in high resolution, meaning that I want people to really be able to see the details, because I need the*

Fig. 31. *To Fall Down / Caer*, stills from *For You / Para usted*, 1999.

Fig. 32. Stills from *Matinee / Matiné*, 2009

eyes of the figures to stand out, so that I can film them with space around them. The sequence will be thought out so that one segment will affect the one that comes after, etc. I have to manipulate the emotions of the viewer, so to speak.

IK With the videos, I feel that something has happened in several senses. First of all, I think it's remarkable that an elderly person and a grandchild can sit down to watch these videos and you can find them both doubled over laughing—a situation that is practically nonexistent in the case of most good contemporary art. I am really impressed by the fact that the videos are sophisticated and accessible at the same time, as well as inter-generational. On the other hand, we all know that humor does not function so easily in art. Laughter itself is somewhat prohibited, and in that sense your work has the ability to cross certain lines in a very intelligent way. You might say that your work has a self-reflexive kind of humor.

LP Well, I'm glad to hear that. . . . In reality I think the humorous part of the work is precisely the sad, dramatic element. To give you a few concrete examples: in the first film, when the penguin falls, the audience laughs, but it isn't funny at all [Fig. 31]. The laughter is a bit like that laugh you hear when someone falls down—it covers up the feeling of embarrassment. And everything happens very fast. Speed is a basic element of humor. The piece doesn't give you much time to think, it goes straight to the gut and then immediately moves on to the next scene. The relationship with music is also important. For example, there is a section in my latest video, *Matinee / Matiné* [2009], which I originally called "Accidente" [Accident], which features the torso of an innocent porcelain boy that is suddenly bonked on the head by a hammer and decapitated . . . [Fig. 32]. That segment came right after another one entitled "Insomnio" [Insomnia], which shows a little stuffed duckling "sleeping" on a rock with its eyes open. In that segment the music was from "Mambrú se fue a la guerra." And so, looking at the video proofs with Sylvia Meyer (who works with me on the music for the films), we realized that the decapitated boy was clearly Mambrú. So the image becomes even more terrible when it's combined with the song and the insomnia situation in the previous mini-segment, because while the little duck can't sleep, he asks himself "When will Mambrú be coming back?" And one knows, evidently, that Mambrú is not coming back.[15]

IK What is your collaboration with Sylvia Meyer like?

LP The first time I worked with her, for my first video, *For You / Para usted* [1999], the video was edited and ready to go and I didn't have the slightest idea of what kind of music could go with it. So Sylvia said to me, "Give me the video, I'll put music to it, and you can tell me what you think." When she brought it to me, it was very easy for me to decide what worked and what didn't. And from there I was able to start asking for what I wanted.

I was so inspired by that first experience of working with her, I conceived my second video, *Drum Solo / Solo de tambor* [2000], anticipating the inclusion of music. Our working process is like this: in the last film, *Matinee / Matiné*, there is a part entitled "Ver rojo" [To See Red], which is rather dramatic: a kind of red waterfall drags human figures, horses, objects, soldiers, etc. When Sylvia first suggested very dramatic music, I understood that in this case the image would be much more effective with a totally different kind of music. With that in mind, Sylvia came up with a version of "Moon River" that is just heartbreaking.

IK Why are there so many decapitations, accidents in which big rocks fall on people, lost bunnies, etc. in your video work (as in *Where Are You?* [1999])?

LP Because just when you think that everything is perfect . . . bam! You get blindsided. When you get distracted by life . . . bam! Suddenly you're forced to experience death. You seem healthy, healthy, and . . . bam! The rock on the head. The little bunny was there with me, and suddenly . . . where did he go [Fig. 33]? And that's how it is: between life and death, between what you receive and what you lose. That, I presume, is the game: I am a realist.

15. "Mambrú went to war" is a popular song of French origins that was composed by French soldiers during the eighteenth century to ridicule the Duke of Marlborough, John Churchill (1650–1722), a prominent British soldier who had repeatedly defeated the French armies. The burlesque song, "Marlborough s'en va-t-en guerre," was popularized in the palace of Versailles, where the nanny of Marie Antoinette sang it to their children. The Spanish troops, who were allied with the French, brought the song back to Spain with the pronunciation of "Mambrú."

IK The Argentine critic Miguel Briante spoke of an "exasperating, cruel objectivity"[16] when describing your work in the 1970s. I assume he was talking about the intense literality implicit in the way you represented objects. Interestingly, that cruelty has resurfaced, been transfigured, and is deployed quite openly in the videos, as if over the years you progressively abandoned your inhibitions and allowed yourself to express a horror that surges from behind the tenderness.

LP Until now there was cruelty with laughter, but in the last movie, *Matinee/ Matiné*, the dramatic element appears without humor, as in the segment I just mentioned, "To See Red." And I think that has to do with the fact that a moment arrived when everything on television was horrifying: the tsunamis, the environmental catastrophes. . . . Evidently I was affected by the news of these events. The television aspect is related to the aesthetic of my segments, because you see the drama and then immediately they cut to a Coca-Cola ad. They are like little slices of horror that you don't know how to digest.

Fig. 33. *Where Are You?*, 1999.

IK As we were discussing earlier, photography, and then later video, resulted in a significant change in the way that you relate to the knowledge of technique. First the three-dimensional objects appear, primarily small figurines resting against shelves, which implies a radical shift in technique. In this sense, what does the term "well done" mean for you now?

LP It seems to me that every proposal has a good solution, a solution that is kind of bad, and one that is brilliant, technically speaking. Even if you decide to leave everything dirty, that is still a formal solution to a problem. What I mean is that it is impossible to extract oneself from the question of form; the idea isn't enough.

IK And for you, in your work, what has to be particularly "well done?" What do you pay the most attention to?

16. Miguel Briante, "Liliana Porter: obra en marcha," *Confirmado* (Buenos Aires, 1977): 49.

LP It's hard to say, but you know when something works or doesn't work, from the perspective of the composition: if it's good there on the left, or if it has to go more toward the right, or whatever. Everything has meaning. I think a lot about this issue with respect to art students, because it is a matter of learning: what is the measurement, is this the right space, why is this piece hanging instead of resting against a wall, etc. In other words, starting way back and then finally wondering why the canvas has four pegs, and if another support might be better. In this light, what is "well done" encompasses, in the most fundamental way, the medium, the technique, the presentation, the content, everything that one learns little by little. And at a certain point you don't even realize you're doing it.

IK How do you think art should be taught?

LP In art schools, courses are usually taught from the perspective of technique: sculpture, painting, drawing, and there are more and more techniques all the time. With this approach, even if you spent your whole life on it you wouldn't be able to learn everything there is to learn. A much better format, I think, would be to have an ideas workshop, so that afterward you could get to technique, and you could even invent a technique for each new concept.

IK Can you imagine what that concept workshop would be like for students who have no previous knowledge of art?

LP I think the important thing would be to motivate them to be conscious of how strange the phenomenon of art is, to be aware of the elements they use and why; and if they are breaking away from a tradition, to ask themselves why.

IK How do you envision your future work?

LP I realize that all my life I've done the same thing, and I doubt I will stop doing it: the same question phrased in a different way. The good thing about my age is that you know that you are always going to end up being yourself, so you don't have to worry about being consistent. What most appeals to me right now would be to develop a theater piece and produce it in video. I don't know the first thing about doing theater, but I think that in some sense it's an advantage not having learned the technique, because you do things more easily, without any awareness of whether or not you are breaking away from tradition.

RECURRENCES AND OBSESSIONS

IK In your work there are various themes that repeat themselves over the years: corrections, reconstructions, and repetitions, among others.

LP Regarding corrections, it's hard for me to remember when I started. I think I began with a piece that is called *Four Corrections* [1991], which is made up of four canvases, of which the fourth is a bit taller, so I correct that little piece, marking it with a line. I also made a scribble "corrected" in red. The idea is that it is impossible to correct a scribble, because a scribble, one assumes, is the only thing that, conceptually speaking, cannot be wrong. What interests me about this is that correcting it is very similar to what we do all the time when we are trying to grasp something, searching for a theory for things, which is actually sort of funny because it is simply impossible. What I mean to say is that we never know what the final result will be, and our obsession with knowing ends up being a kind of involuntary exercise in humor. Another thing that fascinates me about the scribble is that it reminds me of school, when they would correct something in math that I didn't understand (and I seriously didn't understand), with that steady, sure hand that was so. . . .

IK Totalitarian.

LP Exactly.

IK I wonder if you could tell the story about the attack on the painting *The Witness* when it was exhibited at MoMA, since it is so connected to the topic of the scribble and the correction.

LP *The Witness* [1990] is a painting that features a mirror and a Mickey Mouse looking at himself in the mirror. Then there is a three-dimensional shelf with a crayon resting on it. In other words, the crayon is on our side, and Mickey and the mirror are in the virtual plane of the picture. The crayon resting on the shelf was used to scribble something on the canvas.

The piece was included in the exhibition *Latin American Artists of the Twentieth Century* [1993] at MoMA. The day the show opened, a man came, ripped out the crayon that was affixed to the shelf, and scribbled something next to the scribble that was already there. Can you even picture it—the

Fig. 34. *The Correction*, 2003.

museum people called me, beside themselves, and when I went to see what had happened, I decided that the man's scribble was better than mine (more spontaneous, more rushed . . .), and so I just signed the canvas again and that was that.

IK Does the scribble represent something like the image of what an artist does?

LP Yes, it is a gesture that represents art [Fig. 34].

IK The same gesture appears in those works that feature a little man drawing a long line, much larger than his own body.

LP There is a tiny pedestal stuck to the wall with a tiny little man who must be about a centimeter tall, who drew a huge scribble on the wall.

IK I think it's quite telling that this specific image would be the image of art for you: something that could be "anything," an image that can't be corrected because there are no real criteria. Another recurrent theme in your work is that of reconstruction.

LP That's right, and I continue to invent other versions, other reconstructions. The first one was a photo of a broken Mickey, comprised of pieces of Murano glass. Standing on a shelf next to the photo was the same Mickey, but whole, untouched, perfect. The piece is like a magic trick that presents the possibility

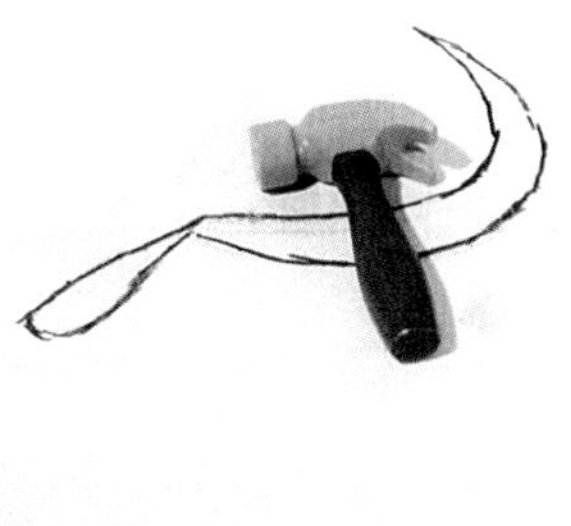

Fig. 35. *Drawing with Plastic Hammer*, 1993–95.

of turning back the clock, or of fixing something so perfectly that it shows no scars or marks at all. In other words, two ideas that are very optimistic, but simultaneously impossible. For me, these reconstructions are metaphors for things that you do that can't be fixed, that can't change. I'm not sure, but I think it was Borges who said that to repent is to alter the past. Anyway, I love that argument, and I recreated it with penguins, with a salt shaker, with different characters and in different formats.

IK Why is it that when you find an idea that interests you, as in the case of these two that we just discussed, you revisit it in so many pieces, over such a long period of time?

LP For me to make an isolated artwork would be completely odd; in general I feel the need to go back and do it again, to go back and say it again, either because I didn't fully digest it or because I still have more to say. And maybe it happens because I started out as a printmaker: when you make a print and execute it forty times, the image becomes a mantra.

IK In your work, other kinds of repetitions appear, as well: different versions of the same image done in different techniques and on different supports, as in the case of the hammer and sickle [Fig. 35].

LP In that case, I think I did the photo in preparation for a painting, and then I did it as a photograph, and in silkscreen. The possibility of having three versions of the same image is interesting, because they each have a different value. That is, the painting is expensive (because it is an original), and the photo and the print have a number of copies. It is the same exact image, but the convention of the canvas makes it more expensive, which I think is brilliant; even when the image in question is that one in particular, the reconstruction of a symbol, the drawing of a sickle and the photo of a little plastic hammer.

IK Did you conceive that image as one of the dialogues?

LP As a dialogue of meanings: an image that means something and nothing at the same time. I am drawn to those symbols in the same way that I am interested in Che's face. I think it's incredible how you find such a motley assortment of people walking down the street wearing T-shirts with Che's image, and many of them don't even know who he was. I am intrigued by the way that image is transformed and takes on another meaning. For some people, it is an image that is familiar and at the same time unfamiliar. Isn't that interesting?

IK Yes, but unlike the figure of Che—now such a popular image—the hammer and sickle do not enjoy such a massive kind of circulation, and, in that sense, the fact that you chose that image and reconstructed it with what you had at hand (a pencil line and a toy hammer) seems to me to be a singular and tremendously powerful political act, because of both the persistence and the meaninglessness that it conveys. Is there something of nostalgia or belief in the selection of that image?

LP What mattered to me was the fact that it is impossible not to recognize it as the symbol of Communism and yet at the same time it is, as the title indicates, a *Drawing with Plastic Hammer* [1993–95]. So the image can either be highly charged with meaning or absolutely stripped of meaning. That interest has to do with the difference between the moment of the utopias and a more present moment in which utopias have been weakened. I did the piece precisely at a juncture in which there was a shift in values.

IK Repetition also has an essential place in the works themselves; as we see in several pieces you did in the 1970s and 1980s, when an image appears repeated on different levels of representation. This is the case, for example, of that painting [*The Riddle,* 1987] where we find drawings of a triangle, a sphere, and a cube, and then the same images, but three-dimensional, resting on the edge of the stretcher. We also see this in those geometric wooden objects with drawings of the geometric figures on their surfaces.

LP I was trying to understand what they were about, and that's why I said the same thing in different ways, to see if I could find a way to define the thing.

Fig. 36. *To Go Back*, 2001.

It's a bit like the Kabbalists' quest: somewhere among the letters of the Holy Book they searched for the name in capital letters; a formula that finally spoke the name, God. And then there is that fantastic poem by Borges, "The Golem," that talks about this, too. The conclusion, for Borges, is that we will not arrive at the archetype, and our actions are ultimately rehearsals. The interesting thing here is that this problem has to do with art, because the model, in art, is really a representation.

IK The images of the little house, the road, and the figure walking are significant in your work, even from the metaphorical point of view, and they are very connected, I think, with empty space, another seminal element of your work [Fig. 36]. The empty space has a fundamental compositional quality as well as a philosophical quality: it is space, the enormous, empty, solitary world that the characters must traverse on their way to or from that image of the little house. The house and the empty space are, as such, two essential emotional nuclei of your work.

LP The little man (or any of the characters) is always leaving and returning to that little house, the place where he is safe, the place of knowledge or truth. It may sound corny, but it's kind of like the traveler who walks through life, yet knows that the possibility of going home is always there. I made many versions of that image. One, for example, features a jug with the little house sketched on its surface, and the line representing the path goes from the jug to the floor, suggesting the idea that the traveler has to cross through various virtual spaces in his trajectory.

IK The traveler crosses through impossible borders, like an Alice in Wonderland. In addition to the obvious figure of the little traveling man, suitcase in hand, sometimes I get the feeling that all the characters in your work are voyagers traversing those empty spaces until they run into a portraitist—you—and sometimes other characters, a whole range of types.

LP I should add that the image of the house is something that I very clearly share with my mother, who was also a printmaker and had lost much of her family to a fire in her house.

IK Your mother was a printmaker?

LP Actually, my mother was a writer; but when I got married she began making prints, and she even won a top prize at the Salón Nacional in Buenos Aires. Since she was from a Romanian family, she had that style of little, intricate, *naif* sorts of things, and she was always drawing images of the house. In her case I imagine that this recurring image had to do with the fact that she lost most of her family in a fire. A few years ago the Fundación Andreani [Buenos Aires, 1999] invited me to put together a show, and they suggested that I exhibit my works along with works by my mother. It was an incredible experience: as I explored my mother's work while organizing the exhibition, I questioned what her work had in common with mine, which I believed to be somewhat more conceptual and emptier. Suddenly I understood that she had had quite an influence on me, especially with regard to the image of the house.

IK It's very revealing that, in some way, the house takes on another meaning, even more so when one considers your life as an immigrant in the United States. Having arrived at this point, I think it would be very useful for us to talk about romances, which are a subtheme in the dialogues you create with your figures, and valuable in the ethic that they exude.

LP Yes, especially in the film, there is a segment entitled "Besos" [Kisses], in which impossible pairs of characters are shown kissing. For example, a soccer player with a postcard of a bishop from the Italian Renaissance. Then there is Minnie kissing Che, a Nazi kissing a dog that is actually a little doggie bank, and a little woman with a potato. To engineer these encounters, I had to do a number of tests first. In the case of the dog and the Nazi, the incredible thing is that one senses that the Nazi changes expression with the kiss, as if the man was worried and said to himself, "What a mess I've gotten myself into!" Honestly, I don't know which of the two is more worried, the Nazi or the dog! What matters is that you clearly perceive that these two figures have fallen in love. In a way, it's as if we've all gone to heaven and everyone has made peace with one another.

IK The *Dialogues* series, which you began in the early 1990s, has the same starting point: the encounter between beings that are different in the sense of species, status, condition.

LP Yes. For example, the dialogue between Christ (which is a plastic gold lamp with a plug) who shares a complicit gaze with a wooden penguin [*Dialogue (with Penguin)*, 1999], in which you feel that Christ, from the great beyond, is dispensing advice to the worried penguin. . . .

IK Is the Forced labor series (from 2004), executed with tiny, three-dimensional figures, a continuation of the theme of the work presented in the video *Drum Solo* [2000]?

LP In some way, yes. The first one I did was the one of the little man shoveling black dirt, which always made me laugh, because the black earth situated in an exhibition space was, for a long time, a cliché of the work of a Latin American artist in New York.

IK Until now you have only mentioned your exhibition at MoMA's Project Room as a milestone in your earlier years, in 1973, but following that there were a number of important solo and group shows. Of these, which do you feel were especially meaningful because they gave you a chance to reflect on your own work, or because they gave you a recognition that you hadn't enjoyed previously?

LP One was the exhibition at the Bronx Museum in New York [1992], curated by Marisol Nieves with Mari Carmen Ramírez. It was very well done and allowed me to see my whole body of work all at once (there was a huge number of pieces that I hadn't seen in a long time that they borrowed from Argentina and from museums). It's like publishing a book: they are learning experiences that allow you to move on to the next phase.

On the other hand, the invitation to exhibit at the New Museum in dialogue with Marcel Broodthaers [2011] was one of the most moving experiences I have

Fig. 37. Installation view of *Museum as Hub: The Incongruous Image—Marcel Broodthaers and Liliana Porter*, New Museum, New York, 2011.

had in recent years. The structure of the exhibit itself, incredibly, was very similar to that of my dialogues, in which I force two characters of different origins and temporalities to confront each other and connect [Fig. 37]. In this show, I found myself facing an artist I had never met personally, whom I had not studied in any depth, and who, on top of it, thought in French. And suddenly, in this exhibition, the connection with him became natural and the conversation easy: we both liked Magritte, the idea of the voyage, the appropriation of infantile images. . . .

I also remember the exhibition at the Fundación San Telmo [Buenos Aires, 1990]; yet for me the most relevant of all was the one you curated [Centro Cultural Recoleta, Buenos Aires, 2003], because it included the films and many other pieces I hadn't exhibited in years, especially the black-and-white photographs of the original sets, and through these works people could see where the images of the paintings and the prints had come from. Recently, in 2009, Tobias Ostrander curated *Línea de tiempo*, a solo exhibition at the Museo Tamayo in Mexico City. The previous solo exhibition in Mexico was my first show at Galeria Proteo when I was seventeen years old, so this show, fifty years later, was for me a very moving and important experience. I was pleased with Tobias's intelligent concept of the show and its wonderful presentation.

IK Beyond the curatorial hypothesis, that exhibition at Centro Cultural Recoleta made a big impression in Buenos Aires; it was at that moment that your work became known on a more massive scale and ultimately became quite influential among new generations of artists.

LP I think so. That was total happiness. In fact, I think every exhibition helps me to continue, forces me to think. In public, you transform a bit, create some distance between yourself and your work. One activity that brings great, great joy is showing the videos, especially when I show them in places like Uruguay or Argentina, because in some way the audience is like me and laughs when I laugh. (This happens a lot when I go to universities here [in the United States] to give a talk, show a video. . . . Here I observe a very different reaction. This is important. It's as if I've done a different piece.)

IK One of the most curious surprises to come out of these conversations is your relationship with Argentina. Until now, I had always thought that the fact of living for so many years in the United States had distanced you from your home country.

LP For me Argentina represents very personal presences: my childhood, my adolescence, my family, my friends, the language, and all of that is more or less in order inside of me. And I don't have an impermeable position with regard to the context in which I live. On the contrary, I feel that I don't have any filter at all—sometimes I go to Buenos Aires and I forget the codes. For example, that ambiguous relationship one has with one's doctor in Argentina. Instead of telling you that he's going to have to cut off your arm, he'll tell you that everything's fine and then he'll go and tell the truth to your aunt. Here in the United States, that doesn't exist, things are literal here, and people are used to that. In that sense, I like the literal approach better. It's a lot less work.

And yet, even though I have spent forty-eight years of my life in this country, at the university I always had such a hard time remembering students' names, but if there was a Latino named Pérez or García I always retained it right away [Fig. 38]. In short, the great advantage one has in situations like mine is that you have a much larger world, or a house with many more rooms. And without a doubt your work needs all those early experiences that make you who you are.

IK Precisely. One axis that you explore in your work is translation, the problem of the many different ways one can say the same thing, as if your displacements (your years in Mexico and then your move to New York) determined your questions about the world in a very definitive way. It almost seems as if that initial surprise at the existence of different parallel worlds and the way of

Fig. 38. Liliana Porter teaching at Queens College, New York, c. 1998.

saying things in multiple ways eventually became one of your most essential concerns. Without nostalgia, I should add.

LP Yes. Nostalgia is something that doesn't appeal to me. I don't think, for example, about how I had a childhood, and then became an adolescent, and now I'm an adult. The sensation I have, instead—and this is strange—is that everything is happening at the same time, or I carry everything with me.

ART AND HAPPINESS

IK Going back to the question about the process of producing your work that we discussed at the start of this conversation, I want to ask you, with regard to the objects, the toys: How does the process of conceptual or performative construction occur in the encounters you create with your figures? Do you start to play with them until something appears, or do you have a preexisting idea or image that you then carry out?

LP Let me give you an example. The other day in San Telmo, I found an old Bakelite doll with a rifle. If you place it, standing, alone on a table, something has already happened . . . and it's ready. People are always telling me, "You have to see *Toy Story*, you're going to love it," things like that, but it's the opposite that interests me, the objects I choose already come loaded with their plots . . . I add almost nothing. The essential thing is the encounter with those elements, though I couldn't explain exactly what I find in them. What I am trying to say is that everybody has their own plots, almost like a repertoire of themes, these notions are not alien to who I am—on the contrary, in fact, they are inseparable from who I am and they repeat themselves over and over. They are common ideas: horror, falling, basic things, but when you tease them out of their circumstances, they create something that is different from what happens when you add a script.

The object and its characteristics come together (the face, the colors, the way it's made, its childishness, its violence) with attributes that do not jibe.

And so I choose them without thinking too much. On the other hand, finding a place for an object depends on a whole process, an order: I have to find the perfect day when I really feel like working, and one of the conditions I need to work is to generate a place of well-being. The process is very pleasant: I prepare the camera, I bring the objects, and I begin to practice until suddenly something happens. It's fantastic!

Each case is different. Some are very clear from the outset and others require more tests or complexities, as was the case with the Kennedy car in the last video. . . . I didn't know where that image was coming from or what it was asking of me, but it was very clear that something was going to happen. Finally the music appeared, the superimposition of the sound, and that opened another door that lent significant meaning to the image. Music is very manipulative.

The essential thing is that what you do has to be enjoyable. There are times when I am truly moved. I remember a large painting [*The Resemblance*, 2007] of a landscape and a tiny little house against an almost white background. I took a photo of a little house, framed it, placed it sideways, and then took a photo of the whole thing sideways [Fig. 39]. Then I affixed a little shelf on the canvas, rested the framed photograph against it, and took another photo of that image. In other words, on top of the shelf, in the end, there was a framed photo that represented a framed sidelong photo that featured the image of the house. Then I sat down and on the canvas I began to paint that landscape, the same landscape I was looking at in the photo, as if it were my model. That entire process, for me, is so moving. . . .

IK What is it that moves you? That your model has ended up so far away, beneath so many layers of representation?

LP First, there is a great pleasure in doing it. But simultaneously, the matter of time emerges and, through the gesture of copying the image, it seems that there is some logic at work that you understood. What stirs me emotionally is realizing, finally, that one is always touching the surfaces of things. That's where it is, that's the heart of what moves me emotionally. The solitude of the object, what gets lost . . . everything is focused on one instant of pleasure: the paint and the workshop smell nice. . . . You like it, and everything blends together, the raw and the subtle, everything at the same time.

IK The emotion that the object conveys is related to a human feeling: animism is an essential aspect of your work.

LP Totally. My work couldn't possibly be any more animistic!

IK In your life, you practice a very particular kind of philosophy. You always say that to be happy you have to invent or create that happiness, as if happiness had a lot to do with faith, but with a faith driven by will. In that sense, it's quite interesting that your work deals with life issues that are not necessarily happy. How do you think through that relationship between the dramatic scripts of your life and your way of living?

LP I think that this has a lot to do with my mother. She had eight siblings who died, one after the other, one each year. And when all she had left was a sister, her father, and her mother, this sister and her father died when the house caught fire. And yet the house that I lived in as a child was a happy house: the garden,

Fig. 39. *The Resemblance* (detail), 2007.

the fireplace, the games. Whenever we invited friends over, my mother would get the house ready and make delicious food. How she managed to overcome the pain of losing her family is a mystery to me, and yet everything she did was aimed at making us happy, which was a fundamental lesson for me, for my own life. My paternal grandmother, who was Jewish, for example, was not at all happy about my mother not being Jewish, but my mother included her in our life and always spoke kindly of her. I should add, too, that my mother was not denying or blocking out the things that she went through. She just believed that it was possible to build something in spite of tragedy.

IK Do you feel Jewish?

LP Yes. My parents were atheist when they were young, but I participated in a Jewish way of eating, thinking, and looking at the world. Whenever I cross paths with someone who is anti-Semitic, it makes me angry because it's like speaking poorly of my grandmother. I sense that my reaction goes beyond religion or ideology, or maybe it hits closer to home, I don't know. The Jewish side is embedded in many aspects of my life. As is being Latin American, in the sense that you can go to a five-star restaurant with the director of a New York museum and be waited on by a Peruvian or Mexican waiter, and the truth is that you feel more sympathetic to the waiter than to the person you're eating with.

IK Let's go back and pick up the thread when we were talking about your theory of happiness, your relationship with your mother, and the terrible tragedies that take place in your work.

LP My work derives from the reflection that we do not understand anything and that we will never solve the basic question of why we are on this planet, and from the horrifying realization that if a man can be dismembered in a wartime situation, I can also be the person doing the dismembering; I could learn how to use a chainsaw. On the other hand, hearing incredible music or seeing a splendid work of art makes me feel that I also have the potential of being sublime. I feel that in some way I am guilty of the horror of the former as well as the wonder of the latter.

IK With regard to this, I'd like to return to a theme that emerges in the dialogue pieces. In these works, you propose encounters between beings that communicate despite vast differences: figures that speak from several planes of representation, that share conversation despite belonging to different species, who fall in love from the place of their essentially impossible communication. I interpret those encounters as the assertion of a philosophical, political possibility in connection to recognition and the encounter with the "other."

LP What you say is interesting, because some people interpret them as the opposite.

IK As the staging of an impossibility?

LP Exactly, but I don't agree. Like you, I think that the idea is actually rather hopeful. With regard to the relationship between my life and my art, I would say that I have a hard time separating the two in my mind. During the crises I have gone through in my life (illnesses, separations, etc.), art was always the most constant, solid thing I had within myself; something that accompanied me and provided a coherence, a structure, a means for being firmly connected with the task of staying alive without collapsing.

Making art or envisioning life from the perspective of art, at least for me, allows for a certain degree of sanity. In this sense, I am interested in being as healthy as possible and, as a consequence, as happy as possible—maybe because

I think that the most normal thing is to be completely crazy and very unhappy. And if you manage to achieve the opposite, you win. It's a kind of game.

I think we can agree that life is basically terrible. The easiest thing in the world is to be on the verge of tears, always. Evidently everything is very, very strange. You just turn up here, all of a sudden, and you have a very short window of time to figure it out. What human beings do with their time here turns out to be quite touching: one man decides to be a cook, another becomes a watchmaker, someone else spends time collecting bottle caps, etc. And the distractions crop up very fast: norms, situations, trends, relationships, forms to fill out, etc., which distract us from the essential issue. And sitting down to ponder what life is really about seems like a kind of bourgeois luxury, a pastime.

So, on this point, I would have to say that what art gives me is awareness. Awareness of this short period of time that we have, on one hand, and on the other hand, a way of understanding reality. It may sound corny or dramatic, but for me art is a form of salvation.

IK It's an idea that seems very serious, and even idealistic, for someone who is so immersed in art as a professional career, with all the cynicism that is attached. How, then, does this concept of art as salvation coexist with the concept of art as a career?

LP Well, of course, you have to be very careful. Art also infiltrates, very quickly, that "distractive" structure. I'm referring to paperwork, a willingness to fill out forms. The work of art, in its personification as object, enters immediately into that whole "logical" world: market, fame, collectors, measurements, technique, publications, history, restoration, dates, interviews, etc., that unwittingly separates art from what is essential. Despite all of that, art helps us to think, to structure a possible language for communication amongst ourselves. Of course, I ask myself: Can this be true? Because, let's be frank: What is it that we need to communicate? Or: What is it that we call "essential"?

IK Which historical artworks do you feel connected to? Which artworks embody what you refer to as "pure substance"?

LP I recently visited the Thyssen-Bornemisza Museum, in Madrid, to view those tiny portraits from the 1400s, which are truly incredible: *Portrait of a Man*, *Portrait of a Young Man*. Extraordinary! And when you look into the eyes of those models, they seem so alive, so present. And you can imagine the painter who painted them looking at their faces as he painted, and you feel that there

Fig. 40. *Levitating Rabbit*, 2008.

is an important moral lesson behind the experience of seeing this. But what? I feel that a part of you is somehow reconciled. At the museum there is a small oil painting by Morandi. I look at it and I feel the urge to start crying. It's like seeing the Three Wise Men and confirming the fact of their existence. That—quite incredibly—they exist, and what we were told as children was true!

IK The question of the relationship between art and life has to do not only with the content of your work but also with the way in which you relate to everyday life, when you are working or talking with friends. In this sense, anyone who knows you, knows that you have a very keen sense for objects that surround you (a connection that allows you to reclaim the simple imaginary world of childhood to illuminate the complexity of the adult world, a lucid quality like that of María Elena Walsh[17]), and I believe that this comes through in your work in a totally fluid way.

LP I suppose that being an artist is like having a lens through which one sees everything: everybody has their own particular obsessions and they tend to see only what they really find interesting. In other words, if you are a colorist painter,

17. María Elena Walsh (1930–2011) was an Argentine poet, writer, musician, singer-songwriter, playwright, and composer, especially famous for her children's works.

you notice colors, and if you are fascinated by light, then you gravitate toward Rembrandt, etc. In my case, I think that humor is an important factor; because of humor, I can express a certain degree of compassion.

IK Beyond the series of drawings of the little boat that you did when you were in the middle of a personal crisis, in 1977, do you consider your work to be autobiographical?

LP Yes. In each of my pieces you can find a correlation with personal experiences, and the way those experiences affected me. For example, in *Levitating Rabbit* [2008] sometimes I think that it's me trying to keep my head above the general calamities that strike this earth. It is not a realist portrait; it must be a portrait of rabbit desire or intention [Fig. 40].

With regard to my way of feeling and thinking, I think that both are well summarized in the segment from the *Matinee/Matiné* [2009] video called "Chicken Salad." It's funny and tragic at the same time, naturalist or literal, but incomprehensible. It is basically a dislocated situation in every sense: the "chicken" is actually a duck, though it's not really a duck but a windup toy; the lettuce acts like a missile, a kind of bomb that falls onto this duck unexpectedly, without warning, and everything is connected to or recalls, for a brief moment, a chicken salad—an inedible salad, of course. It's pure metaphor. Its violence inspires laughter, though in reality it's quite tragic.

IK In what way do you think that your work, particularly the more recent pieces, no longer represents your feelings, your life, but rather collective life and history itself?

LP I think paintings like *Levitating Rabbit* and *Untitled with Fallen Chairs* [2009], as well as a series of works on paper that feature these kinds of "tsunamis"—great waves that drag furniture, people, all kinds of things—have to do with the environmental disasters and wars that we see every day in the news media. Especially if one's everyday life is far removed from that reality, a conflict is generated between the personal possibility of pleasure and tranquility and the horrific misfortune of others. Human experiences cannot be separated so easily: "This is mine, this is yours." There is something in every experience that makes it common or collective. And so I interpret these works as coming out of a desire to live, or reflect, even though it's just through art, the disaster that feels very close, too close. . . .

Fig. 41. Liliana Porter in her studio, Franklin Street, New York, 1980s.

IK Do you think that way of conceiving a work of art might extend to other pieces that are not necessarily related to anything tragic?

LP Yes. I think that what makes a person read a book or look at a painting, in other words what makes someone interested in something, has to do with what I was talking about before: that nothing is entirely yours or entirely mine. It almost seems as if you seek to listen to what, maybe, in some way, you need to say [Figs. 41 & 42].

Fig. 42. Liliana Porter in her studio, Rhinebeck, New York, 2008.

INTRODUCCIÓN

Este libro, el séptimo de la serie Conversaciones/Conversations de la Fundación Cisneros (FC)/Colección Patricia Phelps de Cisneros (CPPC), explora la trayectoria de Liliana Porter desde la década de los sesenta hasta el presente y revela su proceso de producción a través de una brillante conversación con la curadora Inés Katzenstein. Puede que el lector se sorprenda al observar que sus trabajos, tan rigurosos e intelectuales, evidencian con frecuencia un sentido del humor que va desde lo ingenioso y gracioso hasta a la comedia intelectual. Su obra, desde los múltiples y el 'arte de correo' creados en el New York Graphic Workshop [Taller Gráfico de Nueva York], fundado en los sesenta con Luis Camnitzer y José Guillermo Castillo, hasta sus más recientes videos, merecen nuestra meticulosa consideración, y apreciaremos cómo las técnicas utilizadas, ya sean de grabado, dibujo, fotografía, pintura o video, están específicamente determinadas por las ideas que desea expresar.

La aguda introducción de Gregory Volk enfatiza la tendencia tanto hacia la inventiva como hacia el intervencionismo en el trabajo de Porter y su habilidad para reconciliar dialécticas opuestas: la sensibilidad con sofisticación, la esperanza con el dolor, lo diminuto con lo inmenso, lo común u ordinario con lo inusual, el silencio con la comunicación. Estas aparentes contradicciones son las que convierten sus creaciones en algo "humanamente rico".

Inés Katzenstein describe la obra de Porter como un acto de conocimiento que emplea el humor como metodología. En su extensa conversación con la artista, Katzenstein extrae importantes matices de la biografía de Porter, sus métodos de trabajo y procesos conceptuales, sus asociaciones personales y profesionales, sus influencias artísticas, su identificación con su nativa cultura argentina, y su apreciación por la ciudad de Nueva York, su hogar adoptivo durante los últimos cuarenta años, ese lugar donde "todo es posible". En el transcurso de la charla, queda claro que para Porter, puede también decirse que "todo tiene posibilidades"—los objetos y gestos y las convenciones del proceso de hacer arte son transformados a través de yuxtaposiciones, reconstrucciones y re-contextualizaciones efectuadas por la artista.

Le estoy profundamente agradecido a Liliana Porter por permitirnos la realización de este documento. Nos proporciona profunda gratificación sumar su voz a las otras de esta serie con el fin de cumplir con la misión de la Colección

Patricia Phelps de Cisneros: preservar de primera mano las historias de artistas e intelectuales latinoamericanos líderes. Inés Katzenstein, una antigua promotora del trabajo de Porter, ha probado ser una extraordinaria interlocutora, y Gregory Volk, quien ha escrito con gran conocimiento y precisión acerca de Liliana Porter en otras ocasiones, ha contribuido a crear un excelente marco para las propias palabras de Porter, las cuales nunca habían sido publicadas a esta escala. Extiendo mi sincera apreciación a Satoshi Tabuchi, el bibliotecario de la CPPC, por su diligencia para investigar el magnífico material adicional para la versión electrónica de esta publicación. Los libros electrónicos *(e-books)* son un nuevo y estimulante proyecto que ofrecerá la labor y las palabras registradas en Conversaciones / Conversations, a un público más numeroso y con mayor profundidad. Quiero también agradecer a Donna Wingate e Ileen Kohn por concretar la misión de la CPPC a través del programa de publicaciones y extender mi reconocimiento una vez más a Marquand Books por su dedicación en la producción de impecables volúmenes.

Gabriel Pérez-Barreiro

Director, Colección Patricia Phelps de Cisneros

UNA TERRIBLE SIMPLICIDAD
Acerca del arte de Liliana Porter

Gregory Volk

Muchos de los trabajos claves de Liliana Porter de los años sesenta y setenta surgen de su relación tenaz, desafiante y experimental con el grabado y con lo que ella llama "arte boludo" o *dumbass art* en esta entrevista con Inés Katzenstein. Para Porter, el arte boludo consiste en utilizar materiales extremadamente simples, cotidianos y aparentemente sin importancia, en lugar de cosas hermosas, extravagantes o repletas de contenido. Estos objetos mundanos (un clavo, un tornillo, una línea dibujada, un trozo de hilo colgado) retienen su normalidad y paralelamente adquieren un contexto nuevo e inquietante, en un marco de asombro, humor y catarsis, y en especial cargados con la consideración e inteligencia usual característicos de su estilo. Una pieza temprana, de 1968, titulada *Wrinkle* [*Arruga*], consiste en diez grabados que registran las etapas sucesivas de una hoja de papel que fue plegada, doblada, arrugada y estrujada en una bola. Un papel arrugado es extremadamente banal, es un gesto que hacemos con frecuencia. Pero, preservar, registrar y transformar cuidadosamente este objeto descartable, es harina de otro costal. En los grabados de Porter, la destrucción proyecta una belleza sutil. Una simple hoja de papel deshecha, encapsula una transformación; al tiempo que sugiere topografía y geología, los paisajes de planetas distantes vistos a través de poderosos telescopios, fotografías ampliadas de los contornos de la piel e incluso los diferentes estadios de la vida humana, desde la tersa juventud hasta la vejez arrugada. En respuesta a esta serie, Emmett Williams, el tremendo poeta-artista de Fluxus, la comparó con: "naturalezas muertas de *action painting*", "una naturaleza muerta con un proceso dinámico", "terremotos", "ondas en el agua" y "las montañas de la Tierra arrugada y los valles de la luna".

En la década de los setenta, Liliana Porter intervino libremente famosas e históricas imágenes de arte. Parte de la gracia de esta acción involucra extrañas sensibilidades y constituye una investigación sofisticada de originales y reproducciones, pinturas y grabados retocados. Para su grabado *The Magician* [*El Mago*] de 1977, Porter tomó una reproducción de una pintura de René Magritte titulada *The Magician (Self-Portrait with Four Arms)* [*El Mago (Autorretrato con cuatro brazos)*] de 1952 en la que Magritte se halla comiendo, cortando carne en un plato y sirviéndose una copa de vino todo a la misma vez, y ella sobre impuso su propia mano sosteniendo un tenedor con el que intenta darle a Magritte una pequeña porción de pastel de verdad. Hemos visto la obra de Magritte docenas y posiblemente cientos de veces; por lo general en tarjetas, afiches y reproducciones en libros, lo cual demuestra cómo una pintura original se convierte en un objeto encontrado, reproducible y común. El intento absurdo de Porter de dar pastel a una imagen famosa reinventa la trivialidad de la imagen en algo alocado y único, que deriva en una conflagración descabellada de lo práctico y lo fantástico, al incrementar aún más lo que ya es de por sí una exageración surrealista. Es además, una escena sumamente graciosa.

Cuando uno coteja estos trabajos relativamente tempranos con su producción de la década de los ochenta y los noventa, se nota cómo ha migrado gradual pero decisivamente desde grabados (ya sean excéntricos y experimentales) hacia una práctica expandida que incluye fotografías, pinturas, dibujos, esculturas, videos e instalaciones; sobre todo una práctica marcada por constantes riesgos y exploraciones, una especie de juego "de todo o nada". En los ochenta es de particular importancia su decisión de emplear, de diferente modo, una variedad ecléctica (y siempre en expansión) de figurines, juguetes, animales, caricaturas y enseres insólitos del hogar encontrados en mercados de pulgas, tiendas de antigüedades y tiendas de *souvenirs*. En el estudio de Porter, varios anaqueles están densamente poblados por este elenco de personajes y objetos que incluye: osos, patos, vaqueros, soldados alemanes, botellas escondidas dentro de atuendos tejidos, pequeñas bailarinas, bailarines de tango a cuerda, un zorro que toca el tambor, pingüinos, cerditos, payasos, budistas japoneses, revolucionarios chinos y el Che Guevara, entre muchos otros.

A veces, los diversos figurines se presentan realmente como objetos incorporados en su obra. Otras veces son sujetos en fotografías, pinturas o dibujos, y en otras se revelan como actores de sus videos. Puede que los muestre solos (lo cual enfatiza el aura de soledad que generalmente impera en el trabajo de Porter), en pares o en grupos. Curiosas figuritas de humanos y animales suelen operar en un espacio inmenso y vacío, sin referencias o elementos que provean cierta guía o dirección al espectador. Esto lo logra con recursos mínimos, por ejemplo: fotografiando los materiales en contra o dentro de un espacio vacío (por lo general una hoja de papel en el taller) o colocándolos sobre un estante blanco. Estas simples acciones conllevan un impacto profundo. Sus pequeñas figuras parecen estar atrapadas por las distancias, atormentadas por inmensidades; en tanto que lucen pensativas, decisivas y desconcertadas en un mundo tan grande que excede cualquier tipo de comprensión o sentido de orden.

Wind [*Viento*], 2011, por ejemplo, es una fotografía de un pollito mullido de juguete, solitario, de pie en un espacio blanco y rodeado de pedacitos de papel supuestamente esparcidos por el viento. El observador registra que es un mero juguetito en un entorno manipulado; sin embargo, notamos algo penosamente conmovedor en este pollito, parado de esta manera en particular: es valiente y vulnerable a la vez, esperanzado y triste, y parece estar suspendido de camino hacia un destino incierto. Esto es exactamente lo que en realidad me afecta del arte de Porter. Una imagen que podría ser cursi e irónica, no lo es en absoluto. Por el contrario, es hermosa, intensa y misteriosamente impregnada de humanidad. Responde a nuestras aspiraciones y frustraciones colectivas, nuestra capacidad para el asombro y la consternación, nuestro interés en la libertad y nuestra dolorosa experiencia acerca de las limitaciones, restricciones y dudas.

Hay un gran momento en esta excelente entrevista, cuando Inés Katzenstein pregunta: "¿Qué es lo que tiene Nueva York que te dejó esta gran impresión?" A lo cual Porter responde: "Lo que más me impactó era esa sensación que da a veces Nueva York de que 'todo es posible', que si había inconvenientes para hacer algo, estas imposibilidades estarían más en mí misma que en el contexto". Ella se refiere a su experiencia como una joven argentina recién llegada a Nueva York, energizada por la ciudad exuberante; mas esta conciencia (o influencia o logro) de que "todo es posible" también caracteriza su arte. En otros pasajes de la conversación, Porter revela parte de su evolución y de sus ambiciones artísticas. "Igual tengo que pasar por esa etapa en la cual siento que estoy haciendo otra cosa, una acción imprecisa que no entiendo del todo, algo que está por revelárseme", anuncia. Luego declara, " . . . lo que me da el arte es conciencia. Conciencia de este corto plazo que tenemos, por un lado, y por otro, un medio para entenderme con la realidad. Aunque suene un poco cursi o dramático, te diría que para mí el arte es una forma de salvación".

Al leer lo que Porter tiene que decir acerca de su proceso artístico, y en particular su comentario donde afirma que el arte es una "forma de salvación", me sorprende no solamente cuánto esta expatriada argentina se conecta con el espíritu de la ciudad de Nueva York en donde "todo es posible", sino también con una veta visionaria en la literatura y en el arte americano que se origina en el siglo diecinueve con Ralph Waldo Emerson. Este notable poeta filósofo trascendentalista fue una figura de gran influencia sobre escritores y artistas de su entorno en Concord, Massachusetts –como Henry David Thoreau, Margaret Fuller, Walt Whitman, los pintores de Hudson River Schoool [la Escuela del Río Hudson], los pintores del oeste norteamericano y los luministas– e igualmente con artistas y escritores más tardíos como Edward Hopper, Barnett Newman, Agnes Martin y Sol LeWitt. "Los artistas conceptuales son místicos más que racionalistas", escribió LeWitt en *Sentences on Conceptual Art* [*Oraciones sobre el arte conceptual*], sonando francamente emersoniano. "Llegan a conclusiones donde la lógica no llega o alcanza". Ya que Emerson, un ex-ministro unitarista, gravitaba hacia la poesía y el arte en su búsqueda espiritual, tendía a hacer enormes reclamos sobre el arte, tomándolo como parte inseparable de preguntas sobre el carácter individual, el crecimiento psicológico, la revelación y la redención. Emerson desdeñaba el arte que no surgía de la inspiración galvanizada que perseguía; por el contrario, abogaba por una especie de ferocidad sin trabas, una fusión orgánica entre el arte y el ser, y una voluntad tenaz de tomar riesgos. Él creía que el formalismo en sí mismo no solucionaría nada; sin embargo, "la dependencia instantánea del formalismo con el alma", como escribió en 1844 en su ensayo "The Poet" [El poeta] (por cierto, la primera gran afirmación en los Estados Unidos acerca de las estrategias radicales y experimentales para hacer arte), podría ofrecer muchas posibilidades –formas artísticas flexibles que tomarían el talante de la psiquis del artista; un arte cerebral, apasionado, riesgoso, experimental y extraordinariamente abierto al mundo, dispuesto a descubrir nuevas formas (sin importar cuán poco ortodoxas) y capaz de transmitir ideas generadoras[1].

También en "The Poet", Emerson comenta sobre el uso de materiales y temas artísticos, al anunciar que "el pensamiento hace que todo pueda ser utilizado", –y luego agrega– "los objetos pequeños y humildes sirven tanto como los grandes símbolos . . . Estamos lejos de haber agotado el significado de los pocos símbolos que usamos. Todavía podemos llegar a usarlos con una simplicidad terrible"[2]. Aunque no es precisamente un precursor del siglo diecinueve al Pop, al Minimalismo ni al arte conceptual (tendencias que influenciaron a Liliana Porter y su obra); en realidad, Porter y Emerson no están lejos el uno del otro. Para Emerson, las cosas familiares, humildes e inconsecuentes podrían ser materia para un arte particularmente inquisitivo, cargado psicológicamente (y tal vez espiritualmente). Un parecer cercano a la búsqueda de Porter, quien emplea con frecuencia una variedad democrática de "objetos pequeños y humildes" (como el pollito de juguete) al igual que "grandes símbolos".

A un nivel, esta extensa colección de chucherías internacionales luce *kitsch* y devaluada: *souvenirs* baratos comprados en tiendas para turistas, algunos *tchotchkes* queridos por una tía vieja pero un tanto repulsivos, premios olvidados obtenidos en algún carnaval local, decoraciones plásticas para pasteles de bodas . . . Mas Porter encuentra una riqueza y potencial emocional en estos objetos inusuales que de otra manera serían enseres producidos en masa pululando por el mundo. Uno puede sentir que ella los adora y que se comunican

1. Ralph Waldo Emerson, "The Poet" [El poeta] (1844), en *The Portable Emerson* [*El Emerson portatil*], (ed.) Carl Bode, en colaboración con Malcolm Cowley (Nueva York: Penguin Books, 1981), 242.

2. Ibid., 245.

misteriosamente con ella. Uno percibe que los ha guardado por mucho tiempo, los ha analizado, estudiado sus expresiones, los ha tratado como individuos y ha compartido su vida con ellos. Son mudos pero muy comunicativos. En realidad no cuentan sino emanan historias, o mejor aún, pasajes y trozos de cuentos silenciosos, pistas de recuerdos, fragmentos de sueños. Es absolutamente cierto que Liliana Porter trabaja con objetos encontrados, además lo hace con una devoción e intensidad extraña y peculiar. De suerte tal que pueden funcionar como substitutos y embajadores utilizados para explorar las variables de la psiquis, la niñez y la memoria, conexiones y alienaciones de y con los otros, el amor (y su ruptura), el propósito, la alienación, los temores, la alegría ocasional, la cruda experiencia de crisis políticas e injusticias. El arte de Porter nunca es abiertamente autobiográfico, pero parece estar animado por una profunda búsqueda psicológica y social: la profundidad del ser en relación a una sociedad fraccionada y en conflicto.

En *The Explanation* [*La explicación*], 1991, dos figurines se encaran: un hombre solemne con traje negro y sombrero y un patito amarillo, tierno, con grandes pestañas. Aun cuando connotan diversos entornos, mundos y universos diferentes, intentan lograr algún tipo de entendimiento. Lo mismo sucede con *Dialogue with Alarm Clock* [*Diálogo con reloj despertador*], 2000, donde una mujer con un traje rosado (que sugiere haber sido arrancada de un pastel de bodas) simula estar conversando animadamente con una mamá cerdita y su lechoncito, que de hecho es un reloj despertador. Estos encuentros interpersonales, sorprendentes e inusuales, abundan en los trabajos de Porter. A la par, la empatía rebosa en ellos y es asombroso cómo uno siente ternura y afecto por estos personajes, a pesar de ser pequeñas chucherías.

Cuando uno contempla su producción de los ochenta y noventa y compara con la de los años sesenta y setenta, más concentrada en grabados, resulta tentador dividir su obra en un 'antes y después': antes, los grabados; después, los juguetes encontrados e incorporados de varios modos. Sin embargo, esta división simplista tiende a oscurecer la consistencia (y tenacidad exploradora) al acercarnos al enfoque desarrollado por Porter a través de los años. Se puede establecer una conexión con lo que sugirió brillantemente Inés Katzenstein en la introducción a esta entrevista. Katzenstein escribe: "En mi opinión, el trabajo de Porter exhibe su relación con la vida en un terreno artístico específico", y pasa a discutir cómo esta correlación apunta hacia varias preguntas: "¿A dónde vamos y a dónde pertenecemos? ¿Cómo vamos a relacionarnos con las personas que se cruzan por nuestras vidas? ¿Cómo podremos lograr una comunicación entre nosotros, si somos esencialmente seres distantes? ¿Cómo es posible que funcionemos a nivel social a través de códigos tan artificiales sin cuestionarlos? ¿Qué es la sabiduría? y ¿Cuál es la relación entre la práctica artística y la felicidad?" Inés Katzenstein está en lo correcto: estos siempre han sido los temas detrás de las inquietudes de Liliana Porter y, aun cuando ha utilizado diversas formas de explorarlos, permanecen como parte esencial en su arte. Otra conexión importante tiene que ver precisamente con cómo utiliza estos elementos de manera maravillosamente idiosincrática y visionaria, al crear una poesía visual profundamente humana, elaborada, entre otras cosas, mediante herramientas rudimentarias y baratijas a las cuales impregna de una curiosa doble identidad, resueltamente cotidiana y silenciosamente dramática.

De hecho, los objetos, tal cual son o transformados, coexisten. Está a cargo del observador, el movimiento constante entre estos dos contextos, el mundano y el otro, soslayado, raro, a veces humorístico y psicológicamente complejo. A primera vista, *Scratch* [*Rasguño*], 1974, un grabado y aguatinta, revela un clavo penetrando el soporte de papel y registra la sombra proyectada por el clavo. Es difícil imaginar una imagen más banal que ésta. Nos cuesta descubrir ese solo rasguño (real, no impreso) que va del comienzo del punto de penetración, en ángulo a través del papel y el passe-partout que lo rodea; una "rotura" visible y táctil que podría haber sido provocada por el clavo afilado, que incluso aparece lustroso y hasta enjoyado. Presencia y ausencia, agitación y reposo, todo converge, mientras que el clavo, la sombra y el rasguño sugieren la apariencia de un reloj. Una de las tantas referencias al tiempo a lo largo del trabajo de Porter.

Key Ring [*Llavero*], 2011, una fotografía mostrada hace poco en Hosfelt Gallery en Nueva York, es igualmente maravillosa. Un llavero (con llaves adjuntas) luce una miniatura plástica de Jesús con una túnica blanca y faja roja. Este Cristo en forma de baratija, este Redentor de bolsillo que arrastra una llave agobiante a través de una extensión blanca y vacía, es fascinante. La fotografía de Porter destaca lo absurdo de un Jesús reducido a un objeto práctico producido en masa y también logra que se perciba extrañamente sagrado, además de profunda y dolorosamente humano. La llave es una carga pesada, casi del tamaño del cuerpo de Jesús, y a la par una gran promesa: "Las llaves del Reino de los Cielos" (Mateo 16:19), una imagen que resuena en nuestras vidas a medida que nos movemos por el mundo en busca de belleza, pero sobrecargados de recuerdos, preocupaciones, pérdidas y temores.

La teoría del carnaval del crítico literario ruso Mikhail Bakhtin, también ilumina ciertos tipos de arte visual –y puede ser útil con respecto a Liliana Porter[3]. En términos de Bakhtin, el "momento carnavalesco" o la "situación carnavalesca" es aquel en el cual las reglas normales, los valores, las jerarquías

3. Todas las citas de y referidas a Mikhail Bakhtin son de *Problems of Dostoevsky's Poetics* [*Problemas de la poética de Dostoievsky*], (ed. y trad.) Caryl Emerson (Minneapolis: University of Minnesota Press, 1984), 122–24.

y modos de aprehensión se suspenden temporalmente a favor de un nuevo tipo de libertad, que puede a la vez ser absurdo y estimulante, desconcertante y liberador. Los excesos, las hipérboles, la exuberancia y la parodia son intrínsecos a estas situaciones carnavalescas que no pretenden trascender la vida normal, no intentan substituir una nueva consciencia por una enervada.

Por el contrario, la vida mundana y la carnavalesca coexisten y uno se mueve entre ambas e ingresa a la situación carnavalesca exorbitante o distorsionada con el fin de ser evaluado y transformado para pronto retornar a la vida normal –tal vez sacudido y con mayor profundidad– y quizás con cierta sabiduría ganada. No estoy sugiriendo que Porter esté en deuda con Bakhtin, que en definitiva no es tan importante. Estoy proponiendo que una inclinación carnavalesca y excéntrica –una que implica un juego de espíritu libre y bufonería, lo cual en términos de Bakhtin "combina lo sacro con lo profano, lo elevado con lo bajo, lo grandioso con lo insignificante, lo sabio con lo estúpido" y que temporalmente reemplace la vida normal con todas sus reglas, categorías, jerarquías y estratificaciones– es esencial en su producción, y es asimismo uno de los grandes motivos por el que sus obras, que hacen referencia a objetos familiares y encontrados, son tan atractivas, catárticas y liberadoras. Si bien Liliana Porter no es una artista obviamente política en el sentido de abordar un tema en particular o un equívoco social, existe una profunda e implícita operación política en su trabajo, que tiene mucho que ver con (en palabras de Bakhtin) la jubilosa suspensión de "desigualdades socio-jerárquicas", así como con un interés fundamental en la libertad. A lo anterior se suma el hecho de que muchos de sus proyectos manifiestan una atracción y excitación carnavalescas, que se complementa con ostentosos vestuarios, máscaras, animales revestidos con atributos humanos y viceversa, procesiones, actuaciones, y maravillosos y desafiantes eventos.

Consideremos la fotografía *Dialogue (with Penguin)* [*Diálogo (con pingüino)*], 1999, que muestra un encuentro poco factible entre Jesús y un pingüino. En la fotografía, Jesús (que en realidad es una lámpara de plástico envuelta en el cable eléctrico) mira a un pingüino de madera con grandes ojos, que le devuelve la mirada en una mezcla de asombro, nerviosismo, vergüenza y excitación. En un nivel, este encuentro no es tan extraño; ambos interlocutores son figuras producidos en masa, por lo tanto comparten un contexto determinado. En otro nivel, el encuentro es francamente caprichoso ya que presenta a un Salvador y un ave de la Antártida. Sin embargo, esta situación incongruente o fantástica evoca viejos conflictos y dicotomías: religión y naturaleza, humanos y animales, el cielo y la tierra, nosotros y ellos, tú y yo. Jesús, que luce calmado y con la mirada baja, parece emanar una serenidad sabia, a pesar de estar truncado, inmóvil y claramente ridículo, mientras que el pingüino, ligeramente inclinado hacia adelante, es "todo ojos y orejas".

En este raro encuentro, llevado a cabo en un espacio vacío, advertimos algo cómico y cautivante a la vez: es la insólita humanidad de la imagen que afecta al observador. Esta imagen extravagante de Porter nos remite a nuestra incomodidad frente a los otros, la extrañeza y el misterio de otras vidas, las fisuras que por lo general existen incluso entre amigos, familiares o amantes, y la fluidez comunicativa que acontece cuando dichas fisuras se reparan.

Esta fotografía de una lamparilla plástica en la forma de Jesús Cristo, que aparenta estar discutiendo con un pingüinito, enfatiza exactamente lo que este Jesús y este pingüino son en realidad: chucherías, piezas *kitsch* compradas en una tienda. Son objetos, y la fotografía realza el hecho de que son objetos, de manera muy similar a su producción más temprana cuando acentuaba la objetividad de un clavo o un tornillo. Al mismo tiempo, la composición de ambos objetos en un encuentro intenso e interpersonal los transforma totalmente, y ambas figuras son percibidas –en contra de toda evidencia y lógica– como seres vivos, inquisidores, con sus propias y complejas vidas internas, pensamientos y emociones. Apreciamos algo querible y amable en este Jesús-lámpara, al igual que vemos esperanza, fragilidad, temor y entusiasmo en este pingüino de juguete. Si bien sabemos que estamos observando una fotografía de dos chucherías de plástico, nos llega un sentimiento muy especial y evocativo acerca de estas dos figuras, que parecen haber pasado milagrosamente a otro plano de existencia y comprensión.

Durante varias décadas Liliana Porter ha estado exhibiendo un arte idiosincrático y admirable, con una riqueza y un peculiar efecto humano, y esa maniobra nos ayuda a vivir de forma más armónica en un tiempo (como todos los tiempos) penoso y esperanzador, enloquecedor y atractivo. Su arte lidia con preguntas difíciles y permanentes, a la vez que transita por el asombro al cual nos acercamos, no solamente para deleitarnos, sino también en busca de alimento y sabiduría.

Partes de este ensayo aparecieron originalmente, con ciertos cambios, en "Five Sections for Liliana Porter [Cinco secciones para Liliana Porter]", *Liliana Porter: Línea de tiempo* (Ciudad de México: Museo de Arte Contemporáneo Internacional Rufino Tamayo, 2009).

LILIANA PORTER

EN CONVERSACIÓN CON

INÉS KATZENSTEIN

PRÓLOGO

"La significación es obra de la voluntad".
—Jacques Rancière, *El maestro ignorante*

Cuanto más se profundiza en la producción de Liliana Porter, se evidencia que cada una de sus imágenes resulta de un movimiento de interrogación acerca del mundo. Por eso, el objetivo de esta conversación fue desplegar el pensamiento de una artista que asume la construcción de su obra como un acto de conocimiento, abrirlo para intentar comprender esa relación con los objetos que su obra refleja. Así, si el diálogo con Liliana Porter que aquí se presenta por momentos peca de biográfico y anecdótico, lo hace reconciliado con su pecado: en la creencia de que las historias le dan una vitalidad especial a los recuerdos, y que, a través de la reconstrucción de la experiencia de su autora, se puede definir mejor la perspectiva artística y ética implícitas en las obras.

A lo largo de seis capítulos organizados con una dirección a grandes rasgos cronológica, el relato de Porter se acerca y se aleja de las obras, va y vuelve del contexto social y cultural a la reflexión sobre las técnicas, y de las técnicas a la vida privada. Considerada ésta como un ejemplo particular, pero modélico, de cómo vive y piensa una artista latinoamericana radicada en los Estados Unidos por más de cuarenta años, durante el periodo de emergencia, auge y crítica al multiculturalismo. Sin embargo, y esto es lo distintivo del vínculo arte y vida en Liliana Porter, deja claro que la suya es una vida caracterizada por la decisión de ir construyendo una expresión propia, y de persistir en el trabajo artístico con el convencimiento de que el arte encarna una posibilidad real de comunicación y hasta de comunión con los objetos, las ideas, la realidad y las personas.

La entrevista se desarrolló en varias instancias. Comenzó con una secuencia intensiva de reuniones durante cuatro días en la casa de Porter en Rhinebeck, Nueva York. Durante esos días, nuestra charla fue mutando del relato familiar al análisis histórico, de la confesión a la teoría. En cada una de esas modulaciones, Porter provoca una chispa entre chiste y verdad, entre detalle y moraleja, entre vida personal y política, que espero se refleje en esta edición. Después de esas primeras sesiones, la plática continuó en algunos encuentros en Buenos Aires, pero fundamentalmente se desarrolló por correo electrónico, formato en el cual intenté mantener la frescura y la intimidad de las tertulias que tuvimos cara a cara, incluso imponiéndome a mí misma, como entrevistadora, un estilo escueto, coloquial, sostenido por la dirección que iba tomando mi curiosidad a medida que se desarrollaba.

Hay descubrimientos importantes, relativos a Liliana Porter, que surgen, para mí, de este diálogo. En primer lugar, me sorprendió la intensidad de su relación con la Argentina y su vínculo pragmático, pero no por ello simple, con Estados Unidos. Por otro lado, y quizás más importante, de estas declaraciones surge la impresión de que Porter es una artista que se aboca a traducir lo que piensa, lo que se pregunta y lo que siente en un código que toma la forma de eso que llamamos arte. Si bien su producción fue cambiando con el tiempo, y sintonizándose con los distintos lenguajes y tendencias de cada coyuntura, cada variación sirve para subrayar sus temas esenciales. Escribo esto y me suena a lugar común. ¿Puede decirse eso de todos los artistas? No lo creo. En mi opinión, el trabajo de Porter exhibe su relación con la vida en un terreno artístico específico. Las interrogantes son pocas y sencillas, fruto de su particular distancia (a la vez inmersión y extrañamiento, ternura y lucidez) respecto del mundo: ¿A dónde vamos y a dónde pertenecemos? ¿Cómo vamos a relacionarnos con las personas que se cruzan por nuestras vidas? ¿Cómo podremos lograr una comunicación entre nosotros, si somos esencialmente seres distantes? ¿Cómo es posible que funcionemos a nivel social a través de códigos tan artificiales sin cuestionarlos? ¿Qué es la sabiduría? y ¿Cuál es la relación entre la práctica artística y la felicidad? Otra vez, suenan a preguntas elementales, casi *clichés*. Pero no lo son. La verdad es que no muchos artistas se ocupan de ellas. Hay, en esta historia, una reflexión permanente sobre estos tópicos.

Intuyo que es esta peculiar relación entre arte y vida lo que descoloca a Porter de sus colegas y coetáneos. Porque si bien es una de las artistas más laboriosas e integradas al sistema del arte que uno pueda conocer, destaco el hecho de que su obra funciona siempre con un grado alto de diferenciación respecto a la de sus contemporáneos. Podemos situarla en distintos ismos, trazar sus influencias y glosar su contexto. Sin embargo su trabajo produce un contraste en referencia a las formas más comunes del arte, que la posiciona en un raro margen: una marginalidad que no tiende a la oscuridad y el hermetismo, más bien se aleja de lo central o canónico por su tendencia hacia el horizonte de la comunicación.

Esa diferenciación radica, pienso, en el componente teatral de sus estrategias. Desde siempre, la actitud de Porter no fue directa, sino acaso retórica. En su primera etapa de artista consolidada (que sitúo desde mediados de los años sesenta hasta fines de los ochenta), aparece un tono pseudo-pedagógico en sus obras. Me refiero a una voluntad ya no de hacer una imagen por su apariencia (formal), sino para mostrar, con dedo chistoso de "maestra Siruela" o con mirada de alumnita ingenua, algún descubrimiento. Algo que la propia artista simula no comprender del todo, pero que adivina importante. Pensemos, por ejemplo, en la serie de *Magritte*. La artista expone su sintonía con la imagen, quiere expresar qué sabe, qué entiende. Esa cualidad demostrativa también es clave para la concepción de sus pinturas de los años ochenta. En esas obras, cuando Porter pinta, es decir, cuando hay materia, la gestualidad es tan convencional en su "expresionismo" y el tratamiento matérico aflora tan sorpresiva y enfáticamente, que se vuelven paródicos. Aquí Porter pinta actuando de pintora. Y cada cambio técnico del cuadro existe para corroborar su divergencia con el resto. Y cuando deja de ser paródica o pedagógica, empieza a trabajar un tipo de "objetitos" de mercado de pulgas, devaluados de entrada, anacrónicos, y los pone en funcionamiento en clave teatral (donde la foto o el video son la representación de ese teatro), proponiendo a los espectadores establecer relaciones de animismo usualmente reprimidas o acotadas al espacio de la infancia. Aquí hay algo de sociológicamente experimental, que igualmente me suena a suavemente disruptivo de las convenciones estéticas del arte.

Finalmente, quizás lo más transgresor sea la puesta en funcionamiento del humor como metodología de conocimiento, como metodología emancipadora, en el sentido que apunta Rancière cuando habla del "borramiento de la frontera entre aquellos que actúan y aquellos que miran"[1]. Cuando hay risa, en Porter, ésta logra eliminar toda desigualdad entre artista y espectador. La comunión se produce inmediatamente. Así, el humor provoca un posicionamiento fundamental y radical de la artista, consistente en la corporización de los problemas filosóficos inherentes a la obra en el nivel de lo cotidiano. Pero no hay traducción desde lo alto de la filosofía hacia lo bajo de la risa. Más bien la aventura de vivir todo junto.

Inés Katzenstein

1. Jacques Rancière, *The Emancipated Spectator* [*El espectador emancipado*] (Nueva York: Verso, 2009), 19.

PRIMEROS PASOS

INÉS KATZENSTEIN ¿Cuál es tu primer recuerdo como artista?

LILIANA PORTER Quizás haya sido en el año 1958 cuando todavía era alumna en la Universidad Iberoamericana de México y salieron algunas notas en los diarios sobre mi trabajo [Fig. 1]. Como ves, me acuerdo de cuando los demás usaron la palabra "artista" refiriéndose a mí; pero yo misma auto-definiéndome, eso sí que no me acuerdo. Es que "artista" es una palabra que no se sabe bien si es a favor o en contra, ¿no es cierto?

IK ¿Por qué lo decís?

LP Porque la palabra "artista" tiene algo de "actor", o sea algo medio fraudulento, y también de aquel que se autodefine como distinto, lo cual de por sí no resulta muy simpático. Cuando alguien afirma sin dudar: "Soy un artista", enseguida me entra la sospecha de que esa persona debe ser medio tonta, o por lo menos hay gran posibilidad de que la obra sea un poquito mediocre. Es como si alguien contestara a la pregunta: –¿Usted qué hace?, y diciendo "soy sabio".

IK Un aspecto me impresionó cada vez más a medida que te fui conociendo, y es el hecho de que tu mirada sobre el mundo, día a día, es tan intensa, lúcida y humorística como la visión sobre el mundo que manifiestan tus piezas. La sorpresa, inocencia o crueldad que irradia uno de los muñequitos en una de tus fotos, es similar a aquella con la que mirás lo que pasa en tu jardín por la ventana de tu casa. ¿Tu obra es la consecuencia de esa mirada previa de extrañamiento sobre el entorno que te rodea, o más bien fuiste construyendo, cultivando, esa mirada hasta que se transformara en vos misma?

LP Quizás estoy demasiado cerca de mí misma para darme cuenta o analizar lo que me decís. En realidad creo que todo el mundo es así, porque ¿cómo disociar lo que uno es de lo que uno hace? ¡Sería mucho trabajo!

IK Lo que quiero decir es que tu obra, en mayor grado que el arte de otros artistas más formalistas o más contenidistas, parece consecuencia directa, una transposición nítida, de una manera particular de mirar la realidad. A la vez, claro,

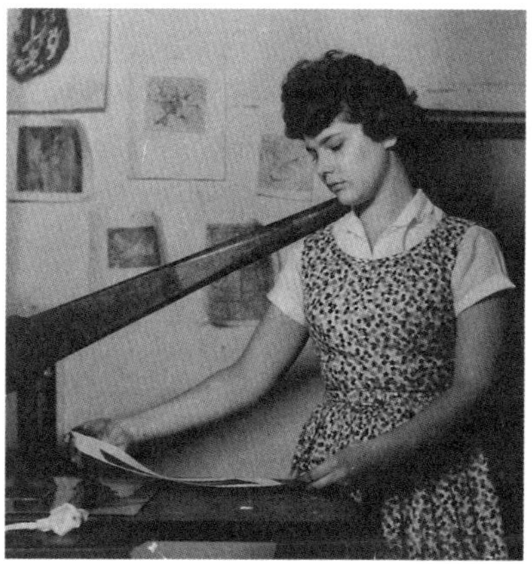

Fig. 1. Liliana Porter en el Taller de Grabado, Universidad Iberoamericana, Ciudad de México, 1958.

Fig. 2. De izquierda a derecha: Julio, Margarita, Luis y Liliana Porter en Buenos Aires, 1955.

uno puede preguntarse ¿hasta qué punto ese modo de percibir el mundo se va retroalimentando de tu propia obra?

LP Debe ser así. Quizás me condicionó muchísimo el ambiente donde crecí, con un papá inteligente, con gran sentido del humor, y una mamá que reinventó su realidad a partir de durísimas experiencias de infancia. Asumo que fue una gran influencia ser testigo de cómo ella, en vez de transformarse en una persona amargada, enojada o negativa, armó su vida con una gran dosis de compasión, con un constante estado de asombro o de conciencia ante (aunque suene cursi) el misterio de la perfección que uno encuentra en la naturaleza, y cómo a partir de allí desarrolló una especie de fe esencial en el ser humano o en la vida, o quizás simplemente una fe esencial, abstracta [Fig. 2].

Pienso que todo eso ayudó a mi percepción del mundo y de las cosas, y, luego, a medida que fui creciendo y desarrollando mi trabajo, fueron surgiendo por sí solos los temas que me interesan, que me interesan en la vida y en la obra al mismo tiempo.

IK Leyendo algunas cartas que escribías a tu familia cuando eras muy joven, desde Nueva York, en 1964, es indudable que ya tenías un sentido del humor muy sofisticado que seguramente provenía, como dices, de tu padre, un famoso escritor y humorista. ¿Podrías contarnos quién era y qué hacía Julio Porter?

LP Según Wikipedia (y es verdad): "Julio Porter (14 de julio de 1916, Buenos Aires –24 de octubre de 1979, Ciudad de México) fue un guionista y director de cine, conocido como uno de los más prolíficos en la historia del cine argentino. Entre 1942 y su muerte en 1979, escribió los guiones de más de 100 películas. Entre 1951 y 1979 dirigió 25 películas".

Era eso y mucho más . . . me llevaba muy bien con mi papá. Era muy divertido e inteligente, y me apoyaba en todo. No era, digamos, un papá arquetípico, en el sentido de alguien que te daría consejos trascendentes o algo así. Ese papel, en todo caso, lo cumplían mi hermano o mi mamá. Mi papá era un personaje famoso en el cine, la radio y el teatro en Argentina. Estaba muy orgullosa de mi familia, de mi casa y de él, y me sentía muy afortunada de ser su hija. A mi papá le encantaban los amigos, las reuniones, los restaurantes, la gente. Era muy divertido, pero también era bastante irresponsable y desaforado. Mi mamá no la pasó siempre tan bien con él, seguramente porque estaba muy enamorada, aun después de que se separaron. Se escribían poemas, cartas, armaban líos, se peleaban, se reconciliaban . . . ¡parecían de película italiana!

IK ¿Recordás situaciones de tu vida de niña que pongan en evidencia el clima de tu casa?

LP Lo primero que me viene a la cabeza es un diálogo que tenía con mi hermano Luis cuando éramos chiquitos y todavía dormíamos en el mismo cuarto (Luis es tres años mayor que yo). Estaba oscuro y cada vez que sentía algún ruido, ya sea que él se hubiera dado vuelta en su cama o algo así, le preguntaba:

—¿Luis?

—¿Qué?

—¿Sos vos?

—No. Soy otro.

—¡No! ¡Dale!!!

—Soy otro.

—No embromés. ¿Sos vos?

—Soy otro. Si no, ¿cómo explicás estos pelos largos negros que me crecen en las manos?

—¡Mamaaaaaaaaaá!!! ¡Mamá!!!

Lo increíble de esto es que era un juego que se repetía igual o parecido de vez en cuando.

Un hecho interesante es que mis abuelitos eran rusos, de la ex Unión Soviética, y a veces, para hacerme dormir, me cantaban canciones en ruso. Y por otro lado, los padres de mi mamá venían de Rumania y mi mamá nos cantaba canciones en rumano. No entendía ninguna de las dos lenguas, pero me imaginaba escenas muy concretas cuando las escuchaba. La primera canción que compuse en el piano se llamaba *Los indios rusos*. Me desconcertó cuando mi abuelita me dijo: "En Rusia no tenemos indios".

IK Esa relación con lenguajes extraños que no nos permiten acceder al sentido y nos separan de la supuesta verdad de las cosas, y a la vez esa articulación tan potente entre lo "gracioso" y lo "horripilante" son claves en tu obra actual. ¿Hasta qué punto creés que el mundo de tu infancia te determinó como adulta?

LP Para mí, el mundo que uno vive en la infancia, sin duda, determina la personalidad que uno asume como adulto. Por lo menos en mí, todas las primeras vivencias en mi casa, en la escuela, con mis padres, con mi hermano, mis amigos, están muy presentes.

IK Y cuando finalmente aparecen los juguetes en tu obra, a partir de los años setenta, pero de manera protagónica en los noventa, ¿creés que ese mundo de tu infancia se muestra de modo más evidente? Es decir, ¿los juguetes te ayudan a recuperar parte de tu infancia?

LP La verdad, aunque suene raro, no asocio los juguetes o esos objetos que uso en mi obra con la infancia. Es decir, no los relaciono con nada pasado, si se entiende pasado como lo que ya no existe más. Eligiendo trabajar con estos elementos no siento que "recupero" nada. Más bien estimo que soy ahora, simultáneamente, todas las etapas de mi vida. Como si no hubiera perdido nada realmente, sino más bien acumulado experiencias, sin necesidad de sustituir una fase por otra en forma consecutiva. Incluso pienso que mi relación con los objetos no es infantil. No hay nostalgia. En todo caso, se trata de algo más analítico. Me enfrento al objeto y me tomo el tiempo de verlo.

IK Empezaste a estudiar arte cerca de los doce años, en un bachillerato artístico. ¿Cómo fue que decidiste tan temprano tu vocación? ¿Qué modelos de artistas mujeres te eran cercanos?

LP En esa época se podía ingresar directamente a Bellas Artes después de la escuela primaria. A mí me encantaba ir, y eso que hasta los catorce años vivía en el barrio de Florida, bastante lejos de la escuela. Realmente no recuerdo bien eso de "querer ser artista". Lo que sí recuerdo es que me encantaba dibujar, pintar y el ambiente de la escuela. La sala de proyecciones donde impartían Historia del Arte era antigua, con cortinas de terciopelo rojo oscuro, toda de madera, y olía a piano.

En ese periodo, no recuerdo haber tenido ningún modelo en particular de artista mujer, salvo haber escuchado que existía Raquel Forner[2]. Me gustaban [Lino Enea] Spilimbergo[3] y los dibujos de [Juan Carlos] Castagnino[4], y más adelante descubrí el arte moderno. Me interesaban Braque, Gris y Picasso.

IK Antes de seguir adelante con tus inicios, quisiera hacerte preguntas generales que espero abarquen toda tu trayectoria, y que sirvan de introducción a tu manera de pensar y trabajar. ¿Los tuyos son procesos de búsqueda que culminan en una obra, o más bien chispazos, encuentros? ¿Hay un intervalo de juego que en un momento se detiene y constituye la obra final?

LP A esta altura ya estoy entregada de antemano a los temas que, ya lo sé, vuelven siempre. Entonces el método es más bien "solo dejar que pase algo". Dar lugar a que los acontecimientos sucedan de por sí, y luego "acomodo todo" lo menos posible.

Por ejemplo, en alguna ocasión, tuve una pre-idea de hacer una película porno. Bueno, no es porno, pero llamémosla por ahora así. ¿Cómo proceder en este caso? Ni idea de lo que podría resultar al final, tampoco tengo muy claro el porqué me interesaría hacer eso. Solo sé que me gustaría armar situaciones de tal manera que, a cierta altura, aun cuando uno muestre una cucharita o cualquier objeto normal, el espectador lo perciba como medio porno. Porque lo que hay que transformar no son los objetos, sino la mirada del espectador. Bueno, ¡vaya a saber cómo se hace eso! A pesar de la dificultad, digamos, lo programo en mi cerebro. O sea que si hay señales de algo que sirva para eso, voy a estar atenta. Empezaría de esta manera: mirando a los personajes de mi colección de muñecos y, al verlos con atención, se me mostraría qué picardía podría hacer alguno, con quién o cómo. En esta actividad podrían participar amigos. Sería divertido que otros sugirieran escenas para la "materia prima".

Luego se supone que llegado a un punto, la pieza se sofistica y uno empieza a comprender para qué sirve lo que está haciendo y cuál es la moraleja oculta. Si la obra es "exitosa", se me va a revelar por sí misma. Cuando uno comienza a entender lo que hace, allí puede manejar el aspecto formal para potenciar la idea.

Ya sé que el resultado va a ser coherente con la obra anterior; sin embargo igual tengo que pasar por esa etapa en la cual siento que estoy haciendo

2. Raquel Forner (1902–88), pintora y escultora argentina.

3. Lino Enea Spilimbergo (1896–1964), pintor y grabador argentino.

4. Juan Carlos Castagnino (1908–72), pintor y dibujante argentino.

otra cosa, una acción imprecisa que no entiendo del todo, algo que está por revelárseme.

IK ¡Me rio de imaginarte parada frente a los estantes de muñecos, mirando con perspectiva libidinosa a tus pobres esclavitos! Pero, este "dejar que las cosas sucedan", ¿era similar a cuando, por ejemplo, disponías objetos para tus naturalezas muertas de los años ochenta? ¿La dimensión narrativa e incluso sentimental de esas obras volvía su proceso diferente a éste que me estás contando?

LP Encuentro que el procedimiento era similar. Estaban esos elementos "preferidos" en ese momento (ciertos libros, los barquitos, postales) y yo los iba acomodando hasta que me parecía que todo estaba bien, que todo era verdad, digamos.

IK Los procesos técnicos de tu producción se modificaron de modo considerable, especialmente si comparamos los cuadros de la década del ochenta (donde esos procesos innumerables y complejos que incluían foto-grabados, objetos, dibujos, pinturas, etc., eran centrales para el sentido de la obra) y las fotos de la década de los noventa, mucho más simples técnicamente. Me pregunto si el procedimiento de concepción de la obra también fue cambiando con el tiempo.

LP Cada técnica te pide un tipo de esfuerzo diferente. Las condiciones de trabajo van modificándose. Cuando empecé a hacer video tenía absolutamente claro lo que quería hacer, así que me fue muy fácil conseguir asistencia especializada. Las fotos me dieron más problemas, ya que como nunca estudié fotografía y quería tomarlas yo misma sin ponerme a aprender el significado de esos numeritos en las cámaras, las fui haciendo un poco por instinto. Fue un misterio el cómo me fueron saliendo. Aprendí lo que necesitaba aprender pero de una manera muy parcial y medio absurda. Volviendo al concepto, en las pinturas había más complejidad técnica porque estaba tratando de hacer una deconstrucción de los múltiples niveles de representación. En las fotografías, por otro lado, esos niveles se resumen a uno, y ese uno está contenido en el objeto. Y, por supuesto, el gesto se vuelve técnicamente menos complicado y el objeto tal vez más complicado.

IK Compartiste vida y trabajo con otros artistas (con Luis Camnitzer y Alan Wiener, y más recientemente con Ana Tiscornia). ¿Qué lugar ocupa su colaboración en tu vida como artista, y cómo la pensás en cada uno de esos casos, sin duda muy distintos?

LP Luis y yo éramos muy jóvenes cuando nos conocimos. Yo tenía veintidós años y él veintiséis, así que fuimos creciendo juntos. Los dos éramos muy trabajadores y nos complementábamos muy bien, nos apoyábamos y teníamos conversaciones útiles sobre el quehacer de cada uno. Podía inventarle obras a él (y viceversa) sin ningún problema. Nuestra producción individual siempre fue muy diversa, pero uno entendía muy bien la obra y la mentalidad del otro, así que nos podíamos ayudar muchísimo. Fue una unión muy positiva. Las cosas nos salían muy bien. Con Al Wiener la relación no se centraba en el arte. Incluso, a Al no le interesaba realmente "ser artista". Sin embargo, podía perfectamente hacerme una crítica, no tanto desde el punto de vista formal o conceptual, sino como desde más lejos, abarcando más aspectos de mi personalidad y del contexto en el cual vivíamos. Al era alguien que, como ninguna otra persona que haya conocido, vivía en el absoluto presente. Es decir, no miraba para atrás ni planeaba nada para adelante. "Baste al día su afán", como dice la Biblia. Aprendí muchísimo de ese raro atributo de Al.

A Ana Tiscornia, artista uruguaya, la conocí en 1990 cuando fuimos invitadas a ir a Cuba como jurados del concurso Joven estampa en la Casa de las Américas. Trabajando esos días nos hicimos entrañables amigas. Más adelante nos encontramos en Uruguay y luego, cuando Al y yo nos separamos, la llamé por teléfono a Montevideo desde Nueva York y le dije: –¿Por qué no venís? Desde entonces vivimos juntas.

Ana está familiarizada con mi obra, mi manera de pensar y mis gustos, a tal grado que a veces sabe con antelación lo que intento hacer. Ella es más ordenada y más sistemática, aparte que ha tenido una educación más formal (arquitectura, semiótica y otras yerbas). A veces, refiriéndome a algo que acabo de hacer, le pregunto: –¿Y esto qué es? Y ella me lo explica, parece que sabe antes que yo la respuesta.

Aunque nuestras obras y actividades son diferentes, ella me ayudó muchísimo cuando hice los videos, y en los dos últimos, de hecho, es co-directora, porque realmente se metió muy de lleno a trabajar conmigo. Además hemos concretado obras de arte público y juntas concebimos dos exposiciones que fueron experiencias extraordinarias, porque en realidad ninguna de las dos sacrificó nada, lo que hicimos fue superponer los dos mundos y armar así un tercero que resultó ser nuevo para ambas [Fig. 3].

IK Sin embargo, es indudable que siempre elegiste compartir tu vida con personas que estuvieran involucradas más o menos en lo mismo que vos, y que formaran con vos algo así como un equipo. ¿Por qué creés que es así?

Fig. 3. Ana Tiscornia y Liliana Porter, Galería Casas Riegner, Bogotá, 2011.

LP Nunca lo pensé, pero creo que compartir la vida en sus diversos aspectos es, por lo menos en mi caso, consecuencia directa de preocupaciones, pensamientos e intereses comunes. A decir verdad, la mayoría de mis obras las hago sola. Hice un solo trabajo en colaboración con Luis Camnitzer y José Castillo [en la exposición *Information*, en 1970], y en los últimos años, algunos con Ana. Pronto vamos a presentar nuestra tercera muestra de obras hechas en común y estamos escribiendo un texto para un libro sobre arte del futuro. Además, juntas hemos creado un heterónimo: Alicia Mihai Gazcue[5], que sigue vivita y coleando y que cada vez está más activa y por consiguiente nos da quehacer. De todas formas, lo que más me gusta es trabajar con otros haciendo cosas alrededor mío, aun cuando cada quien esté en su propio proyecto. Es estimulante interrumpir una actividad, discutir e intercambiar ideas.

IK Mirando retrospectivamente tu trayectoria, es evidente que sos una artista tremendamente activa, prolífica y comprometida con tu quehacer. Sin embargo, ¿tuviste momentos de "depresión" creativa?

LP Me parece que el periodo en el cual trabajé menos fue cuando cumplí el rol de "madrastra". Al, mi segundo esposo, tenía un hijo de su matrimonio anterior, y como yo no había tenido hijos, me daba ilusión que Eric viniera a vivir con

5. Este personaje surgió de una invitación de la revista *Otra Parte* (Buenos Aires, verano 2007–2008), a crear un artista inventado para un número dedicado a Crítica-ficción. Porter y Tiscornia crearon las imágenes, y yo escribí un pequeño texto sobre la vida de Alicia Mihai Gazcue. A partir de entonces, Porter y Tiscornia continuaron dando vida a "la artista", que ha participado de diversas actividades, exposiciones y publicaciones.

nosotros. Así sucedió y durante esos tres años creo que hice menos obras. Eric era un niño medio triste. Y yo quería que estuviera feliz y hacía lo imposible por lograrlo. En ese tiempo mi cabeza estaba muy metida en esa relación; pero "depresión creativa" no recuerdo haber tenido nunca realmente.

IK ¿Nunca pensaste en hacer otra cosa, nunca descreíste del arte?

LP No. Todas las otras cosas que me interesan están dentro de lo que llamamos arte. Me parece que me hubiera gustado ser escritora.

NUEVA YORK EN LOS SESENTA
Una crítica al grabado

IK A los dieciséis años te trasladás con tu familia a México. ¿Por qué se fueron y qué te dieron tus años de permanencia en ese país?

LP A mi papá le gustaban los juegos de azar. Y por azar se jugó la casa, y hete aquí que la perdió. Era un gordito complicado. Pero como él siempre tenía las estrellas a su favor, enseguida consiguió un contrato para trabajar en México y así fue como terminamos allá.

Esos años en México me dieron mucho. En principio, la experiencia de conocer por primera vez otro país, con otra geografía, otras costumbres, otro modo de ver la vida. Luego, la amistad con José Emilio Pacheco y Carlos Monsiváis, quienes tenían también más o menos mi edad, y que ahora son reconocidos escritores. Asimismo traté a Juan José Arreola, Emilio Carballido, José de la Colina, Homero Aridjis, Juan García Ponce, Octavio Paz, Alfonso Reyes, y otros . . . Y por supuesto, a los artistas plásticos de la época. Cuando llegué a México frecuenté a Antonio Seguí porque íbamos al mismo taller de grabado en La Ciudadela.

Fig. 4. Liliana Porter y Juan José Arreola en la inauguración de la primera exposición individual de Porter, *Óleos y grabados*, Galería Proteo, Ciudad de México, 1959.

Fue en México donde desarrollé la técnica del grabado, y fue en esa ciudad donde mostré mi primera exposición individual a los diecisiete años, en la Galería Proteo [Fig. 4]. Los mexicanos fueron muy generosos conmigo. Yo era muy joven, pero igual me sacaron numerosas notas en los periódicos. Me tomaban en serio. Tengo una nota preciosa de Juan José Arreola que hasta me la sé de memoria. En ese tiempo, la señora Margarita Nelken, la crítica de arte de moda en ese momento, escribió varias veces sobre mi obra. De esa fase tengo tres diarios personales, así que puedo reconstruirla casi día por día. Cuando los releo me asombra que trabajaba continuamente en mi obra, igual que ahora.

IK ¿Por qué decidiste volver a la Argentina, incluso si tus padres y tu hermano se quedaron en México?

LP Regresé porque extrañaba muchísimo a mis amigos, mi ciudad, todo. Así que a los diecinueve años, tres después de haberme ido, volví a Buenos Aires y me fui a vivir a la casa de mis abuelitos (los papás de mi padre). Regresé también a la Escuela de Bellas Artes (ya era la Escuela Nacional de Bellas Artes Prilidiano Pueyrredón) y mis profesores eran Ana María Moncalvo y Fernando López Anaya, buenísimos profesores y magníficas personas [Fig. 5]. Tenía una relación excelente con mis abuelos. Mi abuelo era formidable, un hombre muy dulce, que en su tiempo había sido dueño de la imprenta Porter Hermanos que publicaba a jóvenes escritores y que además imprimió la célebre revista *Martín Fierro*. Siempre contaba anécdotas maravillosas y me regalaba muchos libros. Mi abuela era una rusa divina.

Fig. 5. De izquierda a derecha: Fernando López Anaya, Liliana Porter, Eduardo Levy y Ana María Moncalvo, Galería Galatea, Buenos Aires, 1961.

IK Nueva York es una ciudad a la que llegás como turista y donde te quedás a vivir toda tu vida adulta. ¿Quedarse fue una decisión de una vez y para siempre o una serie de decisiones? ¿Fantaseaste con volver a Buenos Aires o quizás a México?

LP En 1964, mis padres ya habían vuelto a Buenos Aires, pero mi hermano se había quedado en México terminando la carrera de Arquitectura. Fui a México a visitarlo y Guillermo Silva Santamaría, quien había sido mi profesor de grabado, me aconsejó ir a Europa a ver los museos. Yo tenía veintidós años. Antonio Seguí estaba en París, así que el plan era que él me iba a guiar en esa primera visita a Europa. Estando en México, un ex-compañero de Bellas Artes en Buenos Aires, Carlos Stekelman, que vivía en Nueva York con sus hermanas (Ana, bailarina, y Marta, médica), me invitó a quedarme una semana con ellos para que pudiera ver la Feria Mundial y los museos antes de partir hacia Europa. Acepté y tal fue el impacto que me produjo la ciudad que decidí postergar mi viaje a Europa y quedarme una temporada en Nueva York.

IK ¿Cómo fue eso?

Fig. 6. De izquierda a derecha: Luis Camnitzer, Liliana Porter y Luis Felipe Noé, en Nueva York, c. 1965.

LP Al cuarto día de llegar fui a inscribirme en el taller de grabado Pratt Graphic Arts Center, que estaba en Manhattan. Allí conocí a Luis Camnitzer y, a través de él, a Luis Felipe Noé, pues compartían un departamento en el West Village, en Sullivan Street. Admiraba muchísimo a Noé, desde siempre, pero no lo conocía personalmente, así que fue maravilloso. Los tres pasábamos juntos mucho tiempo: veíamos exposiciones, conversábamos sobre arte, y demás [Fig. 6]. Luego Luis y yo empezamos el romance, y en 1965 nos casamos. Luis siempre decía que estábamos de paso, nunca había un propósito de quedarnos y vivíamos la estadía con carácter transitorio. En realidad, jamás nos planteamos regresar a Argentina o a Uruguay.

La única vez que me pasó por la cabeza irme de los Estados Unidos fue en 2001, cuando se cayeron las Torres Gemelas. Sin embargo, decidí quedarme. Lo que sí me planteé desde el principio, consciente o inconscientemente, fue mantener mi relación viva con Buenos Aires. No perder mi condición de argentina, aunque esa definición sea totalmente abstracta y subjetiva y bastante difícil de explicar. Más bien es como si dijera "mantener mi apellido", no sé.

IK ¿Qué fue lo que te impactó de la ciudad? ¿Qué fue lo que te decidió, en ese año de 1964, a quedarte? ¿Qué muestras recordás que te hayan impresionado especialmente?

LP Lo que más me impactó era esa sensación que da a veces Nueva York de que "todo es posible", que si había inconvenientes para hacer algo, estas imposibilidades estarían más en mí misma que en el contexto. Es decir, la sensación de estar en un lugar donde sobraban estímulos, cosas para ver, estudiar,

Fig. 7. Liliana Porter en frente de su *Instalación de la ambientación Arruga*, Museo de Bellas Artes, Caracas, 1969.

experimentar, aprender, y también la sensación de estar en el siglo veinte. De vivir en lo que en ese momento era el presente. Las exposiciones que más me impresionaron fueron las de la galería Leo Castelli, las obras de los artistas *pop* y las de los minimalistas.

IK Cuando llegás a Nueva York se produce en tu trabajo una rápida transformación. Podría decirse que dejás de ser una estudiante de arte y adoptás un lenguaje y una concepción de obra más reflexivas. ¿En qué consistió ese cambio y a través de qué artistas, de qué obras o de qué nociones llegás a él?

LP Considero que llego desde el grabado. Es decir, al darme cuenta de que las revoluciones en el arte, los nuevos movimientos y conceptos siempre se dieron desde la pintura o la escultura, y raramente desde el grabado. Y al examinar este tema, concluyo que el problema consiste en la trampa de la técnica, que en el grabado es mucho más evidente. Quiero decir que el grabador tradicional, a veces, no es más que un técnico excelente, ese es su mérito. Luis y yo investigamos precisamente eso, en una circunstancia en la cual estábamos por sucumbir a ese problema: Luis haciá esos linóleos gigantescos de imágenes influenciadas por el Expresionismo alemán, y yo mis planchas de grabado cada vez más grandes e igualmente complicadas técnicamente. Ambos analizamos cuáles eran las características más importantes del grabado, y llegamos a la conclusión de que era su condición de generar múltiples, y así surgen todas las ideas que desarrollamos en el estudio del New York Graphic Workshop [NYGW].

Como sucede con todos los movimientos de la historia del arte, hay un contexto que requiere un lenguaje determinado. Y en ese momento estaba en el aire la gestación del *Pop*, del Minimalismo y del Arte conceptual. El *Pop* enfatizaba la serialización de objetos de consumo masivo, del mercado, por ejemplo, las sopas Campbell de Warhol eran un perfecto múltiple. Notábamos que solamente un artista como Warhol, que no era grabador, podía tener la libertad mental de elegir la técnica serigráfica, totalmente coherente con su concepto. Una técnica usada en la industria y desdeñada por "las bellas artes". Por otra parte, teníamos ideas políticas (sacar al arte de una elite), y para ese fin, nada más adecuado que la eficacia democrática del grabado. A partir de esa visión hice las exposiciones por correo, utilizando técnicas comerciales *(offset)*; las obras desechables (ambientaciones como las que hice con la imagen del papel arrugado en los Museos de Bellas Artes de Chile y Venezuela) [Fig. 7], y más adelante las obras en foto-serigrafía que imprimía en el muro y que eran borradas después de la exhibición. El hecho de poner énfasis en el concepto y no en el procedimiento, o, dicho de otra manera, poner la técnica al servicio de la idea, me fue sacando de la categoría de "grabadora".

IK Una práctica de autocrítica en referencia a la disciplina en la cual enmarcabas tu trabajo.

LP Exacto. Respecto a qué artistas concretamente me influenciaron, sí puedo afirmar cuáles son los que me interesaban: Lichtenstein, Warhol, Oldenburg, Dieter Roth y, más adelante, los italianos del grupo de arte povera.

A la vez el Minimalismo y el *Pop* nos hicieron conscientes de que lo que veíamos era un tipo de arte muy local, no exportable a los países en vías de desarrollo. Una obra típica minimalista era inconcebible, absurda y, diría incluso, éticamente cuestionable si se hubiera gestado en un país latinoamericano. Eran piezas de muy costosa producción resultado de una alta tecnología, posibles solo en una estructura económica que estaba en posición de asimilarlas desde diversos puntos de vista: mercado, sociedad, etc.

Las obras *pop* fueron el resultado directo de una sociedad de consumo hiperdesarrollada. Esos materiales que se usaban para la propaganda en los supermercados o en las calles no existían en nuestros países, en donde todavía íbamos a comprar el pan con una bolsita de tela. Estados Unidos estaba, en cambio, en el apogeo del derroche y el exceso. ¡Lo gracioso es que ahora acá se fomenta la bolsita de tela reusable para ir a comprar el pan! Lo que nuestros países importaron del *Pop* y del Minimalismo fueron solo aparentes convenciones visuales, híbridos influenciados por reproducciones. Una interpretación a partir de lo visual y no del concepto.

En ese sentido, al ver estas exposiciones en el momento que surgieron, reafirmamos la sospecha de que la tesis del arte internacional era una falacia y que aspirar a él para llegar al *mainstream* requería una especie de negación del contexto propio, de ponerse el disfraz y ser validado por la corriente principal. Creo que opté por el mejor de los caminos: seguir siendo quien soy e ir incorporando naturalmente todo lo que resultaba coherente con mi postura.

IK Me gustaría preguntarte acerca de los estereotipos cíclicos que se adoptan relativos al arte latinoamericano en los Estados Unidos. En otra conversación que tuvimos mencionabas la exposición *The Geometry of Hope* y a la primera Feria Pinta de Nueva York (ambas en 2007) como hitos de la historia reciente en el sentido de implicar una nueva mirada de lo latinoamericano desde los Estados Unidos. Una que subraya la tradición constructiva y que por lo tanto se aproxima más a la idiosincrasia argentina, estereotípicamente más racional y europeizante, en contraste con el patrón anterior ligado a lo maravilloso o a la naturaleza. ¿Cómo te sentiste en las distintas etapas históricas de la mirada de Estados Unidos hacia Latinoamérica, en relación con tu obra? ¿Cómo te sentís ahora, con esta nueva tendencia geometrizante?

LP A mí me da igual cuál es la moda del momento para definir desde acá lo latinoamericano. Es decir, me da igual con respecto a la producción de mi propia obra porque, pase lo que pase, voy a seguir haciendo lo que hago. No tengo ninguna necesidad de "diseñar" mi identidad, y no puedo ni me interesa controlar la percepción de los otros sobre quién soy y qué hago. A lo largo de los años he participado en innumerables mesas redondas y paneles alrededor de esos temas, reflexiones a partir de querer definir qué es el arte latinoamericano, la identidad, la globalización y otros tópicos. Por supuesto, hay posiciones divergentes. Lo que definitivamente no me perdonaría es dejar de ser lo que soy para que me acepte el otro. Pienso en español y puedo pensar en inglés. Eso, en mi opinión, es una situación enriquecedora. Lo que empobrece es ocultar voluntariamente lo que uno es por el afán de integrarse al *mainstream*, o lo opuesto, transformarse en el estereotipo para entrar en el *mainstream*. Esos esquemas, por suerte, están siendo superados por las generaciones más jóvenes. En general, siento que hay una apertura hacia la integración de otras culturas.

IK Luis Camnitzer dice que su audiencia es latinoamericana porque cree que cierto nivel de comprensión mutua se genera entre personas que comparten una lengua. ¿Estás de acuerdo con este concepto? ¿Sentís mayor empatía en la comunicación de tus ideas artísticas frente al público argentino o latinoamericano?

LP Cuando muestro los videos (notarás que acostumbro escribir cualquier texto o subtítulos en inglés y español), admito que hay segmentos que se van a captar mejor en este contexto y otras en las que hay que ser argentino para entenderlas. Por ejemplo, en *Drum Solo/Solo de tambor* [2000], el fragmento "Coro argentino" o "Gaucho" obviamente se capta mejor si uno es argentino. Considero que toda obra se percibe diferente de acuerdo con el contexto. Para la Bienal de Sharjah [Emiratos Árabes], la curadora eligió *Forced Labor: Red Sand* [*Trabajo forzado: arena roja*, 2008], y esa obra allá, de golpe, se cargaba de significados que no tenía en Nueva York o en Buenos Aires, ni que yo hubiera previsto.

Contestando la pregunta, mi obra incluye como concepto la conciencia de que las cosas cambian y se resignifican de acuerdo al que las mira y al contexto. Entonces, lo que dice Luis es verdad.

IK ¿Tenías contacto con lo que sucedía en Argentina mientras estabas en Nueva York?

LP Estaba al tanto de lo que ocurría en Buenos Aires, pero estaba enfocada en mi propio trabajo. Muchos de los eventos que pasaban eran lejanos a los contenidos que me empezaban a interesar. Eso no los hacía, a mis ojos, mejores ni peores. Eran cosas que pasaban al mismo tiempo mientras yo pensaba en otras. Esto no quiere decir que no encontrara relevantes ciertos proyectos, como el del Instituto di Tella de Buenos Aires, un lugar muy estimulante y controvertido, un centro que podía tener su lado frívolo pero que también generaba pensamiento. Lo que ocurre es que, en relación con lo que decía antes de Latinoamérica y Estados Unidos, pienso que el concepto esencial del *pop* norteamericano no era exportable. Fue un fenómeno local, absolutamente estadounidense. Lo que se llamó *pop* en nuestros países fue una traducción desde lo formal: los colores primarios, el uso de imágenes de la cultura popular . . .

Recuerdo que cuando llegué a Nueva York en 1964, la fuerza gráfica de los carteles y otros medios de publicidad eran impactantes, igual sucedía en los supermercados con los diseños de los envases de comida. El *pop* se apoderó de ese lenguaje casi literalmente, y simplemente lo puso en el contexto de las bellas

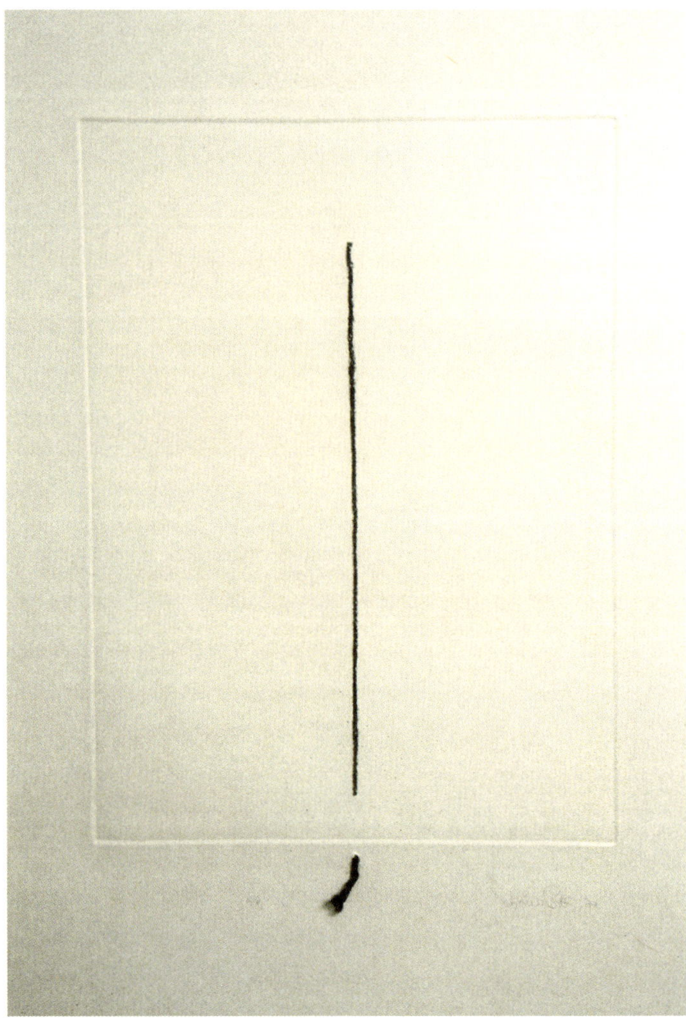

Fig. 8. *Stitch* [*Puntada*], 1970.

artes. Si de por sí la cosa era impactante, mucho más lo era dentro de las paredes de una galería o de un museo.

IK Desde mediados de la década de los sesenta comienza un proceso de progresivo reduccionismo visual en tu obra. ¿Éste ocurre simultáneamente con la crítica al grabado de la que hablabas antes?

LP Cuando tomo conciencia de la trampa de la técnica, decido parar y tratar de plantearme ideas lo menos ostentosas posibles, técnicamente hablando. El mérito de la obra tenía que estar claramente en lo que planteaba, y no en cómo lo decía. Para comenzar, seleccioné imágenes con la menor carga de significado. Me doy cuenta ahora de que esa era una tarea imposible, o por lo menos un poco rara. No obstante, en ese tiempo, para mí, los elementos más "insignificantes" eran objetos encontrados en una ferretería: un clavito, un gancho, un hilito, y también, luego, una esquina doblada en un papel, una pequeña arruga, y después, las sombras para crear ausencias.

Esas elecciones quizás tienen la siguiente explicación: cuando era muy chica, pensaba que las mercancías en las ferreterías eran gratis, porque no podía concebir que nadie tuviera que pagar dinero por un clavo. Debe ser por eso que inconscientemente elegí esos materiales. No se me ocurría nada más banal. En ese punto apareció el espacio vacío, los fondos monocromos blancos. Porque al quitarle el contexto al objeto, no hacía falta un fondo que definiera ningún lugar. Los eventos no sucedían en el ámbito de lo real ni en una copia o representación del espacio real, sino en uno abstracto.

En *Stitch* [*Puntada*, 1970], el hilo real se une a otro hilo representado [Fig. 8]. Una situación mínima, pero que revela temas que me inquietaban y que desde entonces sigo explorando: la cuestión del tiempo, de la substancia de la realidad, de mi relación con las cosas, de los significados. Y así se fueron desarrollando naturalmente las imágenes en la obra.

Pienso que ese voluntario "reduccionismo visual", como vos lo llamás, sirvió para afinar o descubrir cuál era mi mirada sobre el mundo que me rodeaba. Quiero decir que si conscientemente elegía elementos que percibía como insignificantes (en todo el sentido de la palabra), el hecho es que en esas obras, evidentemente, no estaba hablando sobre un clavo o una sombra o un ganchito. Porque la interpretación final no venía de la cosa, del "objetito", acaso de la mirada. Digamos que abría un lugar a un silencio, una atmósfera, una reflexión totalmente ajena a la ferretería.

IK Pareciera que en ese momento hacés un descubrimiento. Que, paradójicamente, es en la supuesta "frialdad" del laboratorio donde ensamblás esos pequeños componentes banales (el blanco de la pared, el blanco del papel intocado, y más tarde, cuando realizás fotografías en la profundidad del vacío del estudio fotográfico) que una cualidad expresiva del objeto se dispara. Escribí sobre ello en el texto de tu muestra en el Centro Cultural Recoleta de Buenos Aires en 2003: "Cuanto más 'objetivo' es el enfoque de la cosa, cuanto más perfecto e irreal es el vacío en el que se encuentra; y cuanto más pequeño es el objeto en relación con el fondo en el que se sitúa, más 'afectiva' se vuelve nuestra mirada frente a ellos. Camnitzer sostiene que «el blanco le da tristeza a los objetos

Fig. 9. *La lune* [*La luna*], 1977.

–incluso a un clavo. [El de Liliana] No es un minimalismo racional sino un intento por destilar la magia que está escondida en la 'cosita'»"[6].

LP A esta altura tengo claro que ese espacio es básico en mi obra. Por un lado, porque saca al objeto de contexto y también de cualquier temporalidad. No sé si eso es del todo posible, pero lo que estoy tratando es de eliminar las distracciones entre "uno" y la cosa. Tampoco sé si esa elección de espacio es intuitiva o racional, o las dos categorías simultáneamente. Lo que sí sé es que cuando se abre el telón, el objeto ya no está sobre la mesa en mi estudio en Rhinebeck. Lo sitúo voluntariamente en otro lugar (o no lugar) porque intuyo que así va a ser más fácil "verlo". Allí, lo subjetivo es al mismo tiempo objetivo. Quiero decir, la conexión que uno establece con "la cosita" se vuelve más real. Si parece "mágica", es porque no estamos acostumbrados a esa forma de mirar. Con respecto a la escala del objeto en ese ambiente, la pequeñez manifiesta lo infinito del "lugar" y lo "solo" de cualquier entidad o persona.

IK ¿Alguna vez te tentó la vía lingüística?

LP Los únicos textos que aparecen en alguna obra son citas de fragmentos de tex-

6. "Conversación con Luis Camnitzer", Nueva York, julio 2003. Citado en Inés Katzenstein, *Liliana Porter: Fotografía y ficción* (Buenos Aires: Centro Cultural Recoleta, Malba-Colección Costantini, 2003), 21.

Fig. 12. Taller de New York Graphic Workshop, c. 1965.

orgullo. Luis estaba haciendo obras muy influenciadas por el Expresionismo alemán y él pasó por un proceso similar al mío: primero el impacto de las posibilidades técnicas que daba Nueva York y luego el gran cambio que significó pensar la noción de edición.

IK ¿En qué sentido creés, como has dicho en varias oportunidades, que aún hoy estás trabajando con el enfoque de la visión quebrada?

Fig. 13. De izquierda a derecha: José Guillermo Castillo, Liliana Porter y Luis Camnitzer, 1970.

LP Un diálogo entre un señor renacentista que está dentro de una postal y "mira" a un personaje de plástico del siglo vientiuno, es una forma de visión quebrada. La línea que empieza en la mano en el espacio virtual y sigue en el papel en el espacio real es visión quebrada. ¡Quizás Noé no esté de acuerdo! Sería una situación típica de visión quebrada . . . [Fig. 11]

IK Desde 1964 a 1970 formás parte del laboratorio de grabado New York Graphic Workshop, junto a Luis Camnitzer y al venezolano José Guillermo Castillo [Figs. 12 y 13]. Leyendo el catálogo que publicó el Blanton Museum sobre el grupo (2008), a uno le queda la sensación de que manejaban conceptos definidos acerca de lo que estaban haciendo, a pesar de que utilizaban los formatos convencionales de los grupos de vanguardia (grupo, nombre, sigla, manifiesto) casi con aires de parodia. Me gustaría que comentes este tema del humor (por ejemplo, el manifiesto y la llamada *cookie*[7] o la noción de *contextual art*), y cuánto había de estratégico en el uso de esas convenciones.

LP Es divertido cómo lo decís. Porque, en ese momento, ser de vanguardia era a lo más que podías aspirar con respecto al futuro. Ahora lo vemos como una convención, pero no en esa coyuntura. Es como si dijeras: "Borges tenía buenas ideas, pero las escribía con lapicera". En ese tiempo todavía se usaba hacer manifiestos. En ese sentido, pues sí, es un poco como decís: lo que hacíamos estaba muy estudiado. Luis venía con las teorías y José con pícaras estrategias y puro cinismo. Creo que José sí era consciente de todas esas convenciones (de los manifiestos, etcétera) y los veía con escepticismo. Él tenía una gran perspectiva para examinar su época, y siento que lo conmovía la seriedad de Luis. Luis venía y se ponía a leer "el ladrillo" (así llamábamos a sus textos analíticos) y José lo miraba divertido y cariñoso y le decía con una sonrisa y acento venezolano: "No te preocupes tanto, chico". Porque él no creía en ninguna teoría filosófica, política o estética en forma definitiva. Aceptaba todo, pero sabía que "no era para tanto". Él era muy lúcido en eso. Intuía, pienso ahora, que todo se convierte en convención y que cualquier afirmación es básicamente de carácter transitorio. Justamente por ser así estimo que a José le hacía bien cierta rigidez de Luis, le equilibraba el sentido de la realidad.

IK ¿Cuáles eran las principales tesis que sostenían al NYGW? ¿Qué era FANDSO?

LP El plan del NYGW ponía énfasis en el factor edición, en la obra múltiple, lo cual incluía el deseo por hacer un arte más democrático. Por otra parte, éramos muy conscientes de que había que poner el acento en los conceptos, en las propuestas y no en el alarde técnico. Los grabadores han sido tradicionalmente muy rígidos con respecto a las leyes del *métier*, y nosotros buscábamos abrir las posibilidades que ofrecía la producción de obra múltiple. Eso nos llevó a las obras ambientales, a las obras postales, a obras tridimensionales, a la utilización de materiales no tradicionales en el grabado y a ideas como las de editar un gesto (por ejemplo: arrugar, mostrado en *Wrinkle* [*Arruga*] de 1968).

FANDSO era, literalmente, *Free Assemblable Non-Functional Disposable Serial Object* [Objetos armables, no-funcionales, descartables y seriados]. Era la sigla para definir el nuevo grabado, una sigla que, quizás de una manera un poquito

7. La *cookie* fue una galleta que los miembros del grupo enviaban por correo en lugar de una postal de navidad. "Hicimos un molde (xilografía) en madera, lo llevamos a una panadería y pedimos que nos hicieran una edición de galletas duraderas. Las pusimos en cajas de cartón para el correo e incluimos el manifiesto de Fandso firmado por los tres". Email de Luis Camnitzer a Liliana Porter, agosto de 2011.

Fig. 14. *Sombra para dos aceitunas* (exposición por correo), 1969.

Fig. 15. *Sombra para boleto de colectivo* (exposición por correo), 1969.

Fig. 16. *Sombra para un vaso* (exposición por correo), 1969.

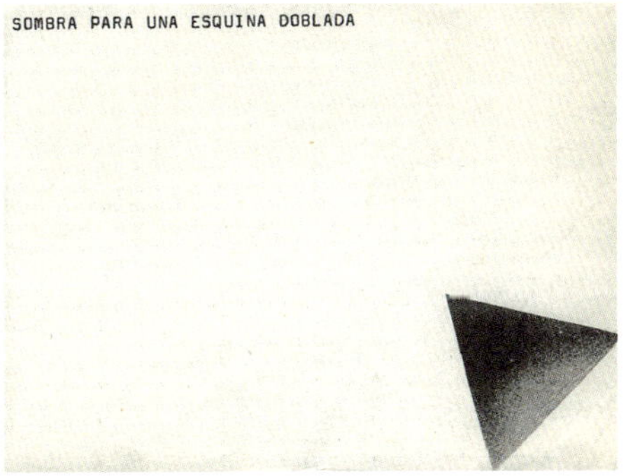

Fig. 17. *Sombra para una esquina doblada* (exposición por correo), 1969.

forzada, reunía los intereses de los tres integrantes del grupo. A José le atraía la noción de los *módulos*, unidades modulares intercambiables como las que presentó en la exhibición del NYGW en el Museo de Bellas Artes en Venezuela en 1972. El *disposable* cubría las exposiciones por correo y las obras ambientales (como mis murales arrugados o los de palabras de Luis en copias Xerox) y los *serial objects* servían para todas las obras múltiples.

IK ¿Por qué empezaron a hacer exposiciones por correo y en qué consistieron?

LP Lo que más me cautivaba era lo poético que había en la acción de mandar sombras por correo. Hoy Luis dice (no sé de dónde sacó eso) que hacíamos arte por correo porque no conseguíamos galería; pero creo que nosotros estábamos tratando de obviar las galerías porque nos parecían antiguas y estábamos en contra de hacer objetos. Ya ves, lo bueno de NYGW era que las distintas visiones del arte podían convivir sin fricciones. José era un tipo muy genial pero un escéptico total, él creía que la cosa no tenía sentido; Luis, por supuesto, pensaba que sí tenía sentido, así que teorizaba y escribía; y yo pensaba que la cuestión no era si tenía o no sentido, sino inventar el sentido. Volviendo a tu pregunta, queríamos hacer obras que no fueran "vendibles", y también, sin querer, el arte por correo era como una extensión o una expansión del grabado al incluir técnicas de producción masiva, como usar el *offset* en lugar de aguafuerte o xilografía. La intención era hacer piezas menos preciosistas.

La primera obra por correo que hice incluía una instrucción-título que decía: "Para arrugar y tirar". Junto a este papel venía otro que tenía impresa la imagen del papel arrugado. Se supone que quien lo recibía debía arrugar el papel y tirarlo. La obra se autodestruía. Era la edición de un gesto en la cual participaba el espectador. Lo que estaba haciendo era mover un poco el sentido del hecho. Normalmente, cuando arrugás y tirás un papel, no pensás. En este caso, ese gesto, dentro del contexto del arte, es decir, de lo inútil, se vuelve poético. Lo importante es que no tiene motivo, está aislado de lo práctico.

Después, en 1969, hice una serie desde el Instituto Torcuato di Tella que consistía en mandar "sombras" por correo: *Sombra para un vaso*, *Sombra para boleto de colectivo*, *Sombra para una esquina doblada* y *Sombra para dos aceitunas* [Figs. 14–17]. En esta obra se revertían los tiempos: inicialmente se veía la sombra impresa que llegaba por correo, luego el que recibía la tarjeta podía, si quería, colocar la aceituna o el vaso o el boleto, encima o al costado de la sombra.

IK ¿Alguien pondría la aceituna?

LP No se sabe, yo la hubiera puesto . . .

IK ¿Qué ejemplos de arte por correo conocían?

LP Conocíamos algunas prácticas pero lo genial es que éramos vecinos de Ray Johnson, que hacía arte por correo mucho antes que nosotros, y ¡en su momento no lo sabíamos! Fue gracioso cuando nos enteramos, porque el cartero opinaba sobre las obras que ambos recibíamos. Se ve que el hombre tomó conciencia de que esos envíos eran diferentes, que tanto los que provenían de la casa de Ray como los nuestros eran otra cosa, y los esperaba con cierta curiosidad.

IK Cuando desde el NYGW inventan la figura de Juan Trepadori surge un aspecto impresionante de la historia del grupo, que tiene que ver con burlarse del mundo del arte, por un lado, y por el otro, solidarizarse entre pares. ¿Podrías contar quién fue Trepadori y cuál era el plan detrás de la creación del personaje?

Fig. 18. Panorámica del proyecto del New York Graphic Workshop presentado en *Información* en The Museum of Modern Art, Nueva York, 1970.

LP Juan Trepadori fue un artista que inventamos en el taller. La historia es así: en un principio, cuando nuestra producción todavía era medio expresionista y hacíamos grabados con color y textura, teníamos editores (*publishers*) que nos compraban ediciones enteras de grabados. Pero cuando comenzamos a ser más "ascéticos" formalmente, nuestra obra no resultaba "vendible", y menos en ediciones completas. Así que en una ocasión, cuando un amigo andaba con problemas económicos, decidimos inventar un artista grabador que respondiera a los deseos estético/comerciales de los compradores. Por mencionarte un caso, uno de estos editores, que se llamaba Barton, quedó encantado con las piezas de este artista inventado, nacido en Paraguay, Juan Trepadori. Eran obras modernas pero comprensibles, sofisticadas y a la vez alegres; en fin, ideales a nuestros fines y a los de ellos.

Así que cualquier amigo que venía y necesitaba dinero hacía un Trepadori, la obra se vendía y el artista conseguía la beca Trepadori, que servía, por ejemplo, para liberar obras de la aduana (ese fue el primer caso), para pagar el costo de algún curso o para comprar materiales. Diversos artistas hicieron obras de Trepadori porque era un estilo fácil de seguir. Lo lindo es que "los cómplices" (desde el primero que lo hizo –un compañero cuya obra era muy dramática, a lo Francis Bacon), cuando hacían estos grabados, totalmente opuestos a su estética personal, se metían en el espíritu de Trepadori y la pasaban muy bien. Trepadori fue cobrando humanidad, se transformó en un personaje querido, un artista bastante derivativo y nada genial; que curiosamente permitía a los artistas, que conformaban el proyecto, la libertad de crear sin presiones y de experimentar cierto inédito e inconfesable placer.

IK La última actividad oficial del grupo fue una participación conjunta en la célebre muestra *Information* en el Museum of Modern Art (MoMA) de Nueva York, en 1970 [Fig. 18]. ¿Podrías contar en qué consistió la obra?

LP Consistía en una página montada en la pared que decía: "The New York Graphic Workshop announces its First Class Mail Exhibition #14". Al lado, había una mesa que tenía sobres y lapiceras para que la gente que quisiera recibir la obra escribiera su dirección en un sobre. Lo que el público recibía no era este mismo cartel, sino uno muy similar que cambiaba la palabra *announces* (anuncia) por *announced* (anunció), o sea, en pasado.

IK Una vez más hacen una obra que intenta burlarse del sistema del arte y simultáneamente producen una donación (en este caso, de la obra al público). El grupo no solo quería regalar la pieza sino, según consta en el libro del NYGW, jugar un juego que supuestamente arruinaría las finanzas del museo, el cual se vería obligado a costear el envío postal de miles de obras. ¿Podrías extenderte en la relación entre circuito tautológico (ya que la gente recibía el anuncio de una obra que consistía en el envío del anuncio), ánimo anti-institucional y el concepto de edición?

LP Veo esta obra menos como burla y más como un juego con el tiempo. Como un juego con lo inmaterial de la cosa. Eso de que al museo le iba a salir muy caro por lo que iba a gastar en el correo, son picardías típicas camnitzerianas, una manera burlona de resistirse a la institución y sus implicancias.

Fig. 19. Casa de Camnitzer y Porter, Lucca, Italia, c. 1971.

IK ¿Hasta cuánto duró NYGW?

LP Como hasta el setenta. El grupo se separó cuando José empezó a trabajar en el Center for InterAmerican Relations [hoy Americas Society], dirigiendo el área de literatura de la institución (Entre otras actividades, él fundó la revista *Review* e hizo traducir a García Márquez al inglés). En ese momento un grupo de artistas hicimos un boicot a la institución porque estábamos en desacuerdo con la política de la sección artística y la política del Center en general. Decidimos que al margen de la relación personal, quedaba raro que siguiéramos como grupo profesional y así nos alejamos de José.

Después del setenta hicimos alguna otra cosa juntos o poníamos el sello del NYGW en alguna obra, pero más bien Luis y yo. José quedó menos conectado.

Fig. 20. Señal de tráfico Camnitzer-Porter, Lucca, Italia, 1975.

IK En 1971, Camnitzer y vos fundan una escuela de grabado en Italia. ¿Cómo surge este proyecto [Figs. 19 y 20]?

LP En 1971, cuando fuimos por primera vez a Europa, paramos en Lucca, Italia, invitados por Gonzalo Fonseca, el artista uruguayo. Allí vimos una casa en venta, un viejo molino de castaños, con un viñedo y un granero junto a un río, y Luis inmediatamente imaginó armar allí una escuela de verano. Me acuerdo que la casa (que Luis conserva todavía) costaba 8000 dólares e hicimos la reserva con 1000 dólares que nos dio el padre de Luis. Volvimos a Nueva York y mandamos a remate dos grabados de la *Suite Vollard* de Picasso y un montón de otras piezas que habíamos conseguido por canje. Así pudimos comprar la casa.

La arreglamos y reformamos, armamos la escuela y empezamos a dar clases los veranos. Teníamos un máximo de doce alumnos, que venían de varios países y dormían en un hotelito cercano o acampaban. Comían con nosotros y trabajaban muchísimo. Era muy intenso. Me acuerdo que Luis era bastante duro con ellos y yo tenía el rol de apaciguar un poco los ánimos.

IK ¿Cómo eran las clases? ¿Intentaban transmitir las ideas del FANDSO?

LP La forma de enseñar era así: primero, analizar con el alumno sus ideas y propuestas desde todo punto de vista, y luego, una vez que llegábamos a un proyecto relevante, estudiábamos sus diferentes posibles soluciones formales y técnicas. Para nada intentábamos que se sumaran a nuestras concepciones o que se influenciaran por nuestro trabajo. Muy al contrario, lo que buscábamos era ayudar a que el alumno encontrara su propio interés, su propia voz, sus propias preguntas y sus propias soluciones.

IK Salvador Dalí tuvo un rol inesperado en tu vida.

LP Era el año 1964. Luis estaba en Pratt Graphic Arts Center y Dalí había llegado a la institución planteando que quería hacer un grabado tridimensional; y como nadie entendía lo que decía (ya que hablaba una mezcla de español, catalán, francés e inglés), llamaron a Luis para traducir y acabó transformándose en algo así como su asistente. La cosa era sin remuneración, pero no importaba. ¡Era Dalí!

Más adelante surgió la posibilidad de hacer grabados para él. Hizo con nosotros la plancha, pero cuando íbamos a imprimir la edición, el editor nos dijo que Dalí se iba a Europa y que no daba tiempo de hacerla y firmarla. Propuso que se estamparan en Europa. Se nos iba una oportunidad buenísima. Entonces, con total espontaneidad, propuse, insólitamente, que antes de partir para Europa él firmara todas las hojas de papel previo a la impresión de los grabados. Sugerí además que se podía preparar una máscara (un esténcil) para que Dalí pudiera firmar siempre en el mismo lugar de la hoja. Imagínate que el editor me miró atónito, como diciendo: "¡Es como firmar cheques en blanco!", Y se empezó a reír. A Luis no le gustó esa risita, así que en ese instante llamó a Dalí por teléfono al St. Regis Hotel (donde Dalí se hospedaba seis meses del año y donde tenía su estudio) y le planteó la idea. Y Dalí, tan espontáneo como yo, dijo: "¡Tráiganme los papeles que los firmo ya!" Y así fue.

Nosotros pensábamos que allí terminaba el asunto, pero él siguió haciendo eso toda la vida, incluso hubo un famoso camión lleno de papeles firmados por Dalí que fue robado y aparecieron en el mercado cientos de *Dalís* falsos. Lo interesante es que la falsedad no estaba en las firmas, que sí eran originales, sino en las imágenes.

IK ¿Cómo se relaciona Dalí con la compra de una primera casa en Nueva York?

LP En esa época nosotros alquilábamos una casa en Locust Valley, Long Island, cerca de la Universidad donde Luis era profesor. Un día viene la persona que nos había tramitado ese alquiler que se había hecho bastante amiga nuestra, y nos dice muy entusiasmada que, muy cerca de allí, había una casa que urgía comprar. Lo único que teníamos era una acuarela de Dalí como de dos metros, que había sido el fondo de una especie de diorama que Dalí estaba armando con ayuda de Luis para la tapa de una revista, y que nos había regalado. Cuando surgió la posibilidad de comprar esta casa, solo tuvimos que conseguir que Dalí nos la autentificara. Y así, de golpe, sin saber cómo, teníamos dos casas, una en Italia, y ésta otra, en Long Island. Así era toda nuestra vida, apenas tocábamos algo se convertía en oro.

IK ¿Tu vida siempre fue así?

LP Sí, pero son decisiones que posiblemente nunca me hubiera atrevido a tomar sola.

IK Necesitás cómplices.

LP Claro.

IK ¿Hasta qué año estuviste casada con Camnitzer?

LP Hasta el 78.

UNA ARGENTINA EN NUEVA YORK
Experiencias de la identidad

IK En 1973 realizás una exposición en el Project Room del MoMA [Fig. 21]. ¿Cómo se originó esa exhibición? ¿En qué consistió? ¿Qué repercusión tuvo en tu posicionamiento en la ciudad?

LP Había expuesto en Milán, en 1972, en la Galería Diagramma, una serie de instalaciones que eran foto-serigrafías impresas directamente sobre las paredes. Eran serigrafías fotográficas de clavos y ganchitos con su sombra, unidas a hilos reales que enganchaba en el piso. Hiperrealistas. Eran situaciones mínimas que engañaban al espectador, sin embargo para mí realmente lo importante no era solo confundir el espacio y la percepción, sino también el tipo de imagen que usaba. Eran elementos que en sí no tenían significado y que instalaba en el fondo blanco, vacío, creando una situación poética a partir de ese espacio de silencio. Después de la exhibición de Milán, entré en la galería Hundred Acres de Nueva York, una galería que me encantaba, cuyo dueño era Ivan Karp y la directora, Barbara Toll. A la semana recibí una invitación de Riva Castleman, curadora en jefe del departamento de grabado del MoMA, para exponer en el Project Room del Museo. Cuando me llegó la invitación, fui a la galería para agradecerles la gestión, imaginando que la propuesta venía a través de ellos, pero lo cierto es que no habían tenido nada que ver. Lo que hicieron entonces fue asignarme una muestra individual en paralelo a la del MoMA, y en vez de un piso me dieron dos. Nunca supe cómo surgió la invitación.

Hay un hecho curioso en relación con esta muestra, y es que en la pared de la sala, en un pequeño texto, dediqué la exposición a la lucha de los pueblos latinoamericanos. En ese momento pensábamos que un latinoamericano tenía que aprovechar una ocasión así para transmitir un mensaje concientizador. La idea no estaba mal. Eran discursos que estaban instalados en la época, como si hoy uno hablase de los derechos de las mujeres o de los inmigrantes. Hay que pensar en el contexto: la Guerra de Vietnam, el movimiento *hippie* y el pensamiento latinoamericano unido, una utopía (ese año [1973] fue el golpe en Uruguay y en Chile). De una manera u otra, los jóvenes nos rebelábamos contra el *establishment,* y como latinoamericanos veíamos como conflictiva toda asociación con las instituciones. Por otro lado, vivía con Luis, que era muy político. Generalmente era él quien estructuraba cualquier discurso que hiciera falta. Así

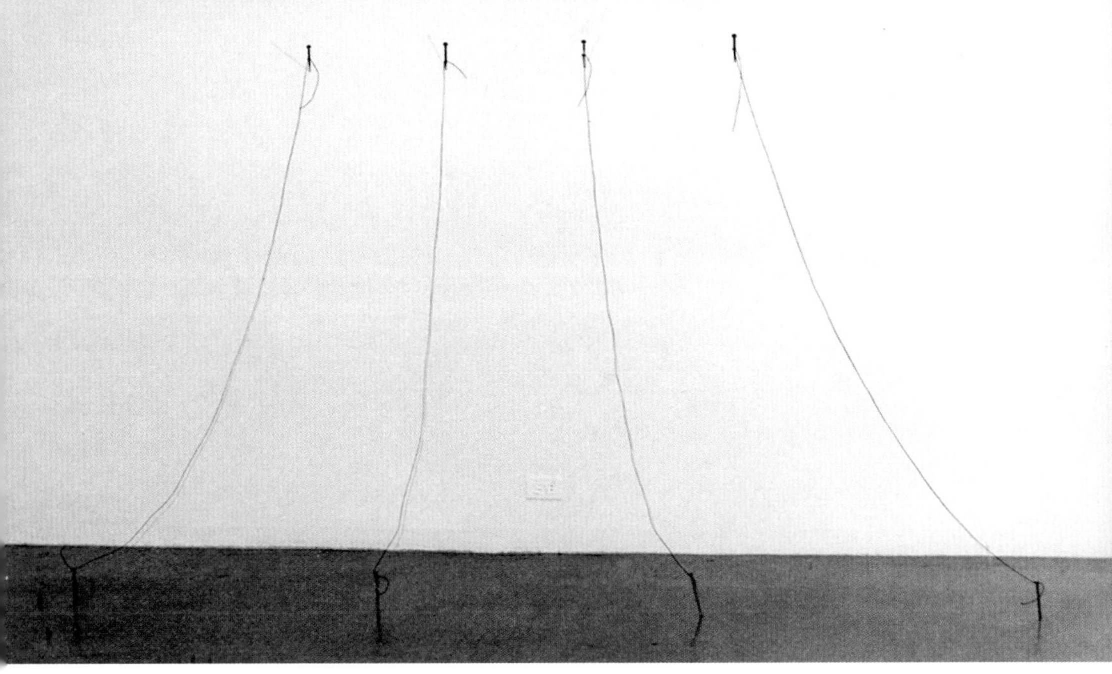

Fig. 21. *Untitled* (Nails) [*Sin título* (Clavos)], The Museum of Modern Art, Nueva York, 1973.

que naturalmente, cuando llegó la invitación del MoMA, él estaba dispuesto a escribir el "ladrillito" en el cual yo rechazaba directamente la proposición.

Por suerte, en medio de eso llegó José Castillo de visita y nos convenció a los dos de que si rehusaba esa invitación, también tenía que rechazar a la galería con la cual acababa de empezar a trabajar, y Luis debía olvidarse de enseñar en la universidad, ya que todo de cierta forma provenía de la misma fuente. Así que terminé negociando y haciendo la exhibición, pero con un "pequeño ladrillo" en la pared.

IK En el libro del NYGW, Camnitzer dice que ese texto decía que eras consciente de que tu invitación al museo estaba condicionada por ser una mujer latinoamericana.

LP El texto se ha perdido y no lo recuerdo muy bien. Lo consulté con Luis y dice que seguramente decía las dos cosas. Hay que tener presente que era una situación muy particular. Viviendo justamente aquí, uno se sentía culpable no solo de estar lejos, además de estar en un territorio que francamente estaba asociado a las dictaduras. Todo acto se volvía simbólico. Por un lado, uno se alegraba de recibir una invitación del MoMA, y por otro, cuestionaba a esas instituciones, puesto que muchos de los miembros directivos estaban implicados en las

Fig. 22. Liliana Porter en su taller en Locust Valley, Long Island, con *The Line* [*La línea*], al fondo, 1973.

políticas de los Estados Unidos respecto a Latinoamérica. Por eso, cuando finalmente decido exponer, lo hago con una proclama que manifestaba la conciencia del conflicto.

De igual manera, internamente en Nueva York se vivía un tiempo de lucha por la integración de las minorías en igualdad de condiciones, y eso estaba forzando a las instituciones a dar cabida a una cuota mínima de estas minorías para mostrarse *politically correct*. Estimo que Riva Castleman estaba realmente interesada en mi obra, pero estoy segura también de que a la institución de algún modo le favorecía esa representación de la doble categoría: mujer y latinoamericana [Figs. 22 y 23]. Mi declaración apuntaba a que no les resultara tan fácil el operativo.

IK ¿Cómo fue la exposición?

LP Había foto-serigrafías impresas directamente sobre el muro y objetos reales. Los elementos impresos eran un clavito, una soga, una sombra, un gancho, que se confundían con los reales.

IK La cuestión del engaño visual, del *trompe l'oeil*, tenía cierta importancia en tu producción de aquel entonces, e incluso lo siguió teniendo en las obras sobre tela que hiciste posteriormente. ¿Cuán importante era ese engaño en sí mismo:

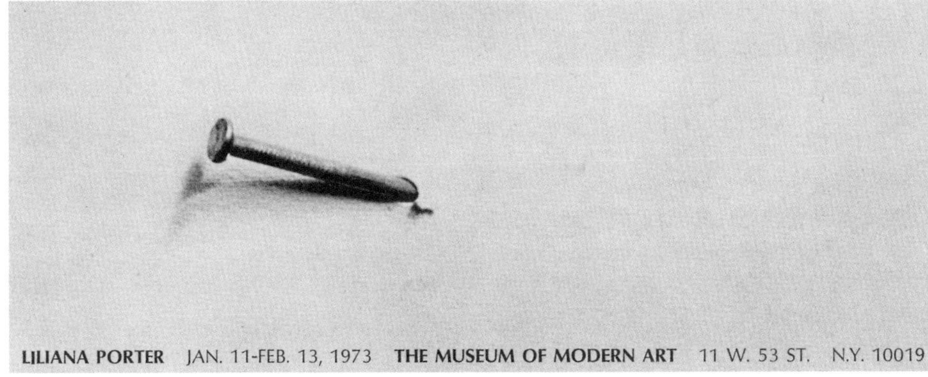

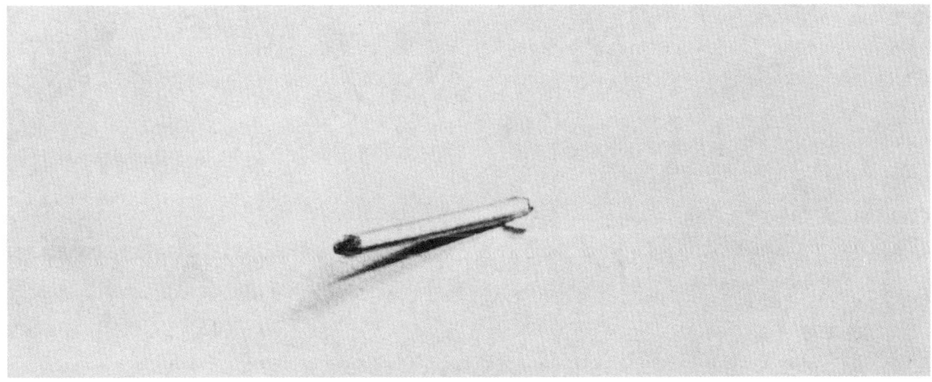

Fig. 23. Tarjeta de invitación (anverso y reverso) para la exposición monográfica de Porter, The Museum of Modern Art, Nueva York, 11 de enero–13 de febrero, 1973.

que el público confundiera la sombra pintada con una sombra real o la serigrafía de un clavo con un clavo real?

LP A mí el truco no me interesaba en sí mismo. Lo que me seducía era ver cómo se unía lo real con lo virtual (la serigrafía del clavo con el hilo real), y la extrañeza o sensación de inquietud que me generaba la desnudez de esas piezas. Un factor que sí empezó a ser muy importante, te diría que protagónico, fue el espacio vacío. Además, creo, son obras que funcionan a partir de una ley importante que es la boludez. El *arte boludo* (así lo llamábamos Luis y yo) consiste en lo siguiente: elegir cosas que no signifiquen nada (lo cual sabemos que es imposible), optar por los elementos menos misteriosos del mundo (aunque de hecho terminen siendo misteriosos). Buscaba lo más neutro, lo menos expresivo: un ganchito, una sombra, un hilito . . .

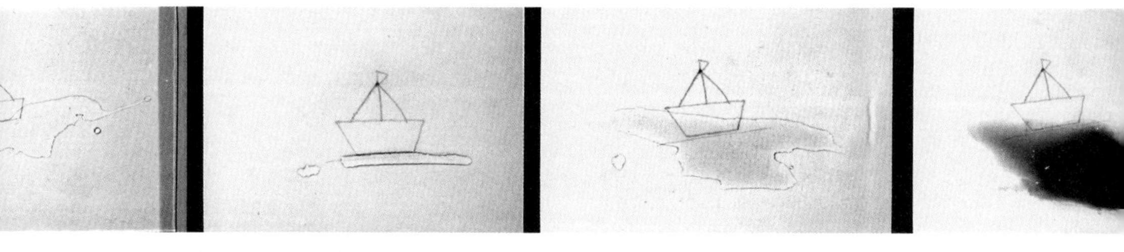

Fig. 24. *Untitled* (contact strip – boat), [*Sin título* (Tira de contacto – barco)], c. 1976–77.

IK De igual forma valorabas la escala de los materiales en relación con el espacio. Por algo los calificás aludiendo a ellos en diminutivo. Hay una expresividad, una poética específica de lo pequeño.

LP La escala es real. El clavo tiene el tamaño del clavo, la soga, el de la soga. Parecen chicos por el espacio vacío alrededor. Recién cambié de escala cuando hice videos, de acuerdo al tamaño de la proyección.

IK Sin embargo hay una expresividad característica que emana de cada componente cuando aparece ubicado solo, en un ambiente vacío, enorme. ¿Podría decirse que esa correspondencia de escala provoca sentimientos en relación a los objetos?

LP El espacio vacío es como un silencio que rodea al objeto y lo aísla de lo demás para que podamos verlo mejor. Estimo que estar solo, sin contexto, enfatiza, potencia la verdadera condición del elemento.

IK En esos años tuviste una crisis personal muy fuerte. ¿Podrías contar qué consecuencias tuvo en tu trabajo?

LP En 1976 tuve serios problemas de salud, que coincidieron con mi separación de Luis. Fue una etapa muy dura, en la cual sentí que me confrontaba con la muerte. Y eso se ligó con la historia trágica de mi mamá y con su manera de ser positiva a pesar de las circunstancias. Esos años en los que tuve que reordenar mi vida me dieron cierta sabiduría, aunque suene pedante. Poco después me casé con Al Wiener, con quien viví doce años. Desde el punto de vista del arte, en esos primeros momentos de crisis empecé a hacer una serie de dibujos, como frases en las que ciertas imágenes reemplazan a las palabras. El protagonista es un barquito como de papel al que le suceden tremendas tragedias: se quema, se hunde, se rompe [Fig. 24]. Visto en perspectiva, esos dibujos no correspondían a ninguna teoría del arte. Era realmente como quien escribe un diario gráfico. No era literatura. No importaba si estaba bien o mal. Era totalmente verdad. A partir de ahí hubo menos control del concepto, menos rigidez, menos ascetismo y más contenido personal. No me importaba demasiado si lo que hacía era arte o no.

IK ¿Cómo era tu posición en el arte neoyorquino de ese momento? ¿Exponías más o menos en las instituciones donde querías? ¿Sentías algún grado de marginación por tu nacionalidad?

LP Hoy me doy cuenta de que, por más que vivás acá mil años, vas a ser extranjero siempre. Si analizás mi curriculum, llama la atención ver que un gran porcentaje de los coleccionistas y exposiciones tienen que ver con Latinoamérica. No hay forma de escapar: aquí la gente está dividida por categoría. Pero ese no es mi problema, ni tengo tiempo para luchar contra eso. Alguien me preguntó hace poco que cuándo me integré, y le contesté que lo interesante de este lugar es que no necesitás integrarte.

Todo el mundo puede seguir siendo distinto, como si estuviera en un país propio, podés inventarte tu propio país. Contestando a tu pregunta, no sé realmente qué papel desempeño ni en qué lugar estoy, sin embargo últimamente siento un reconocimiento más expandido de mi obra.

IK ¿Te referís a un reconocimiento fuera de esas clasificaciones identitarias?

LP Por supuesto. Lo que sí tengo claro, y es bien interesante, es lo que sucede con artistas estadounidenses. Con ellos, uno piensa: "Bueno, el tipo es dueño del lugar". Pero no es así, resulta que ellos te ven a vos como si tuvieras una ventaja, en el sentido de que a mí no solo me conocen en Nueva York, sino también en Argentina, en Perú o en España, cuando por lo general los estadounidenses tienen una repercusión bastante local. En términos generales, diría que aquí el mundo del arte es muy grande y tiene numerosos niveles de integración y reconocimiento, incluso para los locales. De todos modos, sobre mi posición en el sistema del arte en aquel entonces, como le pasa a tantos jóvenes, yo me sentía muy bien: con muestra en el MoMA, con galería . . .

IK ¿Cómo se articulaba la categoría del *arte boludo*[8] con la supuesta intelectualidad del arte conceptual?

8. Ver más en Luis Camnitzer, *De la Coca-Cola al arte boludo* (Santiago de Chile: Editorial Metales Pesados, 2009).

LP La boludez de la que hablamos tiene un costado moral: se trata de un arte boludo pero no tan boludo. La cuestión del vacío y del hilito o de cualquier otro objeto insignificante tenía que ver con descubrir que el silencio es más importante que la palabra, que el silencio puede ser la antesala de una genialidad. Pienso en Giorgio Morandi como modelo. Lo que quiero decir es que no hay nada tan inteligente porque no hemos llegado a la definición de nada. La filosofía se encuentra con ese límite. Entonces, creo yo, lo mejor es encontrar un método para callarte la boca un poco, un método en el que el espacio sea el protagonista, que el objeto sea apenas una presencia.

IK Vamos a ubicarnos en los años ochenta, cuando en Nueva York ocurren dos acontecimientos simultáneos: por un lado, emerge un grupo de artistas críticos y conceptuales (con muchas mujeres a la cabeza) que trabaja con la apropiación de imágenes de la cultura de masas, y por otro, es el contexto de auge de la pintura y el *boom* del mercado del arte.

LP El momento en que vuelve la pintura es relevante, porque a todo el mundo le daban ganas de pintar de nuevo. Algunos de los pintores me interesaban mucho, como David Salle, más que nada por eso de superponer distintas imágenes en una misma tela. Por otra parte, la fotógrafa Cindy Sherman siempre me pareció notable, una artista fuerte. Me encantaba la idea de los estereotipos de las películas y cómo aísla una imagen de un todo narrativo. Me gusta porque no se trata solamente de esa imagen que ves, sino también de lo que no estás viendo, de una narración imaginada.

IK Barbara Kruger, Jenny Holzer y Cindy Sherman son artistas que se apropiaban y usaban lenguajes de la cultura masiva. Se relacionan con tu obra, específicamente con la crítica a la representación que aparece en la utilización, por tu parte, de íconos de la cultura masiva. ¿Qué coincidencias tenías con esa escena?

LP Directa o emocionalmente, nada. Podían hacer exposiciones que te parecieran originales o que te enriquecieran, pero no te puedo decir que hayan sido importantes, como te podría decir que, años antes, me influenció [Luis Felipe] Noé. Los artistas que realmente me afectaron fueron Lichtenstein y Warhol.

IK ¿Eso sucedió puntualmente en los sesenta o continuó?

LP Siguió sucediendo. Lichtenstein continuó haciendo exhibiciones sensacionales, siempre volvía con propuestas nuevas que me sorprendían. Otro artista que me interesaba muchísimo fue Joel Shapiro. Me parecía magnífico que se ocupara toda la vida de la imagen de una persona que está por caerse. Me acuerdo que una vez me acerqué a él, me presenté y le dije que me encantaba su obra y que me parecía increíble que durante tanto años él hiciera, en diversas maneras y posiciones, a ese personaje a punto de caer. Otro artista importante para mí es Richard Artschwager. Me encanta esa mesa inútil que hizo con un cubo que tiene dibujado el espacio de abajo.

IK ¿De Warhol qué te atrae concretamente?

LP En primer lugar, la repetición. Él te hace descubrir que la repetición, en lugar de enfatizar algo, termina anulándolo como sucede cuando repetís varias veces una palabra y de pronto no significa nada. Por otro lado, me gustan muchísimo sus retratos, que en realidad no son retratos de una persona en particular porque son todos iguales. En Warhol se trata de transformar todo en un producto, y en ese sentido, sus figuras son terroríficas. Es el mismo motivo por el cual me entusiasma tanto la imagen de la mujer llorando de Lichtenstein, que es lo más frío que hay desde el punto de vista del lenguaje, pero que puede, a la vez, ser triste.

IK Vos trabajás nociones muy cercanas a esos problemas. No solamente la cuestión del sentido de las imágenes y de los símbolos en su existencia como mercancías (pienso en tus piezas de Mickey o del Che Guevara de 1995), sino también en relación con lo terrorífico que recién mencionabas, que tiene que ver con la contextualización de las imágenes. En tu obra más reciente, es impresionante ver qué pasa con objetos que usualmente vemos en contextos ingenuos, mostrados de tal forma que irradian toda su monstruosidad.

LP Sí, y en el caso de Warhol lo genial es que su obra se vuelve cada vez más dramática sin necesidad de sangre ni de ningún *cliché*. Me detengo en su imagen de Marilyn. Toda la tristeza y el dramatismo están en nuestra cabeza. Así es todo.

IK Bueno, no sé si "todo es así". Considero que es tarea específica del *pop* radicalizar esa conexión entre símbolo y neutralidad.

LP Esa es una buena palabra, neutralidad. Además de Warhol, me gustaba Jonathan Borofsky, así como me encantaban los chistes de Richard Prince. Son chistes, algunos escritos a mano en un papel enmarcado y colgados en la pared. Lo interesante es que son chistes como de bar, racistas, fascistas, machistas o de mal gusto, pero a propósito y en el contexto de una galería de arte se tornan geniales. Él hizo una muestra donde exponía los chistes pintados al estilo expresionista. Ahí la cosa era ya totalmente absurda debido a esa dislocación entre chiste y pintura. ¡Fantástica! Hay una obra muy sugerente de Artschwager, en la cual él utiliza un rectángulo de puntas muy redondeadas, casi un óvalo (lo hizo en plástico, dibujado en la pared o en el suelo), y lo distribuía por toda la ciudad, de tal forma que ibas por la calle y te lo encontrabas, por ejemplo, dibujado en el piso. Lo que me parecía genial era que vos inevitablemente lo reconocías y así se ponía a funcionar una complicidad muy cariñosa entre el artista desconocido y el ciudadano, como si él te dijera: "estoy con vos".

IK Hacia fines de los setenta comenzás a trabajar sobre tela. En ese sentido, quisiera preguntarte, ¿qué sucedió con la utopía de FANDSO? ¿Sentiste que traicionabas el deseo de producir ediciones ilimitadas y el interés por expandir el acceso a la obra de arte por una obra única destinada a un mercado?

LP No. Es que por un lado está la idea y por otro lado la realidad en continuo movimiento. Las concepciones no pueden ser para siempre puntos fijos. Por ejemplo, ¿quién nos iba a decir que, hoy en día, obras concebidas para ser desechables están valuadas en el mercado del arte a un muy buen precio? Alguien podría sentirlo como una traición o como un fracaso del plan original. En cambio, pienso que el propósito original sigue intocado y manifiesto en su propuesta idealista y utópica, y la obra en sí (a manera de ejemplo: las exposiciones por correo), ya no es obra "viva", sino documentos de sí misma. Y, en su calidad de documentos, estimo correcto, natural e inevitable que tengan un precio relativamente alto en el mercado.

IK Igualmente, hacia fines de los setenta empieza el *boom* del Posmodernismo, que tenía mucha similitud con fundamentos teóricos que subyacen en tu obra, sobre todo con la tesis de que cualquier objeto es, inseparablemente, signo y mercancía; es decir, la idea de imagen como espectáculo. ¿Cómo te relacionabas con esa teoría?

LP Personalmente nunca estuve muy de acuerdo con la tesis de que una tendencia o un movimiento viene después del otro, que el que lo dice primero gana y los demás son derivativos, o que si no hacés una cosa de determinada forma estás desubicado. El Posmodernismo en gran medida era lo opuesto al criterio de evolución, y en ese sentido era muy cercano a mi tendencia natural: todo estaba permitido, no había antiguo, moderno o de moda. Así que fue algo muy interesante, incluso políticamente.

IK Hasta ahora mencionaste el texto de tu muestra en el MoMA como un manifiesto claro de la premisa del posicionamiento identitario. Me gustaría que desarrollaras más cómo te afectó la cuestión del multiculturalismo y la lucha por la representación de las mujeres y los latinos, una situación que se dio con tanta fuerza en Nueva York.

LP Fui a muchísimas conferencias, mesas redondas y mítines sobre esos temas y la verdad es que no me sentía representada por las feministas estadounidenses. Yo venía de una experiencia cultural distinta y muchas situaciones me causaban rechazo. Incluso te diría que para mí, las feministas estadounidenses reclamaban el poder de los hombres en lugar de cuestionarlo.

IK ¿Cómo sentís que fueron tus oportunidades como artista profesional, siendo una mujer argentina que vive en Nueva York?

LP En aquel momento sentía que hacía lo que quería y que no se me discriminaba por ser mujer. Pero visto en perspectiva, deduzco que estaba equivocada. Si uno compara mi carrera con la de un artista hombre equivalente, es evidente que el tipo va adelante mucho más rápido. Sin embargo, a mí me parecía que me había ido bastante bien, y tampoco me había sentido oprimida por mi marido ni por nadie. Me daba cuenta de las discriminaciones y diferencias en los sueldos y oportunidades, de los roles que se habían establecido, o que la proporción de hombres y mujeres representada en exposiciones y galerías era abismalmente desigual. Entendía que había mucho por cambiar, pero no me sentía integrada al feminismo tal como estaba planteado en Estados Unidos. Además yo era muy jovencita y bastante inexperta.

IK ¿Qué impresión te provocaba el arte de las feministas?

LP En esa época emerge un grupo de mujeres artistas que hacía obras muy autobiográficas y, en mi criterio, bastante cursis, cosas literales e ilustrativas, y muchas a mi juicio gratuitamente agresivas. En realidad creo que tenía mis prejuicios y no aceptaba bien todas las obras, aun cuando se hicieron piezas muy fuertes que sí me tocaban, como las de Martha Rosler (*Semiotics of the Kitchen*, de los años setenta, que es brillante). Había en el grupo inicial gente muy valiosa como Lucy Lippard, Nancy Spero o Miriam Shapiro . . . Para que se entienda mi punto de vista, lo más interesante que vi de activismo feminista norteamericano fueron las Guerrilla Girls[9], que en realidad aparecieron más tarde, en los años ochenta, y de hecho siguen activas. Me gustaba de entrada que eran inteligentes, tenían humor y eran anónimas. Asistí a muchas conferencias y actividades y no hay duda de que son muy efectivas y muy geniales. Se visten de gorilas para mantener el anonimato y sus varias acciones consiguen realmente hacerte reflexionar sobre los temas de sexismo, la discriminación, la explotación o la corrupción. Son radicales, verdaderas luchadoras por los derechos humanos. Radicales e inteligentes.

Ahora me doy cuenta de que, independientemente de mis propias limitaciones para relacionarme con ciertas obras, yo no estaba de acuerdo con esa idea esencialista de la mujer. Más bien las obras [feministas] que más me impactaban eran las que se aproximaban al asunto desde la perspectiva de una construcción social.

IK ¿Podrías extenderte en el tema de la construcción social de la condición de mujer?

LP Lo que quiero decir es que existe un concepto de la mujer que es el resultado de una construcción social que funciona según intereses políticos y patrones culturales. La propuesta feminista que más me interesa es aquella que revela y a la vez cuestiona esta construcción.

IK En torno a esta situación, ¿hasta qué punto te marcó tu amistad con la artista Ana Mendieta?

LP En esos años fue muy enriquecedor ser amiga de Ana Mendieta, que era feminista y a quien admiraba muchísimo. Hacía una obra valiente y difícil. Una obra que estaba basada en la *performance*, y que por consiguiente no tenía un mercado, ya que todavía no estaba de moda la foto de registro.

Conocí a Ana a través de Hans Breder, en 1965. Él había sido profesor suyo en la Universidad de Iowa y luego habían tenido una relación amorosa. Ana había llegado a Estados Unidos desde Cuba, directamente a un orfanato en Iowa, y en

9. En 1985, un grupo de artistas mujeres, indignadas por una exposición en el MoMA que incluía obras de 165 artistas –de los cuales solo 17 eran mujeres–, fundó las Guerrilla Girls. Autodenominándose como "la conciencia del mundo artístico" produjeron afiches para transmitir información y provocar debate, usando el humor y haciendo declaraciones audaces como por ejemplo: "¿Las mujeres deben estar desnudas para entrar al Met. Museum?" Asumieron los nombres de artistas femeninas muertas y empezaron a usar máscaras de gorila cuando hacían apariciones públicas, para guardar su anonimato. Hasta el momento las Guerrilla Girls han producido más de 90 proyectos, incluyendo afiches, acciones, vallas publicitarias, postales, libros y revistas, en los cuales examinan la discriminación en el arte, la cultura y la política.

1975 dejó esa ciudad para venirse a Nueva York, en ese momento el centro del arte. Ella no le tenía miedo a nada; al principio trabajaba limpiando casas y en un bar y en un restaurant en Soho que se llamaba Food[10]. Ana podía bajarse una botellita de ron sin ningún problema. ¡Todo lo contrario a mí! Siempre contaba que cuando era chica, en el orfanato, pensaba: "Voy a ser delincuente o voy a ser artista". ¡Menos mal que se decidió por lo último! Justamente por ser tan distinta a mí, la admiraba y me sentía, en comparación, una burguesa absoluta.

IK Por lo que decís, es evidente que nunca te llamó la atención participar de situaciones de militancia. ¿Hubo alguna causa que te haya comprometido o conmovido especialmente?

LP Sí, el arte. Considero que el arte es una causa que puede ser vista como política. El arte es una forma de cuestionamiento permanente. Si te entregás a ese proceso, inevitablemente te sitúas delante de la vida y la sociedad.

Hay artistas cuyas obras tratan argumentos directamente políticos. En mi caso, lo político no aparece como tema recurrente, pero pienso que se manifiesta en mi obra de diversas maneras. He intentado ser consistente con los muchos contextos en los cuales hago circular mis trabajos. O sea, cuando había dictadura en Argentina y me invitaban a mostrar representando al país, obviamente no participaba. Se dieron situaciones como la *Contrabienal*[11], en la cual intervine activamente y colaboré escribiendo una declaración [Fig. 25]. Hubo muchas otras ocasiones concretas en las cuales asumí una postura pública, luchas sociopolíticas, como en la actitud opositora que asumí frente a la Guerra de Vietnam. En 1970 hice una serigrafía con una foto que había aparecido en el *New York Times*, del asesinato de una vietnamita, y debajo escribí: "Esta mujer es norvietnamita, sudafricana, puertorriqueña, colombiana, negra, argentina, mi madre, mi hermana, tú, yo" [Fig. 26].

IK ¿Cómo fue tu experiencia en relación con el surgimiento del llamado multiculturalismo?

10. El restaurante *Food* abrió sus puertas en 127 Prince Street, en la esquina con Wooster Street, en octubre de 1971. Sus fundadores eran Gordon Matta-Clark, Caroline Gooden y Tina Girouard. Alrededor de sesenta artistas trabajaron en *Food* como cocineros, camareros y ayudantes durante los primeros tres años de este negocio comunitario, cuyo objetivo era apoyar y ayudar a la comunidad artística de la zona sur de Manhattan. El grupo tuvo éxito, también, cultivando un ambiente creativo: algunos artistas venían al restaurante en calidad de chefs invitados, bailarines venían a bailar, y hasta se hicieron películas dentro del local. Era un lugar donde la gente venía para inspirarse, debatir y producir arte.

11. *Contrabienal* fue un libro publicado para responder a la Bienal de São Paulo de 1971, denominada Bienal de la Dictadura. Organizado por artistas latinos radicados en Nueva York a través del Movimiento de Independencia Cultural Latinoamericano (MICLA) y el Museo Latinoamericano.

Liliana Porter

El artista, como todo ser humano, no está al margen de la realidad social que lo envuelve. La posición de "no comprometido" es en sí un compromiso, pero con la reacción.
Para quien hace arte, la forma de hacerlo, las situaciones en las que acepta o renuncia su exhibición, implican una forma de manifestar una posición política, conciente o inconcientemente.
Participar en esta contrabienal es una forma de precisar esta conciencia, y también una forma de comunicación con compañeros alrededor de esa conciencia.
Quizás, de este enfoque común, puede salir un nuevo lenguaje.

Liliana Porter.

Fig. 25. Portada de la publicación *Contrabienal* y declaración de Porter, 1971.

LP Cuando la galería Bonino estaba en Nueva York, en la década del sesenta, nadie mencionaba si, por ejemplo, Noé era hispano o no. Recién con Nixon tenés que llenar el formulario y poner el asterisco en esa categoría.

Me acuerdo de una anécdota de Luis Cancel, curador del Bronx Museum, de origen portorriqueño, que vivía hacía muchos años en Nueva York. Fue por primera vez a Buenos Aires de visita y cuando volvió me contó que cada vez que él hablaba de los "hispanos", los argentinos le decían que no sabían que hubiera tantos españoles en Nueva York. Él no sabía que nosotros no usamos esa palabra para definir a cualquiera que hable español, ni sabíamos a qué se refería.

IK ¿Pudiste aprovechar positivamente esta nueva situación?

LP Lo que pasa es que los estadunidenses están acostumbrados a esas clasificaciones: si hablás con acento (yo hablo con acento), a veces te hablan más fuerte o creen que no entendés, y muchos se sienten superiores. Eso es muy difícil de cambiar, pero es un problema de ellos. Y si hago una exposición en Houston, y el museo me compra una obra, ésta pasa a integrar su colección latinoamericana, aunque haya hecho toda mi producción en Estados Unidos. Son casilleros muy duros; pero en algún sentido los acepto. ¡Bueno, está bien, yo soy argentina!

IK ¿Ha habido ocasiones en las que tu obra haya circulado en Estados Unidos por fuera de lo latinoamericano?

LP Sí. La galería Hundred Acres, en SoHo, donde ingresé en 1972, no solo no enfatizaba mi condición de argentina, sino que se pasaba del otro lado. Sospecho que incluso les convendría en ocasiones que mi apellido sonara completamente inglés.

También cuando expuse en el Project Room del MoMA en el 73, la invitación surgió porque estaba planteando algo nuevo dentro del grabado. En esa circunstancia en realidad fui yo quien me presenté como latinoamericana.

A veces te invitan a una exposición temática y estás ahí y no es porque seas latinoamericana. Aun cuando en realidad nunca sabés si estás llenando un espacio políticamente correcto . . . Por otro lado, cuando hablo con amigos artistas estadunidenses, puedo notar que muchos de ellos, salvo que sean famosísimos, tampoco se sienten integrados.

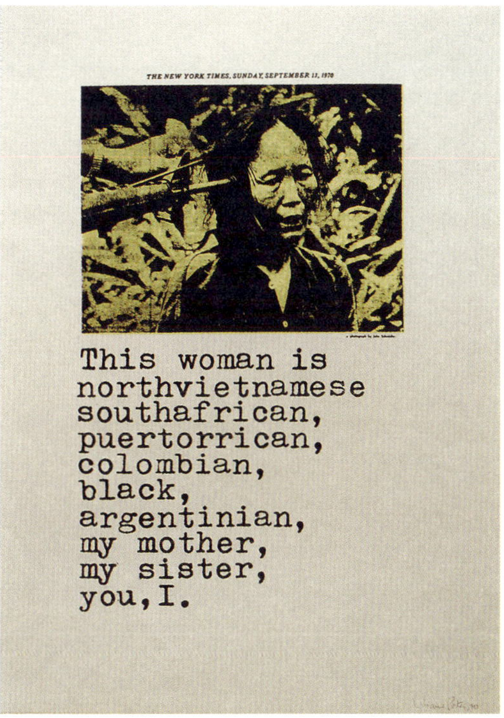

Fig. 26. *The New York Times, Sunday, September 13, 1970* [*New York Times, domingo, 13 de septiembre de 1970*], 1970.

IK Lo que decís es que una característica paradójica de Nueva York es que nunca sentís que estás en el centro.

LP Sí, a menos que seas, qué se yo, Cindy Sherman. Habría que preguntarle . . .

FOTOGRAFÍA Y FICCIÓN

IK Hablemos un poco de la fotografía, tema central de la muestra antológica en la que trabajamos juntas, titulada *Fotografía y ficción,* en el Centro Cultural Recoleta de Buenos Aires en 2003. El objetivo central de la exposición era mostrar cómo la fotografía aparece en tu obra desde finales de los sesenta, concretamente desde 1968 (cuando hiciste tu primer foto-grabado, la obra de la *Arruga*), y cómo esta técnica, con su capacidad de "literalizar" las cosas como diría Baudrillard, definió tácitamente las bases de tu trabajo: una reflexión sobre las relaciones entre los objetos y la reproductibilidad técnica [Fig. 27]. La exhibición permitía entender cómo la fotografía acompañó al desarrollo de tu obra, aunque por más de veinte años haya permanecido oculta en lo que considerabas apenas una fase en el proceso de producción, y tratada como un "adminículo sin pretensión alguna destinado al uso interno"[12], tal como funcionaba en sus orígenes, cuando era utilizada por los pintores como base para sus frescos.

LP Percibía a la fotografía como el tipo de imagen más objetiva posible y como un instrumento que me servía para apropiarme de objetos de la realidad (por ejemplo, un clavo) e imprimirlos en la pared; o luego de armar situaciones, sacarles una foto e insertarla en un grabado. Era una época en la cual todavía la fotografía estaba muy separada del resto de las artes visuales. Entonces la usaba como vehículo para desplazar imágenes hacia y entre mis obras, pero todavía no me atrevía a mostrar las fotos como tales. Así que antes de los noventa solamente expuse algunas, muy pocas piezas con soporte fotográfico. Aún no había un contexto para ese tipo de trabajos. Un poco como le pasaba a Ana Mendieta, las galerías no eran receptivas. Y uno tampoco tenía fe, porque si uno hubiera tenido fe habría dicho ¡esto es una obra y basta!

IK ¿Cuándo hacés una foto-foto por primera vez?

LP Las primeras fotos eran en blanco y negro y las hice entre 1968 y 1977. La mayoría eran fotos que incluían mis manos, ya sea arrugando una foto, como en *Arno* [1968] o dibujándome líneas de tinta que continuarían en el muro o en otro papel, y también están esas fotos donde aparece mi cara y la de Luis con unas líneas de tinta que unían formas en diferentes superficies.

Tengo una enorme cantidad de fotografías, pero las hice para pasarlas a

12. Walter Benjamin, "Breve historia de la fotografía", en *Discursos interrumpidos I* (Buenos Aires: Aguilar, Altea, Taurus, Alfaguara, 1989), 65.

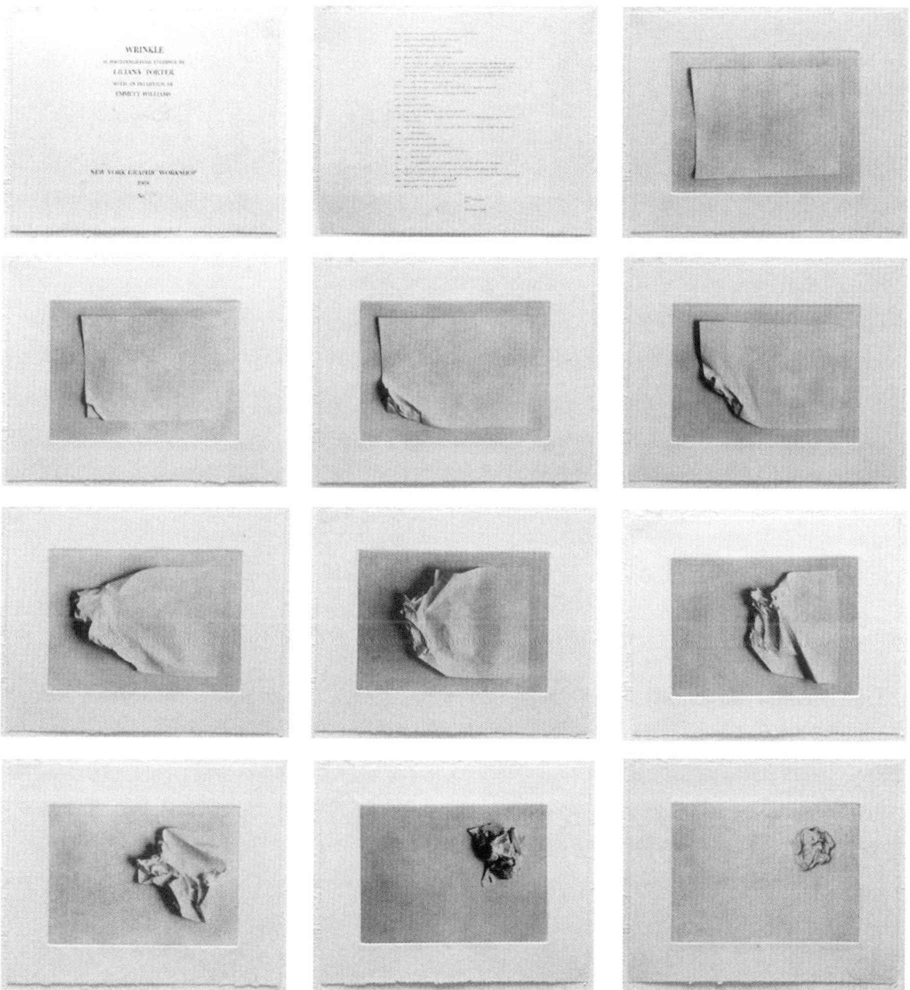

Fig. 27. *Wrinkle* [*Arruga*], 1968.

foto-serigrafía o a foto-grabado. Fue en 1995 cuando decidí usar el medio tal cual. Recuerdo que una de las primeras fotos conforma un tríptico, *Dialogue with Petrus Christus Postcard* [*Diálogo con tarjeta postal Petrus Christus*]. En el año 1994 tuve una exposición con Leandro Katz y David Lamelas en Buenos Aires, en el Instituto de Cooperación Iberoamericana, y mi obra, que era una instalación mural, incluía un estante en donde armé tres "diálogos". Uno de ellos es la postal *Retrato de una joven muchacha,* del pintor flamenco Christus, que mira de reojo a un futbolista brasilero de plástico parado sobre un cubito de madera. A esa escena le hice una foto blanco y negro que, al año siguiente, formó parte del tríptico *Dialogue with Petrus Christus Postcard* [*Diálogo con*

Fig. 28. *Dialogue with Petrus Christus Postcard* [*Diálogo con tarjeta postal Petrus Christus*], 1995.

tarjeta postal Petrus Christus] [1995] [Fig. 28]. Después está *Gaucho* [1995], que originalmente fue una serigrafía, luego una pintura y al final volví al negativo e hice la foto. Decidí sacar la foto porque me di cuenta de que bastaba por sí sola.

Antes de eso tenía el prejuicio de que no podía hacer fotos porque no era fotógrafa. Era un prejuicio artesanal, probablemente derivado de mi formación como grabadora. Pronto comprendí que no era necesario tener el conocimiento técnico perfecto. De golpe la cabeza te libera de ese lío y empezás a entender que si no se piensa tanto en la técnica y uno hace la obra, salen imágenes que en el fondo son más originales que si uno fuera un fotógrafo profesional.

IK Hay una pieza, específicamente una pintura, que me gusta muchísimo. Se llama *La fotografía II*, 1996, y muestra una serie de muñecos posando para una cámara de fotos [Fig. 29]. La imagen es muy graciosa, porque los personajes están posando con toda seriedad, enfrentando a la cámara que aparece representada como si fuese un protagonista más de la escena. Es en realidad un diálogo entre los muñecos y la cámara, que se miran mutuamente de manera solemne. Llama la atención que sea un cuadro sobre tela proveniente de un grabado, que proviene de una fotografía cuyo tema es la fotografía. Otro elemento particular de este trabajo es que, contrariamente a otras obras que incluían tu mano o el pincel como huella del proceso de producción, este cuadro ya no incluye el cuerpo sino directamente la cámara.

LP La historia detrás de ese cuadro es que yo tenía una exposición en la galería de Monique Knowlton en Nueva York. Quería hacer una muestra de fotos pero ella me pidió que por lo menos presentara algunas obras sobre tela, y entonces hice dos que se llamaban *La fotografía*, que documentan una fotografía.

Fig. 29. *The Photograph II* [*La fotografía II*], 1996.

IK Poco a poco empezás a expandir el repertorio de imágenes que incluís en tu obra[13], hasta que en un momento dado algo se enfoca y te transformás en una coleccionista de juguetes. Incluso, más que cualquier otro coleccionista, te convertís en lo que Walter Benjamin definía como una "fisonomista del mundo de las cosas"[14], alguien capaz de extraer toda la potencia metafísica y sentimental de los objetos. ¿Cómo se origina ese itinerario hacia el coleccionismo?

LP Recuerdo que en realidad la secuencia fue barco, libros, conejos de Alicia, Mickey, jarrones, Donald, postales y, muy poco a poco, se fueron agregando otros protagonistas. Aparece por ejemplo José Gregorio Hernández, un médico del siglo XIX que fue canonizado por el pueblo venezolano y colombiano, y que se parece al personaje de Magritte. Es un personaje surrealista. ¡Un santo con corbata! Y allí, creo, comenzaron *los diálogos.*

13. En un texto sobre Porter escribí: "La obra *Objetos familiares* (de la serie de apropiaciones de René Magritte) será fundamental porque, estableciendo un diálogo con ella, será como Porter empezará a extender su repertorio de imágenes. La obra de Magritte presenta un grupo de hombres frente a los cuales Magritte coloca la imagen de ciertos objetos. Porter sustituye esas imágenes por otras, adhiriéndoles la foto de la imagen de ciertos objetos. Reaparecen figuras ya trabajadas anteriormente por la artista como el triángulo, el cubo y la pirámide, pero también aparecen por primera vez el barco, la nube o la luna, un grupo de figuras que se volverá esencial en el repertorio de imágenes de las obras de la etapa siguiente, y, lo que es fundamental: irán adquiriendo status de símbolo". En Katzenstein, *Liliana Porter: Fotografía y ficción*.

14. Walter Benjamin, *The Arcades Project* (Cambridge y Londres: Belknap Press of Harvard University Press, 1999), 207.

Fig. 30. *Minnie/Che,* 2003–6.

IK Aquí confluyen múltiples factores: se amplía el repertorio de objetos, surge la serie de *los diálogos,* empezás a mostrar fotografías y el humor adquiere un protagonismo inédito. Respecto a este último punto, si bien los juguetes que coleccionás remiten al pasado, me da la sensación de que hay un claro abandono de cierto tipo de melancolía y el surgimiento del humor, de la mano de algunos descubrimientos relacionados con los juguetes. ¿Estás de acuerdo?

LP Es verdad. Supongo que el surgimiento del humor fue inconsciente. Las confrontaciones entre objetos, aun cuando se trate de objetos viejos, ocurren en el presente cuando en las pinturas anteriores parecía que los elementos no se podían desligar del pasado.

IK Hay un aspecto muy importante, específicamente durante un periodo de tu producción que tiene que ver con la simbología política de los objetos. Me refiero a esas obras en las cuales utilizás imágenes culturalmente muy cargadas, como en *Minnie / Che* [2003–6], un plato con la imagen del Che [Guevara], sobre el cual aparece acostada, eufórica de amor, Minnie [Fig. 30].

LP Varios factores me seducen de esas imágenes. Por un lado, cómo alguien que en un momento está vivo luego se transforma en un platito, o en la imagen del envoltorio de un queso, como en el caso de un queso que venden acá que se llama *Juana de Arco.* En la obra del Che y Minnie a la que te referís, también están funcionando los lugares comunes. El Che representa el comunismo y Minnie el capitalismo, y me encanta que de repente se enamoren o que Minnie esté robándole un beso al Che. En la película, la obra se presenta en dos tomas: una cuando ella le da el beso y la otra cuando se da vuelta y nos mira, y la música sube de tono, y hasta quizás uno podría emocionarse en ese punto.

En la foto en la que aparece el Che mirando al conejo de Alicia, ambos comparten el hecho de estar en un mismo plano, el plano de la representación, más cerca de la ficción que de la realidad, un plano que podrían compartir con San Martín o Evita [Perón]. Seres que ya no sabés si pertenecen a la historia o a la mitología.

IK ¿Creés que el cambio de medio que hiciste en los noventa, de la serigrafía a la fotografía, transformó tu percepción de la expresividad de las figuras?

LP Claro, la imagen en la fotografía es más concreta que en el grabado, más real. Se podría decir que en el cambio de la fotografía al video, la relación con las imágenes es más directa. Fui acercándome al objeto. Luego aparecen los estantes con los objetos "en vivo", y cuando llegás a ese punto te das cuenta de que continúan siendo una representación.

IK Considero necesario apuntar que es justamente en los años noventa cuando se produce un desarrollo vertiginoso de las tecnologías digitales, la etapa en la cual abandonás la problemática semiótica tal como la venías trabajando en los últimos años (esa experimentación didáctica con los distintos planos de la virtualidad y de la presencia), y ponés en escena otros componentes.

LP Por supuesto, porque la tecnología lo que hace en primer lugar es cuestionar la objetividad de la fotografía. Al aparecer todas las posibilidades digitales se desestabiliza el concepto de lo real. O sea que el espectador se conecta con la representación a tal punto que, si vas a comprar un dentífrico y nunca lo viste en una foto, no lo comprás porque decís: "Eso no existe". Y es que hoy en día, la cosa es un subproducto de la representación.

IK ¿Cómo surge la idea de filmar tu primer video?

LP Surge a raíz de un juguete, un Pinocho que toca los timbales cuando le das cuerda. Lo más lindo es la expresión de Pinocho una vez que acaba de tocar. Y ese silencio solo lo podés representar con el ruido y el gesto anteriores. Fue ahí cuando decidí que lo ideal era filmarlo. Los videos de arte por lo general no me gustaban, pero el elemento temporal me hacía falta.

IK El formato cinematográfico que utilizaste en cada una de tus películas, caracterizado por el montaje de una serie de escenas o *tableaux vivants* precedidas por textos y acompañadas por música, es muy particular. ¿Cómo llegás a él?

LP Llego directamente desde la experiencia de las fotografías a color. Los fragmentos de los videos son como fotografías donde suceden más cosas. Tengo conmigo el álbum con todas las notas, cartas y material de cuando hice *For You / Para usted*, mi primera película [1999]. El álbum comienza con la carta que le escribí a Juan Mandelbaum, quien tiene una productora de video, explicándole lo que quería hacer.

Transcribo el primer fragmento de mi carta a Juan [finales de 1997]:

> *La idea se basa en el siguiente formato: una serie de viñetas o situaciones que van una detrás de la otra y forman así un todo, el cual tendrá un título general. Unas a color, otras en blanco y negro. Algunas serán silenciosas, otras con sonido y seguramente habrá un texto o título que las precede.*
> *Me lo imagino mejor en film o por lo menos me interesa que se vea en pantalla grande, con las luces apagadas. Además es importante que estén en alta resolución, o sea que se vean bien los detalles, porque necesito que se aprecien bien los ojitos de las figuras, para filmarlas con espacio alrededor.*
> *La secuencia va a ser montada teniendo en cuenta que un fragmento afectará al siguiente, etc. Hay que manipular la emoción del espectador, por así decir.*

IK Con los videos, siento que se producen varios eventos que implican diversos significados. Principalmente es muy notable que frente a ellos puedan sentarse un abuelo y su nieto y estar muertos de risa, los dos, por un rato; una situación

Fig. 31. *To Fall Down / Caer*, imágenes extraídas del video *For You / Para usted*, 1999.

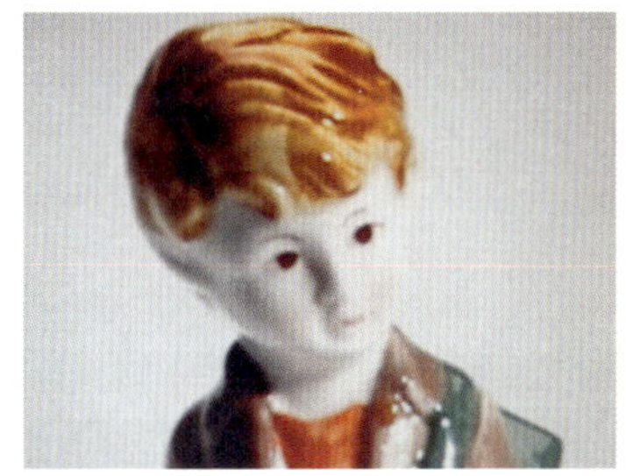

Fig. 32. Imágenes de *Matinee / Matiné*, 2009

que es casi inexistente frente a la mayoría del arte contemporáneo de calidad. Me impacta el hecho de que los videos sean a la vez sofisticados y accesibles, además de inter-generacionales. Por otro lado, sabemos que en el arte el funcionamiento del humor es difícil. La risa en sí misma está un poco prohibida, y en ese sentido tus obras tienen la capacidad de transgredir ciertos límites de una manera muy inteligente. Podría decirse que tienen un humor auto-reflexivo.

LP Pues me alegro . . . En realidad creo que lo humorístico de la obra es justamente lo triste, lo dramático. Vamos a pensar en casos concretos: en la primera película, cuando se cae el pingüino, el público se ríe, pero de gracioso no tiene nada [Fig. 31]. La risa es un poco esa risa de cuando uno se cae, para tapar la vergüenza. Y todo va muy rápido. La velocidad es un componente básico del humor. La obra no te da mucho tiempo para pensar, va directo al estómago y enseguida viene la escena siguiente. También es muy importante el vínculo con la música. Por ejemplo, hay un fragmento en mi último video *Matinee/ Matiné* [2009], que en un principio titulé "Accidente", en el cual se ve el torso de un inocente nene de porcelana que de repente recibe un martillazo y queda descabezado [Fig. 32]. Este fragmento viene inmediatamente después de otro que se llama "Insomnio", que muestra un pollito de peluche, "durmiendo" con los ojos abiertos sobre una piedra. En ese fragmento la música es la de *Mambrú se fue a la guerra*. Entonces, mirando las pruebas del video con Sylvia Meyer (con quien trabajo la música de las películas), nos dimos cuenta que el muchachito descabezado era, indudablemente, Mambrú. La imagen se vuelve más terrible unida a la canción y a la situación de insomnio presente en el fragmentito anterior, porque mientras el patito que no puede dormir se pregunta "¿cuándo regresará Mambrú?", uno sabe que, evidentemente, Mambrú no volverá[15].

15. *Mambrú se fue a la guerra* es una canción popular, escrita por soldados franceses durante el S. XVIII, para burlarse del Duque de Marlborough, John Churchill (1650–1722), un prominente soldado británico que, en repetidas ocasiones, había derrotado los ejércitos franceses. La canción burlesca "Marlborough s'en va-t-en guerre" se popularizó en el palacio de Versailles, donde la niñera de Marie Antoinette la cantó a los niños. Las tropas españolas, aliadas a los galos, trajeron la canción a España con la pronunciación de "Mambrú".

Fig. 33. *Where Are You?* [*¿Dónde estás?*], 1999.

IK ¿Cómo es la colaboración con Sylvia Meyer?

LP La primera vez que trabajé con ella en mi video, *For You / Para usted* [1999], éste ya estaba editado y listo y no tenía la menor idea de qué música se podía incluir. Sylvia me dijo "dame el video, yo le pongo música y vos décime qué pensás". Cuando me lo trajo, me resultó muy sencillo distinguir qué iba y qué no. Y así pude comenzar a pedir lo que quería.

Tanto me entusiasmó trabajar con ella en aquella experiencia inicial que mi segundo video, *Drum Solo / Solo de tambor* [2000], está pensado con conciencia de la inclusión de la música. El proceso es así. Por ejemplo, en la última película *Matinee / Matiné,* hay un segmento que se llama "Ver rojo" que es medio dramático, como una catarata de rojo que arrastra personajes, caballos, objetos, soldados, etc. Sylvia trajo una música muy dramática y allí entendí que la imagen en este caso sería más efectiva con una música opuesta. Y así Sylvia se presentó con una versión de "Moon River" que te parte el alma . . .

IK ¿Por qué tantos descabezados, accidentados que les caen piedras en la cabeza, conejitos perdidos (como en *Where Are You?* [*¿Dónde estás?*] [2000])?

LP Porque cuando uno cree que todo está perfecto . . . ¡zas!, aparece de repente la "mirada oblicua". Cuando uno se distrae con la vida . . . ¡zas!, de pronto hay que vivir la muerte. Uno parece sano, sano y . . . ¡zas!, la piedra en la cabeza. El conejito estaba allí, conmigo, y de pronto . . . ¿dónde se metió? [Fig. 33] Y así todo, entre la vida y la muerte, entre lo que se recibe y lo que se pierde. Presumo que ese es el juego. Soy naturalista.

IK El crítico argentino Miguel Briante había mencionado una "exasperante, cruel objetividad"[16] para hablar de tu producción de los años setenta. Asumo que se refería a la intensa literalidad implícita en el modo en que representabas los objetos. Lo interesante es que esa crueldad vuelve a aparecer, transfigurada y desplegada indiscutiblemente en los videos, como si con los años te hubieras ido desinhibiendo y hubieras dejado que se exprese una especie de horror que surge por detrás de la ternura.

LP Hasta ahora había crueldad con risa, pero en la última película, *Matinee / Matiné*, ya aparece lo dramático sin humor, como sucede en el fragmento que mencionaba recién, "Ver rojo". Y creo que esto tiene que ver con que hubo un momento en donde lo que veía por televisión era espantoso: los tsunamis, las desgracias ecológicas . . . Se ve que esas noticias me afectaron. La de la televisión se asemeja a la estética de mis fragmentos porque ves el drama e inmediatamente se muestra una publicidad de Coca-Cola. Son como tajadas de horror que no sabés cómo digerir.

IK Como veníamos diciendo, la fotografía primero y más tarde el video producen un cambio considerable en tu relación con el conocimiento de las técnicas. Luego aparecen los objetos tridimensionales, en su mayoría pequeñas figuras apoyadas sobre estantes, que implican un desplazamiento radical de los procesos. En este sentido, ¿qué significa hoy para vos lo "bien hecho"?

LP A mí me parece que toda propuesta tiene una solución buena, una medio mala o una genial técnicamente. Aunque se trate de dejar todo sucio, es una solución formal a una problemática. Lo que quiero decir es que es imposible salirse de lo formal, la idea no alcanza.

IK Y en tu obra, ¿qué considerás debe estar absolutamente "bien hecho"? ¿Hacia dónde enfocás tu máxima atención?

LP Es difícil decirlo, pero uno sabe cuándo algo va o no va, desde el punto de vista de la composición. Si está bien ahí a la izquierda, o si tiene que ir más a la derecha, o lo que sea. Todo tiene significado. Pienso mucho en este asunto en relación con los estudiantes de arte, porque se trata de una situación de aprendizaje: ¿cuál es la medida?; si éste es el espacio, ¿por qué está colgado en vez de estar apoyado?, etc. O sea, empezar bien de atrás hasta cuestionar por

16. Miguel Briante, "Liliana Porter: obra en marcha," *Confirmado* (Buenos Aires, 1977): 49.

qué la tela tiene cuatro palitos y si no podría usarse otro soporte. Desde esta perspectiva, lo bien hecho incluye de manera muy fundamental: el medio, la técnica, la presentación, el contenido, todo . . . Poco a poco se va aprendiendo y luego ni te das cuenta de que lo hacés.

IK ¿Cómo pensás que debería enseñarse el arte?

LP En las escuelas tienden a enseñar desde la técnica (taller de escultura, taller de pintura, taller de dibujo) y cada vez hay más técnicas. De esa forma no te alcanza la vida para aprender. Considero que sería mejor si existiera un taller de ideas y que después llegués al procedimiento, incluso que haya que inventar un modo de hacer para cada nuevo proyecto.

IK ¿Te imaginás cómo es ese taller de conceptos para jóvenes que no tienen conocimientos artísticos previos?

LP Creo que lo importante sería estimularlos a ser conscientes de lo extraño que es el fenómeno del arte, cuáles son los elementos que uno usa y por qué; y que si están rompiendo con una tradición, hayan discutido antes sobre ella.

IK ¿Cómo suponés que serán tus próximas obras?

LP Veo que toda la vida hice lo mismo, y dudo que deje de hacerlo: la misma pregunta dicha de otra manera. Lo bueno que tiene esta edad es que uno ya sabe que siempre se va a parecer a sí misma, entonces no tenés que preocuparte por ser coherente. Lo que más me gustaría es llegar a hacer una obra de teatro y evolucionar en lo del video. No sé cómo se hace lo del teatro ni nada, pero pienso que es una ventaja no haber aprendido la técnica porque uno hace las cosas con más facilidad, sin conciencia acerca de si estás o no rompiendo con una tradición.

RECURRENCIAS Y OBSESIONES

IK En tu trabajo hay temas que se repiten a través de los años como las correcciones, las reconstrucciones y las repeticiones.

LP Sí. Sobre las correcciones me cuesta acordarme cuando empecé, creo que comencé con un cuadro que se llama *Four Corrections* [1991], que son cuatro telas de las cuales la cuarta es un poco más alta y entonces yo corrijo ese pedacito, marcándolo con una línea. También hice un garabato corregido con rojo. La idea se centra en la imposibilidad de corregir un garabato, porque se supone que es lo único que conceptualmente nunca puede estar mal. De esto lo que me interesa es que corregirlo se parece mucho a lo que hacemos todo el tiempo al tratar de aprehender algo, buscando una teoría para las cosas lo cual, por ilusorio, es siempre un poco humorístico. Lo que quiero decir es que nunca sabemos cuál es el resultado final, y nuestra obsesión por conocer termina siendo como un ejercicio de humorismo involuntario. Otra cosa que me cautiva del garabato es que me hace recordar la escuela, cuando te corregían esa tarea de matemática que uno no entendía (en serio no entendía), con esa seguridad del trazo tan . . .

IK Totalitaria.

LP Exacto.

IK ¿Podrías contar la anécdota del atentado a *The Witness,* cuando estuvo expuesta en el MoMA, tan ligado a este tema del garabato y la corrección?

LP En *The Witness* [1990] aparece representado un espejo, un Mickey Mouse mirándose al espejo, a su lado hay un estante tridimensional y un crayón de verdad apoyado sobre él. O sea que el crayón está de nuestro lado, el Mickey y el espejo en el plano virtual del cuadro. El crayón que está en la repisa dibujó un garabato sobre la tela.

La obra se mostró en la exposición *Latin American Artists of the Twentieth Century* [1993], que realizó el MoMA. El día de la inauguración vino un señor, arrancó el crayón que estaba pegado en el estante e hizo un garabato al lado del garabato preexistente. Imagínate que la gente del museo me llamó alarmadísima y cuando fui a ver lo que pasó, concluí que el garabato del señor era mejor

Fig. 34. *The Correction* [*La correccíon*], 2003.

que el mío (más espontáneo, más apurado . . .) y entonces simplemente volví a firmar el cuadro y asunto terminado.

IK ¿El garabato podría interpretarse como la imagen de aquello que hace un artista?

LP Sí, es un gesto que representa al arte [Fig. 34].

IK El mismo gesto aparece en esas obras en las que hay un hombrecito dibujando una línea enorme, mucho más grande que su propio cuerpo.

LP Hay un pequeño pedestal pegado a la pared con un minúsculo hombrecito que debe medir un centímetro de alto, que dibujó en la pared un enorme garabato.

IK No deja de ser sugerente que esa, justamente, sea la imagen del arte para vos: que puede ser "cualquier cosa", una imagen que no puede ser corregida porque no hay criterio de verdad. Otro contenido que se repite en tu obra es el de la reconstrucción.

LP Exacto. Hoy sigo inventando otras versiones, otras reconstrucciones. La primera es una foto de un Mickey roto, formado con pedazos de vidrio de Murano. Junto a la foto, está un Mickey parado en un estante, ahora entero, intocado, perfecto. La obra es como un acto de magia, donde surge la posibilidad de

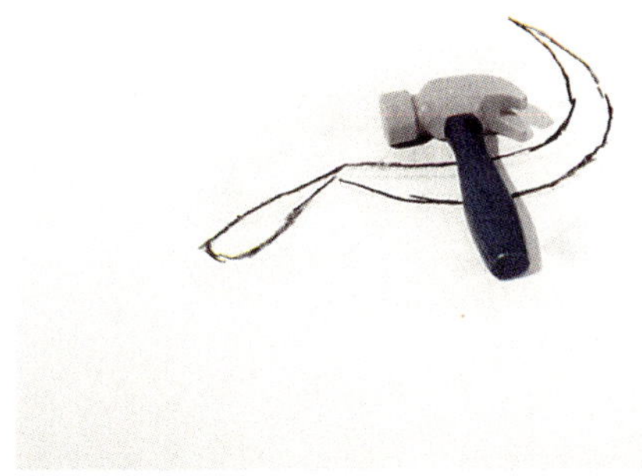

Fig. 35. *Drawing with Plastic Hammer* [*Dibujo con martillito de plástico*], 1993–95.

revertir el tiempo o de arreglar una cosa de manera tan perfecta que no exista marca ni cicatriz de ningún tipo. O sea, dos ideas optimistas, vamos a decir, pero simultáneamente insostenibles. Esas reconstrucciones son para mí metáforas de cosas que uno hace que ya no tienen arreglo, que ya no pueden modificarse. No sé si fue Borges quien dijo que arrepentirse es modificar el pasado. Lo cierto es que ese argumento me encanta y lo recreé con pingüinos, con un salero, con diferentes personajes y en variados formatos.

IK ¿Por qué cuando encontrás una idea que te interesa, como estas dos de las que estamos hablando, la repetís una y otra vez en tantas obras?

LP Para mí hacer un cuadro único es rarísimo, y en general siento la necesidad de volver a hacerlo, de volver a decirlo, o bien porque no terminé de digerirlo o bien porque todavía quiero decir algo más. Y esto quizás sea así porque empecé mi vida como grabadora. Cuando uno hace un grabado y lo imprime cuarenta veces, la imagen se vuelve un mantra.

IK En tu obra aparecen repeticiones de otro tipo, versiones de una misma imagen en múltiples técnicas y soportes, como ocurre, por ejemplo, con la hoz y el martillo [Fig. 35].

LP En ese caso, creo que hice la foto para hacer un cuadro y después lo hice como fotografía y en serigrafía. La posibilidad de tener las tres versiones de una imagen es interesante porque tienen distinto valor. O sea, la pintura es costosa (es un original), mientras que la foto y el grabado tienen varias copias. Es la misma imagen, exacta, pero la convención de la tela hace que su valor aumente, lo cual me parece genial; aun tratándose de esta imagen en particular: la reconstrucción de un símbolo, el dibujo de una hoz y la foto del martillito de plástico.

IK ¿A esa imagen la pensaste como uno de los diálogos?

LP Como un diálogo de contenidos, una imagen que significa y no significa nada al mismo tiempo. Me atraen esos símbolos tanto como me interesa la cara del Che. Es increíble que gente tan diversa ande por la calle con la camiseta con la imagen del Che sin siquiera saber quién fue. Me intriga el cómo esa imagen se transforma y adquiere otro significado. Para algunos, es una imagen familiar pero desconocida a la vez. ¿No es interesante?

IK Sí, pero al contrario de la figura del Che, que hoy es una imagen tan popular, la hoz y el martillo no tienen una circulación tan masiva y, en ese sentido, el hecho de que la elijas y la reconstruyas con lo que tenés a mano (una línea de lápiz y un martillo de juguete), me resuena como un acto político singular, de una enorme fuerza, por la persistencia y a la vez el sinsentido que conlleva. ¿Hay dejos de añoranza o de creencia en la elección de esa imagen?

LP Lo que me importaba era la imposibilidad de no reconocer que es el símbolo comunista y, a la vez, la obra es, como dice el título, *Dibujo con martillito de plástico* [1993–95]; o sea, que la imagen puede estar muy cargada o completamente desprovista de significado. Ese interés tiene que ver con la diferencia entre la etapa de las utopías y el momento más actual, en el que éstas están debilitadas. Hago la obra exactamente en ese intervalo de cambio de valores.

IK La repetición también tiene un lugar fundamental en las obras mismas, como ocurre en ciertas piezas de los años setenta y ochenta cuando una imagen aparece duplicada en distintos niveles de representación. Es el caso de *The Riddle*, 1987, en donde observamos un triángulo, una esfera y un cubo dibujados, y luego las figuras, ahora corpóreas, apoyadas en el borde del bastidor, o en esos objetos geométricos de madera que incluyen su propio dibujo.

LP Lo que quería era entender de qué se trataba, y por eso digo lo mismo de diversas maneras, para ver si encuentro el modo de definir la cosa. Es un poco como la búsqueda de los cabalistas que entre las letras del libro sagrado buscaban el nombre con mayúscula, una fórmula que diga finalmente el nombre, o sea, Dios. Está ese poema genial de Borges, "El golem", que habla de esto. La conclusión, para Borges, es que no llegaremos al arquetipo y que nuestras acciones son, finalmente, ensayos. Lo interesante es que este problema tiene que ver con el arte, porque el modelo, en el arte, en realidad es una representación.

IK Las imágenes de la casita, el camino y el caminante son notorias en tu producción, incluso desde el punto de vista metafórico, y están muy conectadas, creo yo, con el espacio vacío, otro elemento medular de tu obra [Fig. 36]. Ese ámbito vacío tiene una cualidad compositiva fundamental e igualmente una cualidad filosófica: sería el espacio, el mundo vacío, enorme y solitario que los personajes deben atravesar en sus tránsitos hacia o desde esa imagen de la casita. La casa y el vacío son dos núcleos emocionales importantes de tu trabajo.

LP El hombrecito (o cualquiera de los personajes) vuelve o se va siempre de esa casita que sería el lugar donde está a salvo, el lugar del conocimiento o la verdad. Suena cursi, pero es como el viajero que va caminando por la vida y sin embargo sabe que cuenta con esa posibilidad de volver al hogar. Hice muchísimas versiones de esa imagen. Una, por ejemplo, es un jarrón de porcelana que tiene dibujada la casita, y la línea que traza el camino que va del jarrón al piso da la sensación de que el viajero tiene que pasar varios espacios virtuales en su trayecto.

IK El viajero atraviesa fronteras inalcanzables, como una Alicia en el país de las maravillas. Además de la figura evidente del hombrecito viajero, valijita en mano, a veces tengo la sensación de que los protagonistas de tu obra son caminantes transitando por esos espacios vacíos hasta que se encuentran con una retratista que sos vos, y a veces con otros personajes de las especies más diversas.

Fig. 36. *To Go Back* [*Regresar*], 2001.

LP Debo agregar que la imagen de la casa es un elemento que comparto indudablemente con mi mamá, quien también era grabadora y que había perdido gran parte de su familia en un incendio en su casa.

IK ¿Tu madre era grabadora?

LP Mi mamá en realidad escribía, pero cuando me casé ella empezó a hacer grabados y hasta llegó a ganar el primer premio del Salón Nacional de Buenos Aires. Como venía de una familia rumana, tenía ese estilo de cosas chicas, intrincadas, medio *naif*, y dibujaba la casa permanentemente. En su caso, puedo imaginar que esa imagen repetitiva tiene que ver con que ella perdió gran parte de su familia en un incendio. Hace unos años, la gente de la Fundación Andreani [Buenos Aires, 1999] me invitó a hacer una muestra y me propusieron exponer obras mías y de mi madre. Fue una experiencia increíble, porque a medida que iba buscando entre las cosas de mi mamá, me preguntaba qué tenía que ver su obra con la mía, la cual yo veía un tanto más vacía y conceptual. De golpe comprendí que, esencialmente, tenía mucha influencia, curiosamente por la imagen de la casa.

IK Es revelador que de alguna manera la casa cobre otro significado, más aún si se piensa en tu vida de inmigrante en los Estados Unidos. Llegado a este punto, resulta oportuno que hablemos de los romances, que son un subtema de los diálogos que armás con tus figuras, valiosos por la ética que se desprende de ellos.

LP Sí, especialmente en la película aparece un fragmento que se llama "Besos", en el cual se besan personajes imposibles: un futbolista con una postal de un obispo italiano del Renacimiento, Minnie se besa con el Che, un nazi con un perro que es una alcancía y una mujercita con una papa. Para lograr estos encuentros tuve que hacer numerosas pruebas. En el del perro y el nazi lo genial es que uno siente que el nazi cambia de expresión en el beso, como que el hombre se preocupó y dice: "¡Me metí en un lío!" Realmente no se sabe cuál está más preocupado, ¡si el nazi o el perro! Lo que importa es que uno claramente percibe que los tipos se enamoraron. Es un poco como si estuviéramos en el paraíso y todos se hubieran reconciliado.

IK La serie de *los diálogos*, que comienzas a inicios de la década de los noventa, surge de una premisa similar, el encuentro entre seres que difieren por su especie y por su estado o condición.

LP Sí. Por ejemplo, el diálogo entre el Cristo (que es una lámpara dorada de plástico con un enchufe) que se mira con un pingüino de madera [*Diálogo (con pingüino)*, 1999], en el que sentís que el Cristo, desde el más allá, le está dando un consejo al preocupado pingüino . . .

IK ¿La serie de *Trabajos forzados* (desde 2004) realizados a partir de minúsculas figuras tridimensionales son una continuación del tema del trabajo expuesto en el video *Drum Solo / Solo de tambor* [2000]?

LP De alguna manera, sí. El primero que hice fue el del hombrecito paleando tierra negra, que siempre me dio mucha risa porque la tierra negra ubicada en una sala de exposición fue durante mucho tiempo un lugar común del artista latinoamericano en Nueva York.

IK Hasta ahora solamente mencionamos tu participación en el Project Room del MoMA como un hito de tu juventud, en el 73, pero después hubo una serie de exposiciones importantes, individuales y colectivas. ¿Cuáles sentís que fueron significativas porque te ofrecieron la posibilidad de una mirada sobre tu propio trabajo o te dieron un reconocimiento que antes no tenías?

LP Una de ellas es la exposición en el Bronx Museum en Nueva York [1992] que curó Marisol Nieves con Mari Carmen Ramírez. Estaba muy bien hecha y me sirvió para ver toda mi obra junta (había gran cantidad de piezas que no veía hacía mucho y que se pidieron prestadas a Argentina y a los museos). Es como publicar un libro, son aprendizajes que te permiten pasar a otra etapa.

Por otro lado, la invitación del New Museum [2011], acompañada por Marcel Broodthaers, fue una de las experiencias más conmovedoras que me tocó vivir recientemente. La estructura de la muestra en sí, increíblemente se parece a mis diálogos, donde hago que se enfrenten y se vinculen dos personajes que vienen de orígenes y temporalidades distintas [Fig. 37]. Quizá por causalidad, en esta exhibición me encuentro con un artista, con Marcel, a quien nunca conocí personalmente, a quien de hecho no había estudiado profundamente, y quien, para completar, pensaba en francés; y de golpe la conexión con él se vuelve natural y el diálogo fácil: a los dos nos gustaba Magritte, la idea del viaje, las imágenes infantiles apropiadas . . .

Recuerdo también la exposición en la Fundación San Telmo [Buenos Aires, 1990], aunque para mí la más relevante de todas fue la que curaste vos [Centro Cultural Recoleta, Buenos Aires, 2003], porque incluyó las películas y muchas otras piezas que no había expuesto en años, especialmente las fotografías en

Fig. 37. Vista de montaje de la muestra *Museum as Hub: The Incongrous Image—Marcel Broodthaers and Liliana Porter*, New Museum, Nueva York, 2011.

blanco y negro de los sets originales, en las cuales la gente podía ver de dónde provenían las imágenes de las pinturas y las impresiones. Recientemente, en 2009, Tobias Ostrander curó *Línea de tiempo*, una exposición individual en el Museo Tamayo en la Ciudad de México. Por segunda vez exponía en esta ciudad. La primera fue en la Galería Proteo cuando tenía diecisiete años; así que esta exposición, cincuenta años más tarde, fue una experiencia muy emotiva e importante para mí. Quedé muy contenta con el concepto tan inteligente de Tobias y con la magnífica presentación de la muestra.

IK Al margen de la hipótesis curatorial, la exposición en Centro Cultural Recoleta tuvo un efecto en Buenos Aires muy impresionante ya que a partir de entonces tu producción se dio a conocer de una manera bastante masiva y terminó siendo tremendamente influyente en nuevas generaciones de artistas.

LP Pienso que sí. Fue una felicidad total. En realidad, creo que cada exposición me ayuda a seguir, me obliga a pensar. Uno se transforma un poco en público y toma cierta distancia con la propia obra. Una tarea que me causa una gran, gran felicidad, es mostrar los videos, sobre todo en lugares como Uruguay o Argentina, porque ese público se parece a mí y se ríe al mismo tiempo que yo. Me pasa mucho cuando voy a las universidades de acá [de Estados Unidos] a dar una charla, pasar un video . . . Aquí observo una reacción muy diferente. Eso es significativo. Es como si yo hubiera hecho otra obra.

Fig. 38. Liliana Porter dando clase en Queens College, Nueva York, c. 1998.

IK Una de las sorpresas más notables de estas conversaciones es tu nexo con Argentina. Previamente, pensaba que haber vivido tantos años en Estados Unidos te había alejado de tu país de origen.

LP Para mí la Argentina representa presencias muy personales: mi infancia, la adolescencia, mi familia, mis amigos, el idioma, y todo eso está más o menos en orden dentro de mí. Tampoco tengo una postura impermeable al contexto donde vivo. Al contrario, siento que no tengo ningún filtro, y a veces voy a Buenos Aires y me olvido un poco de los códigos. Como esa postura ambigua de la relación con el médico que hay en Argentina, que en vez de decirte que habría que cortarte el brazo se lo dice a una tía y a vos te dice que está todo bien. Acá en Estados Unidos eso no existe, uno se acostumbra a lo literal. A mí, en ese aspecto, me gusta más lo literal. Da mucho menos trabajo.

Y sin embargo, aunque pasaron cuarenta y ocho años de vida en este país, en la universidad me costaba aprenderme los nombres de los estudiantes pero si había un latino y se llamaba Pérez o García, enseguida lo retenía [Fig. 38]. En síntesis, la gran ventaja que uno tiene en situaciones como la mía es que tenés un mundo más grande o una casa con más habitaciones. A la vez no hay duda de que la obra necesita de todas esas percepciones primeras que te hacen ser lo que sos.

IK Justamente, uno de los ejes que manejás es la traducción, el problema de las diversas formas de decir lo mismo, como si tus desplazamientos (tus años en

México y luego tu traslado a Nueva York) hubieran marcado de modo definitivo tus interrogantes sobre el mundo. Pareciera como si esa primera sorpresa ante la existencia de distintos mundos paralelos y ante la práctica de decir las cosas de múltiples maneras se transformó en una de tus preguntas esenciales; pero sin nostalgia, quiero agregar.

LP Si. La nostalgia es un problema que no me gusta. No pienso, por ejemplo, que tuve una infancia, que después vino la adolescencia y que ahora soy grande. Más bien (esto es raro), tengo la sensación de que todo sucede al mismo tiempo, o de que lo llevo todo conmigo.

EL ARTE Y LA FELICIDAD

IK Retomando el asunto sobre el proceso de producción de la obra que hablamos al comienzo de esta conversación, quisiera preguntarte, en relación a los objetos, los juguetes, ¿cómo ocurre el proceso de construcción conceptual o performática de los encuentros entre figuras? ¿Te ponés a jugar hasta que algo aparece, o tenés una idea o imagen preexistente y posteriormente la llevás adelante?

LP Te doy un ejemplo: el otro día encontré en San Telmo un muñequito antiguo de baquelita con un rifle. Si lo parás solo sobre la mesa, ya se arma algo . . . ¡Ya está listo! Siempre me dicen: "Tenés que ver la película *Toy Story*, te va a encantar", o cosas así. Pero lo que a mí me interesa es lo opuesto, los objetos que elijo ya tienen un argumento encima . . . Yo no les agrego casi nada. Lo esencial es el encuentro con esos elementos, aun cuando no pueda explicar qué atrapo en ellos. Lo que quiero decir es que no son ocurrencias ajenas a lo que soy, sino que me son irreductibles ya que vuelven siempre. Son ideas comunes: el horror, la caída, cosas básicas; pero que cuando las desdoblás de las circunstancias, originan una pieza diferente a lo que sucede cuando uno le adjunta un libreto.

Se juntan el objeto y sus características (la cara, los colores, cómo está hecho, su infantilismo y su violencia) con atributos que le son contrarios.

Entonces uno los elige sin pensar demasiado. Por otro lado, encontrarle el lugar a un objeto depende de un proceso, de un orden, empezando por hallar el día perfecto para tener ganas de trabajar. Una de las condiciones que necesito previamente es generar un lugar de bienestar. El proceso es muy placentero, preparo la cámara, traigo los objetos y voy ensayando hasta que de golpe sale algo. ¡Es fantástico!

Cada argumento es distinto. Unos son evidentes de entrada y otros requieren más pruebas o complejidades, como fue el caso del coche de Kennedy en el último video . . . Yo no sabía bien por dónde venía, qué quería de mí esa imagen, pero era obvio que algo iba a pasar. Finalmente apareció la música, la superposición del sonido, y allí se abrió otra puerta importante de significado frente a la imagen. La música es muy manipuladora.

Lo fundamental es que uno disfrute lo que hace. Hay ocasiones en las cuales me emociono. Recuerdo ahora *The Resemblance*, 2007, de fondo casi blanco, que tiene un paisaje con una casita. Hice una foto de una casita, la enmarqué, la puse de perfil y le saqué una foto. Instalé luego un pequeño estante sobre la tela, le apoyé la foto enmarcada y tomé otra foto de esa imagen [Fig. 39]. En otras palabras, sobre el estante, al final, había una foto enmarcada que representaba una foto enmarcada de perfil donde se veía la imagen de la casita. Después me senté y empecé a pintar sobre la tela ese paisaje, el que estaba viendo en la foto, como si ese fuera mi modelo. Todo ese proceso me emociona.

IK ¿Qué es lo que te emociona? ¿El hecho de que un modelo haya quedado tan lejos, debajo de tantas capas de representación?

LP Primero hay un placer muy grande en hacerlo. Pero simultáneamente surge la cuestión del tiempo y, por el gesto de copiar esa imagen, parece que hubiera una lógica que uno entendió. Lo que me emociona es darme cuenta finalmente que uno lo que siempre está haciendo es tocar la superficie de las cosas. Ahí está el corazón de lo que a mí me emociona. Lo solo del objeto, lo que se pierde. Todo está centrado en un instante de placer. La pintura y el taller huelen bien . . . Te gusta, se mezcla todo, lo bruto y lo sutil al mismo tiempo.

IK La emoción transmitida por el objeto se conecta con un sentimiento humano, el animismo es un componente fundamental de tu trabajo.

LP Totalmente. ¡Más animismo que en mi obra no puede haber!

IK En tu vida practicás una filosofía muy peculiar. Siempre decís que para ser feliz hay que inventar o crear esa felicidad, como si la felicidad tuviera mucho que ver con la fe, pero con una fe empujada desde la voluntad. En ese sentido, es bien interesante que tu obra trate temas de la vida no necesariamente felices. ¿Cómo pensás esa correlación entre los guiones dramáticos de tu obra y tu forma de vivir?

LP Esto tiene mucho que ver con mi mamá, quizás. Ella tenía ocho hermanos que fueron muriendo uno por año y un día, cuando le quedaba solamente una hermana, ésta y el padre murieron en el incendio de su casa. Sin embargo, la casa de cuando yo era chica era una casa pensada para ser feliz: el jardín, la chimenea, los juegos . . . Cuando invitábamos amigos, mi mamá preparaba comidas ricas y ambientaba la casa para recibirlos. Es un misterio cómo hizo para superar el dolor de la muerte de su familia, y sin embargo todo lo construyó para que fuéramos felices, y eso fue una enseñanza fundamental para mi vida. Por ejemplo, mi abuela paterna, que era judía, no estaba nada contenta con que mi madre no fuese judía, pero mi mamá la incluyó en nuestra vida y

Fig. 39. *The Resemblance* [*La semejanza*] (detalle), 2007.

nos habló siempre bien de ella. Es importante decir que no es que mi mamá negara o bloqueara lo que le había pasado. Ella creía que se podía construir a pesar de la tragedia.

IK ¿Te sentís judía?

LP Sí. Mis padres de jóvenes eran ateos pero participé de una manera de comer, de pensar y de mirar el mundo que es judía. Y si aparece cualquiera medio antisemita me enojo muchísimo, porque es como hablar mal de mi abuela. Intuyo que mi reacción va más allá de la religión o la ideología, o más acá, no sé. Así que lo judío está metido en abundantes aspectos de mi vida, como ocurre asimismo con el hecho de ser latinoamericana. ¿Viste que vas a un restaurante cinco estrellas con el director de un museo neoyorquino y te atiende un mozo peruano o mexicano y la verdad es que sentís más afinidad con el mozo que con la persona con la que estás comiendo?

IK Para retomar el hilo y concluir, estábamos hablando de la teoría de la felicidad, de la relación con tu madre y de las tragedias terribles que ocurren en tu obra.

LP Mi trabajo deriva de la reflexión de que no entendemos las cosas, de que nunca llegamos a solucionar el problema básico de por qué estamos en este mundo, y de darme cuenta, horrorizada, de que si en una guerra descuartizan a un tipo, yo también soy ese descuartizador y podría aprender a usar la motosierra. Por otro lado, escuchar una música increíble o ver una obra genial me hace sentir que está en mí el potencial de ser eso sublime. Siento que, de alguna manera, soy culpable de lo terrible del primer caso pero también de lo maravilloso del segundo.

IK Y en concordancia con esto, quiero volver a un punto que surge en las obras de *los diálogos*. En ellas propones encuentros entre seres que se comunican en la diferencia más enorme, seres que hablan desde varios planos de representación, que conversan a pesar de pertenecer a distintas especies, que se enamoran desde su incomunicabilidad esencial. Interpreto esos encuentros como la aseveración de una posibilidad filosófica, política, en relación al reconocimiento y al encuentro con un "otro".

LP Es interesante lo que decís, porque algunos los entienden al revés.

IK ¿Los entienden como la escenificación de una imposibilidad?

LP Claro, pero coincido con vos, es lo contrario: la idea es más bien esperanzadora. En referencia al nexo entre mi vida y el arte, te diría que me cuesta mucho separar en mi cabeza los dos proyectos. Por otro lado, durante las crisis de mi vida (digamos enfermedad, separaciones, etc.), el arte siempre fue lo más constante y sólido dentro de mí. Me acompañaba y me permitía una coherencia, una estructura, un medio para estar conectada firmemente con la tarea de estar viva sin colapsar.

Quiero decir que hacer arte o pensar la vida desde el arte, por lo menos a mí, me da cierta posibilidad de sanidad. Me interesa ser lo más sana posible y en consecuencia, lo más feliz. Quizás porque pienso que lo más normal sería estar completamente loco y ser muy infeliz. Y si uno logra lo contrario, gana. Es una especie de juego.

Y es que la vida, convengamos, es básicamente terrible. Lo más fácil es estar a punto de llorar siempre. Evidentemente todo es muy, muy raro. Uno aparece acá, de repente, y tenemos un plazo muy corto para *figure it out* [entenderlo]. Resulta bastante conmovedor lo que hace el ser humano con este tiempo: uno decide ser cocinero, el otro relojero, otro colecciona tapitas de refrescos, etc. Enseguida aparecen las distracciones, normas, situaciones, modas, relaciones, formularios a llenar que nos apartan del tema esencial; entonces pensar de qué se trata la vida hasta parece un arquetipo de lujo burgués, un divertimento.

En este sentido, te diría que lo que me da el arte es conciencia, conciencia de este corto plazo que tenemos por un lado, y por otro un medio para entenderme con la realidad. Aunque suene un poco cursi o dramático, te diría que para mí el arte es una forma de salvación.

IK Parece una conclusión muy seria e incluso idealista para una persona que a la vez está tan inmiscuida en el arte en tanto carrera profesional, con el cinismo que eso conlleva a un cierto nivel de funcionamiento. ¿Cómo llevás, entonces, esta concepción del arte como salvación con el arte como carrera?

LP Indudablemente hay que tener mucho cuidado porque el arte también se mete enseguida en esa estructura "distractiva". Me refiero al ánimo de llenar formularios. Enseguida la obra, en su personificación de objeto, entra en ese mundo "lógico": mercado, fama, artículo, coleccionista, medidas, técnica, libro, historia, restaurador, cita, entrevista, etc., que sin querer la separan de lo esencial. A pesar de eso, el arte, cuando es sustancia pura, nos ayuda a pensar, a estructurar un lenguaje posible de comunicación con nosotros mismos. Claro que aquí me cuestiono, ¿será verdad lo que acabo de decir? Porque, seamos francos: ¿qué es lo que necesitamos comunicar? ¿Qué sería eso que llamamos "esencial"?

IK ¿Qué obras de la historia del arte sentís que te conectan con vos misma, que son lo que llamás "sustancia pura"?

LP Ayer visité el Museo Thyssen-Bornemisza, en Madrid. Realmente son increíbles esos pequeños retratos del 1400: *Retrato de un hombre, Retrato de un hombre joven*. ¡Realmente extraordinarios . . . ! Uno mira a los ojos de esos modelos que se ven tan vivos, tan presentes frente a uno y se imagina al pintor que los miraba a la cara mientras pintaba, e intuye que hay una moraleja importante detrás de la experiencia de ver esto, pero, ¿cuál? Lo cierto es que una parte de uno se reconcilia . . . En el museo había un pequeño óleo de Morandi. Lo miro y siento como el principio de unas ganas de llorar. Es como si uno viera a los Reyes Magos y confirmara que existen. ¡Que increíblemente existen y que lo que nos dijeron era verdad!

IK La correspondencia entre arte y vida tiene que ver no solamente con los contenidos, digamos, de tu obra, sino con el modo en que te relacionás con la realidad, cotidianamente, cuando estás produciendo o charlando con amigos. En ese sentido, para cualquiera que te conoce, tenés una mirada muy especial hacia los objetos que te rodean (una conexión con el mundo que te permite

Fig. 40. *Levitating Rabbit* [*Conejo que levita*], 2008.

recuperar la imaginería simple de la infancia para iluminar la complejidad del mundo adulto, una lucidez un poco como la de María Elena Walsh[17]) que, estimo, se transparenta de manera totalmente fluida en tu trabajo.

LP Supongo que ser artista es como tener un lente a través del cual uno ve todo. Como cada persona tiene una obsesión particular, tiende a ver solo lo que realmente le interesa. Quiero decir, si uno es un pintor colorista, nota los colores, si a uno le fascina la luz, termina como Rembrandt. En mi caso, creo que el humor es un factor importante y así puedo expresar cierto grado de compasión a partir de ese humor.

IK Más allá de la serie de dibujos del barquito que hiciste en plena crisis personal, en 1977, ¿considerás a tu obra autobiográfica?

LP Sí, admito que en cada una de mis piezas podés encontrar la correlación con las experiencias en mi vida, y lo que a uno le afectó de esas experiencias. Por ejemplo, con *Levitating Rabbit* [*Conejo que levita*], pienso a veces que soy yo tratando

17. María Elena Walsh (1930–2011), poeta, escritora, música, cantautora, dramaturga y compositor argentina, conocida especialmente por sus obras infantiles.

de estar por encima de los desastres generales de esta tierra. No es un retrato naturalista, debe ser un retrato del deseo o la intención conejil, digo yo [Fig. 40].

En relación con mi forma de sentir y de pensar, creo que se resumen bien en ese fragmento del video *Matinee / Matiné* llamado "Chicken Salad" [ensalada de pollo]. Es simultáneamente gracioso y trágico, naturalista o literal, pero incomprensible. Es básicamente una situación dislocada: el pollo es en realidad un patito, que tampoco es un pato de verdad, sino un juguete a cuerda; la lechuga actúa como un misil, un prototipo de bomba que le cae a este pato inesperadamente, sin aviso, y todo se asocia o recuerda por un breve segundo a una ensalada de pollo. Claro que una ensalada incomible. Es por lo tanto pura metáfora. Su violencia genera risa, aunque en realidad es bastante trágico, ¿no?

IK ¿Y de qué manera creés que tus obras, sobre todo las más recientes, representan ya no tus sentimientos, tu vida, sino la vida colectiva, la historia?

LP En pinturas como *Levitating Rabbit* y *Untitled with Fallen Chairs* [2009], además de una serie de obras sobre papel que muestran estas especies de "tsunamis", de gran ola que arrastra muebles, gente, cosas varias . . . , supongo que tienen que ver con los desastres ecológicos y de guerra que uno ve diariamente en los medios de comunicación. Principalmente, si la vida cotidiana de uno está muy lejos de esa realidad, se produce un conflicto entre esa posibilidad personal de placer y tranquilidad y la desgracia espantosa del otro. No se pueden separar las experiencias humanas tan fácilmente: "Esto es mío, esto es suyo". Porque hay algo en cada experiencia que se vuelve común o colectivo. Así que me

Fig. 41. Liliana Porter en su taller, Franklin Street, Nueva York, 1980s.

Fig. 42. Liliana Porter en su taller, Rhinebeck, Nueva York, 2008.

gustaría interpretar estas obras como originadas en una necesidad de vivir o reflejar, aunque mas no sea a traves del arte, el desastre que se siente muy cerca, demasiado cerca . . .

IK ¿Creés que esa manera de pensar la obra podría expandirse a otras producciones, no necesariamente relacionadas con lo trágico?

LP Sí. Creo que lo que hace que uno lea un libro o mire un cuadro, es decir, que uno se interese por cosas dichas o hechas por otros, tiene que ver con esto que te decía antes de que nada es del todo tuyo o del todo mío. Parecería que uno busca escuchar lo que quizás, de cierta manera, necesita decir [Figs. 41 y 42].

ABOUT THE AUTHORS / SOBRE LOS AUTORES

Inés Katzenstein has been the founding director of the art department at the Universidad Torcuato di Tella, Buenos Aires, since 2008, where she developed the Artists Program and the Film Laboratory, as well as an exhibition program. She was curator of the Argentine Pavilion at the 52nd Venice Biennial, and co-curator of the *Zona Franca* exhibition at the Mercosur Biennial in 2007. From 2004 to 2008 Katzenstein was a curator at Malba–Fundación Constantini (Museo de Arte Latinoamericano de Buenos Aires). Exhibitions she has curated for other institutions include *Liliana Porter: Fotografía y ficción* at the Centro Cultural Recoleta, Buenos Aires, in 2003; *David Lamelas, Extranjero, Foreigner, Ètranger, Ausländer* at Museo Tamayo, Mexico City, in 2005; and *Televisión, El Di Tella y un episodio en la vida de la TV argentina* at the Espacio Fundación Telefónica, Buenos Aires, in 2010. Katzenstein has written extensively on contemporary art, and was editor of *Listen, Here, Now! Argentine Art of the 1960s: Writings of the Avant-Garde* (New York: Museum of Modern Art, 2004).

Gregory Volk is a New York-based art critic and freelance curator and Associate Professor in both the Department of Sculpture + Extended Media and the Department of Painting + Printmaking at Virginia Commonwealth University, Richmond. His numerous articles and reviews have appeared in publications including *Parkett, Sculpture*, and *Art in America*, where he is a contributing editor. Volk has contributed essays to many exhibition catalogues, including the recent *Sanford Biggers: Sweet Funk—An Introspective* (New York: Brooklyn Museum, 2011), *Ayşe Erkmen* (Turkish Pavilion, Venice Biennale, 2011), and *Andy Warhol: The Last Decade* (Milwaukee: Milwaukee Art Museum / New York: Prestel, 2009), as well he has authored *Vito Acconci: Diary of a Body, 1969–1973* (New York: Charta, 2007). Volk has curated numerous exhibitions in the United States and abroad, including *Outdoor Excursions* at Burlington City Arts, Vermont, in 2011, and *Three Parts Whole* at i8 Gallery, Reykjavik, Iceland, in 2011.

Inés Katzenstein es directora fundadora del Departamento de Arte de la Universidad Torcuato di Tella en Buenos Aires desde 2008, donde desarrolla el Programa de Artistas, el Laboratorio de Cine y el Programa de Exhibiciones. Fue curadora del pabellón argentino en la 52ª. Bienal de Venecia y cocuradora de la muestra *Zona Franca* en la Bienal de Mercosur de 2007. Del 2004 al 2008, se ha desempeñado como curadora en Malba-Fundación Constantini [Museo de Arte Latinoamericano de Buenos Aires]. También ha curado exhibiciones para otras instituciones como: *Liliana Porter: Fotografía y ficción* en el Centro Cultural Recoleta, Buenos Aires, en 2003; *David Lamelas, Extranjero, Foreigner, Ètranger, Ausländer* en el Museo Tamayo, Ciudad de México, en 2005; y *Televisión, El Di Tella y un episodio en la vida de la TV argentina*, en el Espacio Fundación Telefónica, Buenos Aires, en 2010. Katzenstein ha escrito de manera extensiva sobre arte contemporáneo y fue editora de *Listen, Here, Now! Argentine Art of the 1960s: Writings of the Avant-Garde* (Nueva York: Museum of Modern Art, 2004).

Gregory Volk es crítico de arte en Nueva York, curador y profesor asociado del Departamento de Escultura y Medios y del Departamento de Pintura y Grabado de la Universidad de Virginia Commonwealth, Richmond. Sus numerosos artículos y críticas han aparecido en diferentes publicaciones como *Parkett, Sculpture* y *Art in America,* donde contribuye como editor. Ha escrito ensayos para diversos catálogos de exhibiciones, incluyendo recientemente a *Sanford Biggers: Sweet Funk—An Introspective* (Nueva York: Museo de Brooklyn, 2011), *Ayşe Erkmen* (pabellón turco, Bienal de Venecia, 2011) y *Andy Warhol: The Last Decade* (Milwaukee: Milwaukee Art Museum / Nueva York: Prestel, 2009), y publicó como coautor en *Vito Acconci: Diary of a Body, 1969–1973* (Nueva York: Charta, 2007). Volk ha curado numerosas exhibiciones en los Estados Unidos y en otros países, tales como: *Outdoor Excursions* en el Burlington City Arts, Vermont, en 2011 y *Three Parts Whole* en el i8 Gallery, Reykjavik, Islandia, en 2011 entre otras.

IMAGE CAPTIONS / FICHAS TÉCNICAS

Cover [Portada]:
Untitled (Self-Portrait with Square) [*Sin título* (autorretrato con cuadrado)], 1973
Gelatin silver print (Impresión en gelatina de plata)
41 × 28 cm (16¼ × 11 inches)

Title page [Portadilla]:
Red Shoes [*Zapatos rojos*], 2010
Acrylic and collage on paper [Acrílico y collage sobre papel]
32 × 39½ cm (12½ × 15½ inches)

Contents page [Índice]:
Portrait of Liliana Porter in her studio in [Retrato de Liliana Porter en su taller en] Rhinebeck, New York [Nueva York], 2010

Pages [Páginas] 96–97:
To Bring Him Back [*Traerlo de vuelta*], 2010
Figurines, thread, and graphite on paper [Figuras, hilo y grafito sobre papel]
21 × 31.8 cm (8¼ × 12½ inches)

Fig. 1:
Liliana Porter at the [en el] Taller de Grabado, Universidad Iberoamericana, Mexico City [Ciudad de México], 1958

Fig. 2:
From left to right [De izquierda a derecha]: Julio, Margarita, Luis & Liliana in [en] Buenos Aires, 1955

Fig. 3:
Ana Tiscornia & Liliana Porter, Galería Casas Riegner, Bogotá, 2011

Fig. 4:
Liliana Porter & Juan José Arreola at the opening of Porter's first solo exhibition [en la inauguración de la primera exposición individual de Porter], *Óleos y grabados,* Galería Proteo, Mexico City [Ciudad de México], 1959

Fig. 5:
From left to right [De izquierda a derecha]: Fernando López Anaya, Liliana Porter, Eduardo Levy & Ana María Moncalvo, Galería Galatea, Buenos Aires, 1961

Fig. 6:
From left to right [De izquierda a derecha]: Luis Camnitzer, Liliana Porter & Luis Felipe Noé in [en] New York, c. 1965

Fig. 7:
Liliana Porter in front of her [en frente de su] *Wrinkle Environment Installation I* [*Instalación de la ambientación Arruga*], Museo de Bellas Artes, Caracas, Venezuela, 1969

Fig. 8:
Stitch [*Puntada*], 1970
Soft-ground and string [Barniz blando e hilo]
45 × 32.3 cm (17¾ × 12¾ inches)

Fig. 9:
La lune [*La luna / The Moon*], 1977
Photo-etching and aquatint [Fotograbado y aguatinta]
30.5 × 25.4 cm (12 × 10 inches)

Fig. 10:
Luis Felipe Noé, *Introducción al desmadre* [*Prologue to Holy Mess*], 1964
Mixed media [Materiales diversos]
Dimensions variable [Dimensiones variables]
© Luis Felipe Noé

Fig. 11:
Untitled [*Sin título*] *I, II & III*, 1973
Gelatin silver prints (Impresión en gelatina de plata)
Each image [cada imagen] 20.3 × 25.2 cm (8 × 10 inches)

Fig. 12:
The New York Graphic Workshop studio [taller], c. 1965.
© Basil Langdon

Fig. 13:
From left to right [De izquierda a derecha]: José Guillermo Castillo, Liliana Porter & Luis Camnitzer, 1970

Fig. 14:
Sombra para dos aceitunas (exposición por correo) [*Shadows for Two Olives* (Mail Exhibition)], 1969
Offset print and envelope [Impresión en offset y sobre]
Card [Tarjeta] 10.8 × 13.6 cm (4¼ × 5⅜ inches)
Envelope [Sobre] 12.7 × 15.2 cm (5 × 6 inches)

Fig. 15:
Sombra para boleto de colectivo (exposición por correo) [*Shadow for a Bus Ticket* (Mail Exhibition)], 1969
Offset print and envelope [Impresión en offset y sobre]
Card [Tarjeta] 10.8 × 13.6 cm (4¼ × 5⅜ inches)
Envelope [Sobre] 12.7 × 15.2 cm (5 × 6 inches)

Fig. 16:
Sombra para un vaso (exposición por correo) [*Shadow for a Glass* (Mail Exhibition)], 1969
Offset print and envelope [Impresión en offset y sobre]
Card [Tarjeta] 10.8 × 13.6 cm (4¼ × 5⅜ inches)
Envelope [Sobre] 12.7 × 15.2 cm (5 × 6 inches)

Fig. 17:
Sombra para una esquina doblada (exposición por correo) [*Shadow for a Folded Corner* (Mail Exhibition)], 1969
Offset print and envelope [Impresión en offset y sobre]
Card [Tarjeta] 10.8 × 13.6 cm (4¼ × 5⅜ inches)
Envelope [Sobre] 12.7 × 15.2 cm (5 × 6 inches)

Fig. 18:
Installation view of [Panorámica del proyecto del] New York Graphic Workshop's project featured in [presentado en] *Information* [*Información*] at The Museum of Modern Art, New York [Nueva York], 1970

Fig. 19:
Camnitzer & Porter's house [Casa de Camnitzer y Porter en] in Lucca, Italy [Italia], c. 1971

Fig. 20:
Road sign for [Señal de tráfico] Camnitzer-Porter, Lucca, Italy [Italia], 1975

Fig. 21:
Untitled (Nails) [*Sin título* (Clavos)], The Museum of Modern Art, New York [Nueva York], 1973
Silkscreen on wall with string and nails [Serigrafía sobre pared con hilo y clavos]
160 × 228 × 106 cm (63 × 90 × 42 inches)

Fig. 22:
Liliana Porter in her [en su taller en] Locust Valley, Long Island studio, with [con] *The Line* [*La Línea*] in the background [al fondo], 1973

Fig. 23:
Announcement card (front and back) [Tarjeta de invitación (anverso y reverso)] for Porter's solo exhibition [para la exposición individual de Porter], The Museum of Modern Art, New York [Nueva York], January 11–February 13 [11 de enero–13 de febrero], 1973

Fig. 24:
Untitled (contact strip – boat) [*Sin título* (Tira de contacto – barco)], c. 1976–77
Gelatin silver print [Impresión en gelatina de plata]
7.6 × 50.8 cm (3 × 20 inches)

Fig. 25:
Cover of *Contrabienal* and Porter's declaration [Portada de la publicación *Contrabienal* y declaración de Porter] 1971

Fig. 26:
The New York Times, Sunday, September 13, 1970 [*New York Times, domingo, 13 de septiembre de 1970*], 1970
Silkscreen [Serigrafía]
68.6 × 49.5 cm (27¾ × 19½ inches)

Fig. 27:
Wrinkle [*Arruga*], 1968
Ten photo-etchings with text by [Diez fotograbados con texto de] Emmett Williams
Each image [Cada imagen] 21.6 × 29.2 cm (8½ × 11½ inches)

Fig. 28:
Dialogue with Petrus Christus Postcard [*Diálogo con tarjeta postal Petrus Christus*], 1995
Gelatin silver print, triptych [Impresiones en gelatina de plata, tríptico]
42.5 × 92.7 cm (16¾ × 36½ inches)

Fig. 29:
The Photograph II [*La fotografía II*], 1996
Acrylic and silkscreen on canvas [Acrílico y serigrafía sobre tela]
111.7 × 137.1 cm (44 × 54 inches)

Fig. 30:
Minnie/Che, 2003–6
Gelatin silver print [Impresión en gelatina de plata]
20.3 × 25.2 cm (8 × 10 inches)

Fig. 31:
To Fall Down / Caer
Stills from [Imágenes del video] *For You/Para usted*, 1999, 16 mm film transferred to video [Película de 16 mm transferida a video], 16:00 minutes [minutos]

Fig. 32:
Stills from [Imágenes del video] *Matinee / Matiné*, 2009, digital video [video digital], 20:45 minutes [minutos]

Fig. 33:
Where Are You? [¿Dónde estás?], 1999
Ink on notebook paper [Tinta sobre papel de cuaderno]
16.5 × 20.3 × 2.5 cm (6½ × 8 × 1 inches)

Fig. 34: *The Correction [La corrección]*, from the series [de la serie] *Him and Others [Él y otros]*, 2003
Ink on notebook paper [Tinta sobre papel de cuaderno]
20 × 15.8 cm (8 × 6¼ inches)

Fig. 35:
Drawing with Plastic Hammer [Dibujo con martillito de plástico], 1993–95
Hand colored gelatin silver print [Impresión en gelatina de plata coloreada a mano]
27.9 × 35.6 cm (11 × 14 inches)

Fig. 36:
To Go Back [Regresar], 2001
Polaroid photograph [Fotografía Polaroid]
84 × 56 cm (33 × 22 inches)

Fig. 37:
Installation view of [Vista del montaje de la muestra] *Museum as Hub: The Incongruous Image—Marcel Broodthaers and Liliana Porter*, New Museum, New York [Nueva York], 2011

Fig. 38:
Liliana Porter teaching at [dando clase en] Queens College, New York [Nueva York], c. 1998

Fig. 39:
The Resemblance (detail) [*La semejanza* (detalle)], 2007
Acrylic and assemblage on canvas (acrílico y ensamblaje sobre tela)
152.4 × 198 × 11.4 cm (60 × 78 × 4½ inches)

Fig. 40:
Levitating Rabbit [Conejo que levita], 2008
Graphite on paper [Grafito sobre papel]
38 × 28.5 cm (15¼ × 11¼ inches)

Fig. 41:
Liliana Porter in her studio [en su taller], Franklin Street, New York [Nueva York], 1980s

Fig. 42:
Liliana Porter in her studio [en su taller], Rhinebeck, New York [Nueva York], 2008

Titles in / Títulos en Conversaciones / Conversations

Carlos Cruz-Diez
in conversation with / en conversación con
Ariel Jiménez ISBN 978-0-9823544-2-1
E-BOOK 978-0-9882055-1-2

Tomás Maldonado
in conversation with / en conversación con
María Amalia García ISBN 978-0-9823544-3-8
E-BOOK 978-0-9882055-2-9

Jac Leirner
in conversation with / en conversación con
Adele Nelson ISBN 978-0-9823544-4-5
E-BOOK 978-0-9882055-3-6

Jesús Soto
in conversation with / en conversación con
Ariel Jiménez ISBN 978-0-9823544-6-9
E-BOOK 978-0-9882055-4-3

Ferreira Gullar
in conversation with / en conversación con
Ariel Jiménez ISBN 978-0-9823544-5-2
E-BOOK 978-0-9882055-5-0

Gyula Kosice
in conversation with / en conversación con
Gabriel Pérez-Barreiro ISBN 978-0-9823544-8-3
E-BOOK 978-0-9882055-6-7

Liliana Porter
in conversation with / en conversación con
Inés Katzenstein ISBN 978-0-9823544-7-6
E-BOOK 978-0-9882055-7-4

Forthcoming titles / Próximos títulos

Tania Bruguera
in conversation with / en conversación con
Claire Bishop

Waltercio Caldas
in conversation with / en conversación con
Ariel Jiménez

Luis Camnitzer
in conversation with / en conversación con
Alexander Alberro

Alfredo Jaar
in conversation with / en conversación con
Luis Pérez-Oramas

David Lamelas
in conversation with / en conversación con
Christian Rattemeyer

Julio le Parc
in conversation with / en conversación con
Alexander Alberro

FUNDACIÓN CISNEROS
COLECCIÓN PATRICIA PHELPS DE CISNEROS